TO UNDERSTAND A PERSON

TO
UNDERSTAND
A
PERSON

AN AUTOBIOGRAPHY
(of Sorts)

JOHN STRAUSS

Epigraph Books
Rhinebeck, New York

To Understand a Person: An Autobiography (of Sorts) © 2020 by
John Strauss

"Uncertainty Theory" reprinted by permission of The Washington
School of Psychiatry, www.wspdc.org.

Paperback ISBN 978-1-951937-55-3
Hardcover ISBN 978-1-951937-57-7
eBook ISBN 978-1-951937-56-0

Library of Congress Control Number 2020913933

Book design by Colin Rolfe

Epigraph Books
22 East Market Street, Suite 304
Rhinebeck, NY 12572
(845) 876-4861
epigraphps.com

T O

Sarah Kamens, my muse; my kids Jeff and Sarah; my wonderful friend Alain Bottéro, who died so young; Larry Davidson, my mentor; and Anne Ranson, my editor. And to the people barely mentioned here or even not mentioned here at all who have in fact been the very fabric of my life.

Thanks also to Maria O'Connell, Elizabeth Brisola, Kai Erikson, Ashley Clayton, Tom Styron, and Stanley Possick.

C O N T E N T S

CONTENTS

by Larry Davidson

A young woman with a history of serious mental illness whom both John Strauss and I know once said that she had "been chasing real for as far back as I can remember." Having read this book, I think that "chasing real" is a very fit description both for John's professional work as a psychiatric researcher and for the rich, complex, and incomplete life that he so faithfully describes in this autobiography. There is nothing forced, artificial, or extraneous in this book. What we have instead is one person's recollections and honest reflections on a life as lived within a certain historical period and across a number of geographic contexts. What we make of the stories and internal dialogues is up to us, the reader. John is not trying to sell an enhanced image of himself or send an inspiring or cautionary message. He is simply and solely telling tales and inviting the reader into a discussion of how best to make sense of a single human life. Whether that be the life of a person with a serious mental illness or his own life as a grandson, a son, a brother, a lover, a husband, a father, a researcher, and a writer, John invites us to join him on his journey to figure out how best to understand such a life in a way that retains its own richness, its own complexity, and its own incompleteness.

While this is his first attempt at an autobiography, the challenge that John puts forward to his reader is one that he has grappled with himself for over half a century. And he continues to "chase real" just as passionately and uncompromisingly now in his eighties as he did when he first started to conduct psychiatric research in his twenties. What led John to his ground-breaking discoveries about the nature of mental illness early in his career was his conviction that these were conditions that happened *to people*, and that who those people were and what they did or did not do influenced the course and outcome of the disorder over time. To carry out this research, he had to ask his participants to talk about their overall lives in addition to their symptoms and other aspects that fall under the broader rubric of disorder, and then he had to listen closely, actively, and with genuine concern about everything that was "real" about the person. In his later interviews, which became more and more open-ended and narrative in nature over time, John could be heard saying "Wow" in response to stories of uplifting events or tearing up in the face of the poignant stories participants would tell about the horrors and rejections they had experienced due to their illness and its misguided, and at times equally toxic, treatment. In other words, John was real as a person in these interviews, and his realness made it possible for his participants to be real as people as well—in all of their own richness and complexity. While the dense yet unfinished quality of the stories he elicited may have frustrated him as a researcher, it also persuaded him of the need for, and value of, complementing science with excursions into the arts and humanities as additional ways of learning about and understanding human beings. As far as he was concerned, Victor Hugo knew just as much about human nature, if not more, than Freud.

It is just such a search for an all-encompassing framework within which to explore and understand human experience in all of its quantitative and qualitative facets that motivated and undergirds this book. Given its conversational style, it invites the reader to join John on his quest for what's "real" about people; a quest that he passionately pursues both in his personal as well as in his professional life. Students, trainees, postdocs, junior faculty—anyone who is invited to share a meal with John—invariably comes away from this experience having had to confront some fundamental realities in their lives, whether or not these realities have anything to do with their psychiatric studies, research, or practice. As with this book, the confrontation is always a gentle and caring one, and more often than not people leave with more, and more basic, questions than they started with. But this is an effect that is consistent with the nature of the subject matter being discussed; the "real" only gives itself in pieces.

In this way, reading this book is akin to talking a leisurely stroll on a sandy beach filled with glinting seashells. The view is both one of infinite depth condensed into a fading blue horizon and one of infinite complexity as embodied in the intricacies of each single seashell. Life, according to John, is to be captured both in its concrete particulars, its irreducible details, as well as in its overarching yet unfinished trajectories. As he shows us in his autobiography, the John of today is both the same yet also different from the John who was born eighty-seven years ago, as well as from the John of sixty years ago, and so on. It is a great pleasure to follow along with him on this beautifully crafted series of stories, savoring each morsel of this fabulous "moveable feast" while wondering aloud how he, and we, could have been so fortunate as to have been invited.

Where do you get the sheer gall to write a book about yourself? Well, I can tell you how it happened. One day during a conference, my young friend Sarah Kamens, a lovely, kind and intelligent psychologist, asked me if she could interview me about my life and work. I was dumbfounded. No one had ever seemed to have a particular interest in doing that before. But, of course, I jumped at the chance and instantly said yes. I mean how often do you get a chance to talk about yourself like that with a terrific person?

So we had three sessions of about two hours each followed by dinner at a local diner. Sarah recorded the interviews and we had them transcribed. I was sure that I had spoken nothing but wisdom in golden prose, but when I saw those transcripts, appalling! Oh, some of it was okay, but some stuff was all but incomprehensible.

Well, I figured I could do better than that and sat down to write a chronological account of my life. I put that together with the interview transcripts and a bunch of short essays about my experiences that I had written over the years and showed this to my two kids, Jeff and Sarah, to my close friend Larry Davidson and a couple of other people. Their response? "Luke warm" would already be overstating it.

My son, Jeff, then suggested, "Try writing it as though you were giving a talk." It's advice I often give to students but hadn't thought about it for myself. I started again and rambled all over the place. This was not going well.

Finally, someone suggested that I get an editor. I got a whole list of editors, none of whom I knew, and somehow just got stuck and did nothing. Then I was talking to a friend, Stan Possick, over lunch one day and, pretty much in desperation, asked him, "Do you know any editors?" "Yes," he said, "My wife's stepsister who's really good." So I contacted her, we talked, she set about putting some order into all these pieces that I'd been writing, adding some things and deleting a lot of others, and so with a bunch of subsequent revisions, here we are.

What right do I have even to try to write an autobiography? Well, it's true that I worked with Will Carpenter and John Bartko and together we were some of the first people to show with reliable methods that persons with schizophrenia could improve. Why is that a big deal? The concept of schizophrenia, as developed in the nineteenth century when it was known as "dementia praecox," was based on the belief that persons with this disorder never improved and, in fact, most often had a downhill course. The idea of defining a "disease" by its course goes way back to Hippocrates. And this notion, that you can identify a disease process by knowing the course of the disorder and especially by whether people can recover or not, remained dominant in the twentieth century. So our finding messed up the basic underlying view of the disorder and of one of the basic concepts underlying the whole field of psychiatry. Does such a finding warrant an autobiography? Well, in my opinion, no.

Besides the sheer ego trip of trying to write about myself, there is another reason I wanted to do this. I am a psychiatrist, and for about sixty years have been trying to figure out how to think about a person. I have written a bunch of articles with titles like "The Person with Delusions as a Person" in my efforts to try to figure out how psychiatry can be a "human science" dealing both with the rigors of traditional science and the wondrous complexities of individual human experience.

Of course, psychiatrists, psychologists, and many others have tried for centuries to deal with the question of how to reflect what mental illness is and how it relates to the fact of being a person. The field of psychiatry has tried to do that generally either by dodging the issue, claiming that "mental illness is an illness like any other," or by creating a variety of more or less constructivist structures, as with Freudian psychology, for example.

Apart from my selfish reasons, therefore, I have tried to use the process of writing an autobiography as a way to understand what it means to be a human being, and thus, among other things, to understand how better to think about this thing we call "mental illness." That oft-used statement "mental illness is an illness like any other" is catchy enough but not nearly so simple an assumption as it may seem. Some "illnesses," such as lupus, for example, or peptic ulcer, are really complex and very different from others—let's say, certain kinds of anemia or pneumococcal pneumonia. And what if mental illnesses reflect a combination of psychological, biological, and social factors, as when humans try to adapt in certain extreme ways to certain life experiences, then our understanding of what it means to be human must look at the various ways humans have of "adapting" to, or being affected by, and affecting situations.

But if we're trying to figure out what humans do, what a human life involves, how do you do that? How do you even think about a life? What is it they say about stories, a beginning, a middle, and an end. Is a life a story? Does it have a meaning? Is it perhaps many stories? Or no stories at all? Is life perhaps like a Sibelius symphony with many fragments of themes that little by little join together toward the end to be one magnificent theme? Or is it like some twentieth century music that, unlike the eighteenth century sonata form, for example, does not have a more or less predictable progression: statement of theme, development, recapitulation. Perhaps real life rather than reflecting a progression is more like some Asian music that reflects just being rather than directionality. Or do some things in a life continue on more or less, perhaps like a basic building material, while other aspects change more or less radically over time?

So, focusing on this question of how you think about a life, the structure of this particular iteration will involve something built from the three efforts described earlier, the interviews with Sarah Kamens, the chronology I wrote, and the essay-type pieces. I had also discovered the year before I started all this, the wonderful question, "Who are you?" I was teaching an informal session of Sarah Kamens' class of undergraduates at Wesleyan College, and as students drifted into the room, I would ask each, "Who are you?" Listening to the very diverse answers, all of a sudden I realized what an impossible but fascinating question that was. In some sense, this autobiography is an effort to respond to that question. So here we go.

At this point, though, take a few moments and listen to "Try to Remember" from the musical *Fantasticks* and/or "September Song" by Kurt Weil, sung by Lotte Lenya. Both of these are on YouTube.

AN ALL-AMERICAN CHILDHOOD?

ERIE: THE EARLY YEARS

I was born in 1932 at Cleveland, where my family then lived. Dad had come from the village of Loudonville, in central Ohio, had served briefly in the army, had gone to Oberlin for a year, then to Harvard for another year, and dropped out to work in the steel mills of Cleveland when his mother died and his father was hospitalized. In Cleveland, he met and married Mom, who had trained as a teacher. My sister, Susan, was born in 1928.

By 1932, the Great Depression was underway. My father sometimes commented that I was born at the depth of the Depression. People often laughed when he said that, but I sometimes wondered if he was "joking" that I *was* the depth of the Depression. Whatever the case, my father had little money and no prospects so we moved to Erie so he could become manager of an apartment complex in which he had the unenviable position of being a junior owner under Sambo, Mom's dad, the family patriarch. The first home I remember was 1002 Weschler Avenue, which was a side-by-side duplex building, part of Dad's apartments. When I was about five years old I crayoned something resembling an A on the wall of the stairway leading to the cellar. This was judged to be a bad thing, and I never confessed to it. Instead, it was finally decided that the perpetrator was probably Avis Crescent, a friend of my sister's. As you can see, I never forgot that event and have never fully forgiven myself for not owning up and saving the reputation of the innocent Avis. Somewhere inside myself, however, I vowed that I would never do anything like that again.

More innocently, in those years I enjoyed playing "cars" on our joint front porch with my next-door neighbor Dicky Moorhead, who had a little purple Lincoln Zephyr car that I loved. "Cars" involved holding one of our tiny toy cars and moving it around on the front porch while making the sound "vroom vroom." A memory more particular to the time was a bubble gum card that showed the horrible Japanese fighting against the Chinese. This, then, was the time of the Sino-Japanese War preceding the Second World War, a war I remember more clearly.

About Erie, first of all, it may be difficult for people who grow up on the coasts to realize but many cities in the interior of the US are very different from the coastal cities. When I was hitchhiking across the country after my second year in college, it was impressive how comfortable I felt all across the middle of the country, states like Missouri, Kansas, Nebraska, Wyoming, the people there had the same feel as people from Erie. But when I reached California, those people were different. They were more like people from New York or Massachusetts or New Jersey. These people had sharper edges. The drivers were less kind, more aggressive. People talked faster. It was very striking. Certainly, Californians are different from New Yorkers, but both groups have more in common I think than they do with those of us who come from the middle of the country. Those cities in the middle aren't horrible, just different, and the smaller ones there are also very different from the bigger ones like Cleveland, Detroit, and Chicago.

Located 90 miles west of Buffalo New York and 100 miles east of Cleveland, Ohio, the Erie in which I grew up was one of those smaller cities not on either coast. Erie is in a tiny part of the state of Pennsylvania that sticks up between New York state and Ohio, the small part of Pennsylvania that contacts lake Erie. The north side of our town touches the lake. North of that, across what to us seemed an endless expanse of water, was Canada. When I was in high school, at breakfast I would listen to the wonderful Canadian radio station CJBC that played great classical music all the time. When later in life I had divorced, I was a visiting professor for six months in Toronto which is a really fine city. I fell in love with Carrie, a wonderful Canadian woman 25 years younger than I. She was from a tiny town in Ontario, Delhi, which was as it turned out just across the lake from Erie. I think that fact gave us a common way of seeing things so that in spite of the difference in our ages, genders, and nationalities, we had a similar way of being in the world which gave us a tremendous understanding and comfort with each other.

Erie is on "the lake" which is at our north, that in turn means that a large body of water is essentially part of the town. From the house my family lived in when I was in high school, we could see beyond the houses directly overlooking the lake, the water itself and the impressive, huge, long ore boats coming to the Erie harbor to deliver raw materials for our factories.

Jutting out into the lake from the west side of Erie is a peninsula, "The Peninsula" also called Presque Isle which was just a name for us but actually signaled the history of that part of the country as being under French ownership years ago. In the summer after high

3

school I was a lifeguard at the Peninsula which created a bay on its south side but on its north side had miles of wonderful sand beaches. Those beaches also had the greatest small round flat stones for throwing to skip along the tops of the water that exist anywhere. On quiet cloudy days when there were few people at the beach we life guards would spend hours skipping those stones that would sometimes bounce off the water 10 to 12 times before sinking into the waves. Most of us actually got a calloused groove at the tip of the index finger in our right hands from that pastime.

On the south side of Erie the ground rose gradually to become low hills with very fertile soil, excellent for the farming country that extended south and the wonderful orchards of fruit trees. There was a whole life from those farms and orchards of course and some great fairs like the Wattsburg Fair which Dad would take us to, reminding him as it did of his childhood growing up in the farming village of Loudonville Ohio, south of Cleveland.

The "downtown" of Erie was essentially the 20 or so blocks between 6th Street (counting from the lake at the north) and eleventh street and including about four blocks of cross streets, most named after various fruits and trees. We had a department store, the Boston Store, three movie theaters, a hotel, two newspapers, two radio stations, and a bunch of small stores including a planters peanuts store at the very heart of the city at 10th and State. Twelfth Street was industrial with railroad tracks, Bucyrus Erie which made steam shovels for the US and were exported all over the world, and several other factories. And just south of Twelfth Street, on 14th street were the railroad station and a large central post office. We also had a more recent General Electric plant on the eastern edge of town and the Hammermill paper company on the north side right next to the lake, selling paper throughout the country and I imagine the world, and spewing raw chemical sewage into Lake Erie which appeared as a smelly foam all along the shoreline.

We had a small amusement park, "Waldameer", a baseball team, the Erie Sailors, a negro baseball team the Pontiacs, a small zoo with Eva the elephant, and a really pretty square, Perry Square (named after Commodore Oliver Hazard Perry of the War of 1812 fame and the Battle of Lake Erie ("We have met the enemy and they are us" to quote the comic, Pogo that changed the original word "ours" to "us") on the edge of which were the post office and a beautiful old building with pillars, the public library, fancy and wonderful.

On the east side of downtown was "Old French Road" which was just a name like Peach Street or Cherry Street to most of us but actually recalled a time when Erie was French territory (The indians there were called Eriez which of course we pronounced Erie-ez) and a major link between the great lakes and Fort Duquesne (Pittsburgh) 120 miles directly south which then provided a land bridge that allowed connections all the way from the St Lawrence River and Canada to the Mississippi and the Gulf of Mexico. And we had "mad Anthony Wayne's" blockhouse from our days as a British colony, and at the dock was the ship Niagara which I think was Perry's flagship from the war of 1812. Of course we never paid any attention to all that history stuff.

We had one book store, Nash's (The Erie Book Store) and a German-American club the Maennerchor ("mens'choir" in German) which we belonged to and sometimes had dinner at. And we had a great (small) bakery, Kuhneman's that made terrific poppy seed rolls.

The population of Erie was around 130,000, (US population was 130 million, and I think the world was estimated at 2 billion or was it 9?). Erie was 50% Catholic, mostly people of Italian background, and also some Poles, but in many ways the city was run by the aristocracy, Protestant, whose church was the Church of the Covenant (sigh when you say that). There were a couple smallish Jewish centers, our "Reform" Temple of mostly German Jews and the orthodox temple of mostly eastern European Jews. We rarely mixed with each other. In 8th grade when mother had gone to the hospital in New York and our rented house was sold out from under us, our family moved to the lower east side from the more posh south side of the city (but our house was only a half a block from the lake, while not fancy, still a snazzier part of that section of town). That was the year I went to East High (high and junior high) where the kids were mostly from families of Polish and Italian backgrounds. We also had a group of the kids of the Russian dockworkers who lived below 6th street and unloaded the huge ore boats that brought iron ore to our factories. The kids included my friends Chouka Orloff, and Philmore Biletnikoff, lovely people from pretty poor families. In fact, when I think of it now, it's possible to reconsider the national backgrounds of Erie kids I knew by considering family names. To start at "the top", the majority of families who were sort of more in the center of our world, and at the top of the social ladder were the people with "Real American" (i.e., British) family names, Wilson, Crawford, Collins, Thomas, Brown. Then there was a fair number of people with German names, Shrader, Koenig, Fleugel, Griewahn, Kurtz, and can we include Strauss? (well, yes and no). Certainly in terms of numbers there were the Italian names: Scalzitti, Guarniro, Capaziello, Rascatti, Riazzi, Migliori, Spinelli (Barbara, the most beautiful girl in the world ever), and then in smaller numbers, the people with Polish names: Grabinski, Petrowski. On occasions when I went to Cleveland to the west of us, as in the summer after graduating from college, or on the less frequent occasions I went to Buffalo to east of us, I was surprised and disappointed how ethnic groups (Anglos, Italians, Jews) in these big cities seemed to isolate themselves from people of other backgrounds. Although there were I suppose some tendencies towards that in Erie, mostly we were just all in it together and mixed pretty much always and easily. When I worked one summer before college digging ditches for the gas company, our crew of eight or so guys had people of all types of families of European descent. There were no Hispanics in the group, and in the city there were very few Asians, and almost no black people.

I grew up during the second world war and so was exposed to: the Spanish Civil War with the fight for democracy, the leadership of Hitler and Mussolini vs. Churchill and Roosevelt (of course Stalin, Degaulle and others as well), communism vs. (as we saw it) democracy. We were less aware of racism, but more of anti-semitism not just Hitler but also in the US, Father Caughlin, Lindberg, and restrictions against Jews in "tourist homes", summer camp, etc.

Also part of my context in Erie was that of all the friends I had, we and one other family were the only households who had books. My friend Bob would come over to our house even though we lived at an edge of Erie far from his house and our high school, partly to look at our books. We had all kinds, most in a large book case that Bill Reed, Dad's foreman also a master of building and fixing pretty much everything had built in a couple of hours at our house. The bookcase covered two thirds of one wall in the living room. I remember Lee's Lieutenants, Dad had lots of books on the civil War, Black Lamb and Grey Falcon about the Balkans, and tons of others including Kristin Lavransdatter and a complete edition of the Encyclopedia Britannica which of course was great to look things up in for school. We also had a Webster's unabridged dictionary, a huge leather-bound thing about eight inches thick. At dinner, during a conversation, Dad would sometimes say, "I wonder what that word really means", and he'd get up from the table, go into the living room and read what the dictionary said out loud so we could hear it. Often, after dinner, he would go into the living room, sit down at the piano, go through the sheet music he had of Mozart, Bach, Beethoven, Schuman, and others including Gilbert and Sullivan and start to sight read them. If he selected Gilbert and Sullivan, he would often sing little parts as he played.

The books of the other household were owned by Gerta, the wife of Milton Schaffner who owned a meat packing plant. They had a big house in Glenwood, not far from my high school, Academy. In fact there were not a lot of big houses in Erie, the other one in which I knew the people was the house of the Fishes on 38th Street, who sent their sons to Exeter and Princeton. The kids were ok though, and John who was my age and on the swimming team until he went off to Exeter was a really nice person. A couple years ago I met with him and his wife (Sally Wilson) who was also from our high school class, when I happened to be in Chicago where they lived. We had lunch together and they were involved in all kinds of civil rights causes and knew Michelle Obama.

Milton Schaffner was born in the US and rather dull, but Gerta had been born and raised in Germany and spoke with only the slightest of accents. They had two kids, Bertram and Morris. Morris went to work in the meat packing plant and had a small but nice sailboat on "the Lake", but Bertram became a psychiatrist, psychoanalyst and homosexual, at the time the only one I had ever known. (No one ever talked about it of course.) Bertram lived in New York on Central Park South, was a friend of Margaret Mead and wrote a book, "Fatherland", looking at Germany and the rise of Hitler from a psychoanalytic perspective. We had arranged for Gerta to teach me German when I was in junior high and we had several months of lessons. Many of the books they had were like Lessing, Goethe, and Schiller, all in German.

My friend from 9th grade on, Bob, came from a family who had no books, but somehow he was very well read and knew huge amounts about all eras of classical music (and still does). He's trying to write a sequel to the Brothers Karamazoff and I think will never finish it. Bob and I would go to the (only) record store and talk with the sales people about music, and we would go to the radio station (WICU) and talk about all sorts of things with the disc jockey while he was playing a record, and then as mentioned elsewhere, suddenly our "Sunday School" teacher was Frank Fox, salesman at a crumby jewelry store who taught us about Montaigne, Spinoza, Buddhism, ethics, and other things. The point being I guess that I grew up in this non-intellectual world (including my swimming and water polo teams) that was in fact spotted by these wonderful islands of intellectual stuff in a milieu that unlike many places in the US was not anti-intellectual (kids at school didn't tease me when in the halls between classes I would be reading my copy of Spinoza's ethics) and at a time when there were all these extreme political (and intellectual) dichotomies. For me, I guess it was like going to a cafeteria that had all kinds of food including foie gras, canard à l'orange, cheerios and hotdogs, and so no problem just to take the foie gras and canard, along with all the other stuff. I was very lucky.

From high school, I went on to Swarthmore where a lot of the kids were from big cities like New York, Boston and Philadelphia and knew all this stuff about Spinoza, Virginia Woolf, and others. That was the first time in my life I had been in such a milieu and it was both weird and wonderful. (I was on the swimming team as well, so staying in touch with my background).

But, back to my childhood. When I was about six, I started at the Erie Day School, a private progressive school conceptualized and started by my mother and Ross Fink, both of whom were devoted to "progressive education." My first-grade teacher was a Miss Erickson. That year my father took a picture of me that I will never forget and in fact still have. I am sitting on the floor, dressed in my favorite striped tee shirt, and before me on the floor is a jigsaw puzzle consisting of a small number of large wooden pieces. You can see in the photo (my father was a fine photographer) that I have assembled all the pieces for the lower right corner of the puzzle, and separately, all the pieces of the upper left corner of the puzzle. You can also see that I haven't noticed that all I need to do to complete the puzzle is to join the two assembled corners. That photograph represents, in fact, the entire story of my professional life—seeing that two things were separate and struggling with the problem of how they might fit together. About thirty years ago I was a speaker in an American Psychiatric Association symposium. Another of the speakers was Bob Spitzer of DSM-III (Diagnostic and Statistical Manual of Psychiatric Disorders) fame. During the question period someone in the audience asked me why I had proposed the multiaxial structure for that manual, using several "axes" to represent the various aspects of a person with mental illness. I replied that I wanted to include people's level of functioning into the diagnosis as well as their disorder. Bob quipped, "John, you are always trying to put two things together that are difficult to join." I had never realized that before, but he was totally right. And I am still trying to do it. Now, though, I am engaged in the much bigger effort of trying to figure out how to bring science and the humanities together to get a really adequate picture of what we call mental illness—in short, how to make psychiatry truly a "human science."

When I was about seven we moved to a real house at 4717 Upland Drive in Glenwood. This part of Erie was at the south end of town, higher up in elevation and more upper middle class. We had a real yard there and acquired a small cocker spaniel, "Timmy," and a rabbit. My second-grade teacher was Miss Ripley, whom I adored and who gave me a Christmas card with a large fancy S (for Strauss) on it which she had painted herself. She used to read Greek myths to us in class, which I loved (and still do), and had Brewster Price help me to learn how to tell time. We also had some terrific girls in the class—Helen, Alexa, and Babs—and I was also friendly with Jacques Schuler.

A number of kids in that period had French first names because their fathers had fought in France during the First World War and had loved that country. I had a friend in eighth grade, Raoul Riblet, whose name I think reflected the same thing. My father too had been drafted toward the end of the war but was discharged before being sent overseas.

When I was in fourth grade, so nine years old, we had a man in school who was in general charge of maintenance. He also led a kind of phys ed hour for us in which you could take either boxing or gymnastics. All the boys except me took boxing. I didn't like getting hit in the face so I took gymnastics with the girls. Mr. Haskell taught me how to do a back neck stand. You start on your back and then, with a snakelike movement of your spine and pushing with your hands placed one on each side of your head, you are suddenly standing on your feet. I succeeded once but was never able to repeat it. Mr. Haskell was thin and grey and gaunt with sunken cheeks. He had to spend most of his time out of doors since he had been gassed in the war. I liked Mr. Haskell a lot. When I came back to school to start fifth grade after summer vacation, however, he was no longer there. No one ever explained where he had gone, and I think he probably had died, perhaps the result of his damaged lungs.

We always rented houses that were then sold out from underneath us since Mom didn't want to buy a house, always hoping we would move back to Cleveland. (Mom hated Erie and loved Cleveland and being with her family there. My parents would finally move back, but it was pretty much too late for her.) So after a couple of years at Upland Drive we moved about six blocks away to Cherry Street. I think the house was on the corner of Forty-sixth Street (Upland Drive had been at Forty-seventh, 4717).

The Cherry Street house was smaller than Upland Drive but nice enough. All our houses were about a quarter the size of the houses of my friends here in New Haven with families just a little bigger than ours was. Styles change, but we had plenty of room. The year we moved to Cherry Street Mom and Dad took me out of the Erie Day School. It had been so successful that Erie's social elite had pretty much taken it over and its progressive methods had mostly been trashed. (The names of my mother and Ross Fink are unknown to the current Day School administration, which only recalls the names of some of the original financial contributors.) So, beginning in sixth grade I went to Glenwood public school, and I was pretty happy there. The kids teased me for a while saying that at private school we had very long vacations so "never learned anything." But the teasing was never mean. I did fine and made friends, several of whom I got to know even better over the years as, the school districts being what they were, we all went on from Glenwood to Academy (actually a public junior and senior high). I saw many of them much later at our 50th high school reunion, fewer at our 60th reunion, and fewer still at our 65th.

My recollections of those years include many nice things such as going to the "Peninsula," which reached out into Lake Erie. In the summer we had picnics and went swimming there after Dad finished work. On a winter evening the whole family would drive to a large cabin-like structure with a huge fireplace on the Peninsula where there might be forty or fifty people from around Erie drinking cocoa with marshmallows. You could walk out of the cabin on your skates and, lit by the moonlight reflected off the snow, go skating on the ice in the bay between the Peninsula and the mainland. I had "double runners" (skates with two parallel blades) when I was little and then became a pretty decent (but not terrific) skater when I graduated to "single runners." When I was about fifty I was on sabbatical in Toronto one winter and would skate on a pond not far from the apartment where I lived off of Bloor Street and Spadina. The pond was next to an elementary school, and one day as I was skating I noticed kids from the school watching me approvingly from the windows. Having my skating applauded by Canadian kids—that was impressive.

Dougy Young was one of the friends, a good friend, I made in sixth grade. He lived at the house up the hill diagonally behind ours. We skated on the tiny pond in the woods near his house. I went with him on his paper route, and he regularly would come down the hill to the back of our house to call out loudly, "Hey Johnny!" rather than ringing the bell. Dougy and I would listen to "our programs" on the radio: *Jack Armstrong* at 5:30, *Captain Midnight* at 5:45, followed by *Little Orphan Annie*, and *Terry and the Pirates* after that. We walked home from school together at lunch time, back to school after lunch early so we and some of the other kids could play some baseball before class started, and back home after school. After dinner, kids would come to our house and we would play hide-and-seek in the dark. When the Barnum and Baily circus came to town, they set up their huge tents over at the big vacant lot on Peach Street, about a mile from our house. We would walk down and watch them. Not a bad life!

Of course, there was also the time when Dougy and I walked

from school back home by way of the woods. There, a short distance from the path was a small trailer. Dougy said, "That's where Patty Brower lives." Patty was a beautiful girl in our class, very bright, quiet but well spoken, simply but always nicely dressed, her beautiful smooth brown hair hanging loosely to her shoulders. I was in love with Patty Brower, although of course she never knew it. She was so lovely, and yet she lived like this? The world just isn't right!

We were a Jewish family but, like most Jews in Erie, pretty assimilated. My sister and I attended what was called "Sunday School" at the Temple. Sunday School was mostly okay, as were some of the services, but it was pretty peripheral to my life until Frank Fox became our teacher and taught us about Montaigne, Spinoza, Buddhism, and ethics. More about that later.

Most of my friends at the regular school had other religions. About half the kids were Catholic. One asked me when I had had my first communion, and I told her we didn't have that. So I grew up amid multiple belief systems and found that totally normal.

In our family, we had celebrated both Jewish and Christian holidays. We didn't do anything "religious" on Easter or Christmas, but we did get Easter baskets at Easter, and at Christmas we would drive to Cleveland for our big family holiday. On Christmas Eve we would go to my aunt Ruth's house, where they had a large tree with the same decorations every year. My grandfather, Sambo, would give out the presents to my mother and the other three of his four children and to their eight kids (in total), and we would have a great dinner, all eighteen of us (including Nanny, our grandmother, of course).

My mother would have baked Christmas cookies, Pfeffernüsse, Springerli, and Lebkuchen—all made, of course, using Nanny's recipes. The Lebkuchen were especially wonderful, consisting of two thin strips of dough about one inch by three inches, one on top of the other, with a small amount of dark filling between them, and baked just crisp and slightly brown. Sometimes on Christmas morning, sitting around the smaller tree at Sambo's and Nanny's apartment we would get a few more presents. (Sambo and Nanny lived for a time in a very grand house, which figures prominently in my memory and which I am about to describe. Afterward they moved to an apartment.) Then we might have Schnecken made by aunt Rose, one of Sambo's sisters and a terrific baker. You may know Schnecken as cinnamon buns, but these were probably not like any cinnamon buns you have eaten. The ingredients included pecans and raisins, and the dough was raised twice. I have the recipe and have made them a few times myself. They are a hell of a lot of work, but truly magnificent. You will have noticed that the names of all these baked goods are German, but, of course, I never knew that. They just were what they were.

My attempt to describe growing up Jewish in Erie has become an account of Christmas foods eaten in Cleveland. But that's how it was. Mine was an America of various flavors, and I did not become deeply involved with any particular religion. But I developed strong beliefs nonetheless. I came to know that Andy, the man who collected trash with his cart at Dad's apartments, was as important and good a person as any other, that Bill Reed, the foreman at Dad's apartment and a Catholic, was one of the most skilled and fastest workers anywhere, that Montaigne and Spinoza were brilliant, learned men, and, later, that Quaker meetings can provide a remarkable forum in which people share their ideas, their questions, their solutions, and their beliefs.

THE FAMILY

The family in Cleveland, that was my mother's family. Dad loved
Erie. It was bigger than Loudonville but not too big. He was a figure about town, a member of various boards, and regularly had
lunch at the Lawrence Hotel with "the boys," a group of local men
who bantered and shared their stories. But Mom hated the city—it
was too small and provincial and restrictive for her. As a result, we
were always going to her parents' house in Cleveland—not just at
Christmas and for Sambo's birthday but every couple of weeks. We
would drive through Conneaut and Ashtabula and all those other
towns. On the way home, on Sunday night, it would be getting dark
and we could listen to Jack Benny and Eddie Cantor on the radio
before Susan and I fell asleep in the back seat of the LaSalle. (Later,
we replaced the '38 LaSalle with a Ford because Uncle Art in
Cleveland had a Ford dealership. It came with a sparkplug missing,
but we were lucky to have a working car at all in those years just
after the war.) When I was a little older, I could take the train, with
Susan or even by myself, and Nanny would meet me at the East
Cleveland station. At the end of the visit she would take me down
to the station again and put me on the train. Dad and Mom would
pick me up at Union Station when I got to Erie. Every Sunday when
we weren't in Cleveland Mom would call my aunt Ruthie and the
other family members there, always starting her phone conversation with a loud "Hello, how ARE you?" We teased her for that.

Let me tell you about Sambo and Nanny's house. Actually, my
parents always called it "mother's house," meaning Nanny's house.
It was located on Euclid Avenue, and it was huge. You went up
this long front walk from the sidewalk. (Could it have been a quarter mile long? To a small child, it seemed like it.) You climbed the

steps to get up on the front porch with its big pillars, crossed the porch, and there right in front of you was a massive oak front door. It was a double door, I think—if you opened both doors you could bring in a huge table or a lot of guests all at once. I remember that it had huge brass handles and a gleaming brass knocker, with the head of a lion on it, maybe.

We would come by car and find Sambo and Nanny waiting for us. Probably Nanny would open the door, always with a big smile on her face. She was a tall woman, once an opera singer. She would sit down and haul me up to sit on her copious lap, saying "Now Johnny, what would you like for dinner?" By then Sambo would be across the room, sitting in his big chair, talking to Dad, about the Apartments, or the real estate market, or the coming trip to Florida. Mom and Susan would have gone into the kitchen, with its thick counters and solid dark wood cabinets. There they would be putting out the breads that we had brought from Erie, poppy seed breads and rolls from Kuhnemann's. Although Cleveland had rye bread (with lots of seeds) far better than Erie's, its poppy seed bread was nowhere near as good as Kuhnemann's. I would have left my Superman Comic Book, No. 1, in the car, neatly rolled up, but Dad would soon bring it when he carried our grips in and took them upstairs.

To get upstairs you climbed a giant curved wooden staircase, rather like the stairs at Tara in *Gone with the Wind*. It seemed to go on forever. The bannister on the stairs continued in both directions along an open hallway at the top. You could look through (when I was little) or over the top (when I was bigger) of the ballusters to see the hall downstairs. Off the hallway were all the rooms: Sambo and Nanny's room with its big dark wood bed, the room where Mom and Dad stayed, Herb's bedroom (Herb, my mother's younger brother, eventually moved out to his own apartment), the bedroom where Susan and I would sleep (which had been Mom's sisters'), and the bathroom. The last had an exciting scale with a post that came up to your neck and a cross beam on which you balanced the weights. As soon as we got upstairs Susan and I would race to the bathroom to weigh ourselves—the trick was adjusting the weights so that the cross bar was just even, tilting first a little up and then a little down. Then we would run to our room and jump up and down on the beds. When Mom yelled, "Don't jump on the beds," we would stop and go back downstairs.

Actually, the whole house was a little like Tara. If you turned right at the bottom of those stairs, you saw the dining room with its huge table, big enough to sit ten, maybe twenty people. And off to the right of that was the door to the big kitchen with its six-burner stove and a refrigerator that held enough food for everyone for as long as you stayed. To the left at the bottom of the stairs were huge sliding wooden doors. They moved very easily on their rollers so Susan or I could easily open them up, as though we were pages in the royal court, to reveal the massive living room with a big fireplace way at the far end. Mom said that when they were kids and Sambo and Nanny were having a big party, she and her brother and sisters would open those doors just a little so they could see all the guests dressed so beautifully and all the food. That room, like the whole house, was paneled in natural varnished wood.

Off the living room, through another set of huge sliding doors on the left, was another room, almost as large. In there was a black grand piano. Here, Mom's youngest sister, Ethel, practiced before she gave concerts and sometimes Nanny or the other sister, Ruth, would sing to Ethel's accompaniment. Sometimes, too, Dad would play the piano when we were there. He did it for himself, I think, maybe even a little to escape that family. It was a family that he loved and to which he felt he belonged but that in their

Hungarian-German Jewish intensity could drive almost anyone nuts. But not us, not Susan and me, because we were just kids.

Trolley tracks ran along Euclid Avenue out front. When we went to bed at night for a while we could hear the trolleys running, the grind, grind, grind as they started to move changing slowly to a whistle, and their bells, clang clang, and then pretty soon you wouldn't hear them any more because you were asleep.

Out back of Sambo's house was a great tree, apple I think. Susan and I would climb it. Sometimes I would look up at her since she was a much better climber than me and say "I can see your underpants" (under her print cotton dress). Then she would get angry and try to step on my hand hanging onto a branch near her foot, but she was just pretending, she wouldn't ever really do that. Sometimes we would swing on the tire swing. Other times we would just run around the yard.

Next door lived the Rudds—of Chandler and Rudds, the famous candy store. And next to them, is it possible, lived someone named Rockefeller. That family was very rich and very important.

And, of course, Sambo too was rich, if not in the Rockefeller league. But he didn't begin life that way. He had been born in Cleveland, where his mother ran a grocery store. His father deserted the family, and Sambo had to quit school in the "eighth reader" to drive the horse drawn cart with which they delivered groceries. I have no knowledge of what happened after that until somehow he became a violinist in the Cleveland Symphony and then formed several dance orchestras. (When Dad and I were at Sambo's funeral, Dad turned to me and said, "See those men at the back of the room, they are all players from Sambo's orchestras who came after all these years.") Sambo went from his music and dance orchestras into real estate. He became a millionaire when that was even more of a thing than it is today. He lost it all, mostly in a bunch of coal mines during the Depression, and became distraught and depressed, then made it all back. He loved deep-sea fishing with his friend Ed Flanagan in Florida.

Sambo—how did he get that name? Only his family called him that. His real name was Samuel, and his friends called him Sam. His youngest daughter, Ethel, called him "Hambone" when she was little so maybe it evolved from that.

Sambo was a big person physically. He was a heavy-set man, not really fat, about six feet tall, I think. His hair was grey, and, in the time when I remember him most clearly, he had a little trouble walking, though he walked with deliberation anyway. He didn't talk much. He would give occasional directions of what you needed to do, make brief comments about politics, medicine, or whatever ("Those doctors, what do they know?"), and maybe tell some old jokes (A man was asked by the druggist if he should put his order of Carter's Little Liver Pills in a bag, and the man replied, "What do you want me to do, roll them home?"). Yet despite his sparse talking, he was a real presence. I think of him as a nineteenth century Victorian American, a pretty quiet guy but you knew he was the center of everything.

THE ISLAND

Some of my most vivid memories of Sambo come from "The Island" so it is definitely time to introduce you to this incredible place. As I was growing up, we spent at least two, sometimes as many as seven or eight weeks of each summer at "The Island." I started going up there with my family when I was three and went up every year thereafter. I absolutely loved it. When I was in my late teens

I had my canoe there, knew my way among the islands near us, and built a dock for the island "across the way," where Sambo and Nanny—and later I—stayed. I played my flute at the Island (which other people told me they loved to hear), listened to the whippoorwill at sunset, went for a morning swim, and came back late at night from long evenings with Émue sitting on the huge rock at Lee's and talking about *Peter Ibbetson*. I read *Moby Dick* and *War and Peace* on the large screened-in front porch of the Clubhouse. I skinned a rattle snake, having always been afraid of them, went in the woods with Joe, the Indian who worked for us, and canoed with Winnie, a part-Indian girl who taught me some Ojibway and gave me the name of Kiash Koonz (little seagull). I also took people, especially Sambo, out fishing, won the Georgian Bay Creamery Cup awarded for the swimming race at the Parry Sound Regatta, and on and on and on.

The place we called "The Island" was actually a group of three that my grandfather bought in 1918 from the Canadian government. This is the story: In 1918 my grandfather and two of his fishing buddies were looking for a place to go. From Cleveland, they drove up to Penetanguishene, about one hundred and forty miles north of Toronto. How did they know how to go there? How did a Jewish guy who grew up poor in Cleveland get rich enough to even think of going up there? Well, I've told you all I know about that. Mostly it's a mystery and quite extraordinary that three poor Jewish guys, or even fairly comfortable Jewish guys, from Cleveland, should have found their way there. But they did.

They went by way of Toronto, then Barrie, then sooner or later on dirt roads through Orillia and Gravenhurst, a sequence of towns I know by heart since I did it most every year from the time I was three to the time I was seventy or so. At Penetanguishene, more comfortably known as Penetang, the three men rented a boat and traveled up the east side of Georgian Bay (a bay actually the size of Lake Erie, on the eastern edge of Lake Huron) through the 30,000 islands that exist there until they got to the town of Parry Sound. Then they continued by boat across the bay in front of Parry Sound, out to Two Mile Narrows, another bay, and then Five Mile Narrows, a bit farther on, and turned right at Bears Head, an island. Here the channel is technically no longer going out from Parry Sound but heading in, according to the channel markers. That is, the markers (poles planted in the bottom of the channel and poking about three feet above the water with either red flat tops or green pointed ones) changed so that they were no longer "red left out [leaving Parry Sound], red right return [going toward Parry Sound]" but just the opposite. Anyway, our adventurers turned right at Bear's Head, past the Pines, and a little bit farther on but before Moore's, turned right again down a channel. There, past the island called Falthea, were the islands that became known to us as "The Island." These three guys bought the large island and two other smaller ones that formed a kind of bay with it (a total land area of about twenty-five acres, I guess) from the Canadian government for one dollar (Canadian) for each island. The government was essentially giving them away to encourage people to settle there. You just had to build something on each island.

Very soon after that initial trip, Sambo bought out his two partners in what they had called the "Cleveland Island Club." These were business guys from Cleveland, after all, and the year was 1918— you didn't think they'd call it "Paradise" or something like that, did you? But it was paradise. In 1953 I drove Sambo up to "The Island" (or "Canada," as we also called it—sorry!) and then needed to leave in a couple days to sail to Europe, to Paris. Sambo said, "What do you need to go to Paris for? What could be more beautiful than this?" He was right, pretty much nothing was more beautiful than "this," but I needed Paris too.

There is so much to tell you about "The Island." On the main island Sambo built a large building called "The Clubhouse" along with three or four other smaller cabins. Perhaps a hundred yards away was a smaller island where my grandparents had a small house. But it had no facilities of any kind, and when they got older, they no longer stayed there. So, I began to stay there myself. I built a dock for that island, and I had my own canoe, which later became a sail canoe.

The Clubhouse was the center of our activities. It was a very square basic, simple wooden building, dirty yellow in color, consisting most importantly of a huge "living room." Part of that room (beyond some square-shaped wooden pillars helping to hold up the second floor) was a large dining area containing two long simple wooden tables, big enough to seat about twelve people each, and a Buck stove that gave out a prodigious amount of heat, needed when the weather started to get cold toward the end of August. Just to finish the description of downstairs: Next to the Buck stove was an old wind-up Victrola that stood up from the floor, as much a fixture of the place as anything else. Against the wall at the back of this area was a staircase to the second floor, and beyond the wall was the kitchen. That long narrow room had an ice box (not a refrigerator—we didn't have electricity until I was about twelve, so in 1944) and a large wood stove topped with metal plates on which the food was cooked. If I remember correctly, the plates could be lifted to throw in the wood that someone had chopped. Beside the stove was a small sink and a hand pump that drew up water from the "Drink," as we called our area of the lake, which was really a thin arm of Georgian Bay.

Upstairs was a series of small rooms off both sides of a long narrow hall. Each room was big enough for two plain cast-iron beds and two plain wood nightstands. Although the rooms had doors, their walls were just wallboard about seven feet high, not reaching the ceiling (actually the rafters of the roof) and thus really being open to the whole second floor. I slept there for several years after I was old enough to stay separately from my parents. They had one of three simple cottages on the Island, the others being occupied by my aunt Ruth's family, the Markuses, and, in the other direction from the Clubhouse, by the "help." All the cottages were connected to the Clubhouse by a boardwalk.

Other buildings? One section of the boardwalk ended in a Y configuration, the arms leading to two outhouses, a one-holer for the women and a two-holer for the men. I guess the idea was that the women were too proper for two to use the outhouse at the same time. Also, just behind the Clubhouse was another icebox, bigger than the inside one, and snuggled nearby in the woods, was the ice house, a large plain building of blackened wood, about one third full of sawdust many feet deep covering huge blocks of ice. Hanging from a nail on the back of the icehouse door was a large pair of ice tongs, a magical hinged X-shaped tool whose handles you could pull apart to have the teeth on the opposite ends bite into an ice block. If you were strong enough you could carry the block that way by one arm all the way to the icebox.

Across the front of the Clubhouse was a huge screened-in porch. You could sit there and see out along that last channel I took you through, past the Pines, past Mrs. Moore's to the Umbrellas, islands way out there, and then out to the "Open" and beyond to infinity. When I slept upstairs in the Clubhouse, I also had this view from the small window under the eave of the roof—out the channel, past the islands, all the way to the Open. Amazing!

Georgian Bay is too big to be able to see across to the other side.

In our little sheltered corner, however, our three islands formed a kind of large C so that directly across the small bay in front of the Clubhouse you could see the island on which Sambo and Nanny had built their own small house. Early in the morning you could see them coming across to our main island in a small row boat. When the water level was low you could walk parallel to our tiny bay, through the woods and find the shallow spots between the islands that allowed you to walk to "Nanny's Island." Then you could see the Clubhouse from "across the way," a neat thing to do.

Something else to know about the Island: After you leave Gravenhurst to go the fifty miles to Parry Sound the land starts to change from more or less ordinary farmland to what is called the "Canadian Shield." I don't remember the geology, but I think what you are seeing in this landscape of rocks and forest is an exposed portion of the continental crust, a plate of the solid, very ancient rock that underlies all of North America. This is what the islands on the west side of Georgian Bay are made from. So, for example, the Clubhouse sits on a huge mass of rock that extends with various rises and falls all the way down to the water. The "house across the way" (on Nanny's Island) also sits on a huge mass of rock. This is visibly at least a hundred yards in diameter and presumably extends under the moss and then the woods beyond. In sum, you know this place isn't going anywhere. This is part of the stability the Island offered me. You got to know these rocks, where the best places to sit were, where there were depressions to avoid after a rain, things like that. I can still feel it all.

What happened there? As I said, I started going there when I was three. I don't recall anything from that early, but I do from a couple of years later. When I was about five I fell off the dock. Oh, I forgot to tell you that down below the Clubhouse where the high rock it sat on met the water were our docks. They consisted of simple wood planks nailed one next to another on the under-lying wooden framework. There was a slip with two long "arms," between which you put the big boat. Smaller boats were tied to cleats on the outer side of the "arms"—row boats, outboard motor boats, and in my teens my canoe and my Sunfish sailboat. So, my first memory of the Island: aged about five, I was running on the dock and I skidded into the water. It was only about four feet deep there, but I didn't know how to swim. Suddenly I was seized by a pair of hands. Lila Cook, the beautiful young wife of Bob Cook, pulled me out of the water. She had been walking by higher up on the rock, had seen me go into the water, and rushed down to pull me out of the water. She saved my life.

Lila and Bob were friends of my aunt Ruth and came to the Island several years in a row. One year when we were celebrating my birthday, which is in August, the Cooks came out with a case of Best on Earth peanut butter as a present for me. They had brought it up to the Island specially. Funny, what one remembers. I have loved peanut butter for as long as I can remember. I still do. I make my own now. Something else I remember: Several years later, when the Cooks were up again and a few of us were in the water (I could swim by then), the top part of Lila's two-piece bathing suit slipped off. She had beautiful breasts.

When I slept in the Clubhouse after I was 12 or so, I would be awakened in the morning by the sound of Joe, our Ojibway guide, starting a fire in the Buck stove downstairs. Then I would hear music. Joe would wind up the Victrola and play "September in the Rain," "Flat Foot Floogie," or others of his favorites. I can still hear them. And now you can find them on You Tube, the same old music.

And those memories of Sambo on the Island: A special one was going into town (Parry Sound) with him. Every week we would take our wonderful Chris-Craft, the *Scram*, in to buy food and do errands for the twenty or so family members or friends who might be staying on the Island. I loved that boat. It was big, maybe twenty-eight feet, and the fastest boat in the area. Sambo had bought it from some rum runners. But it was a stupid boat to have for us because what we needed was a boat to carry a fair number of people and all the groceries for those people for a week. The *Scram* had two rows of bench seats that could fit maybe three people each. Behind these were the big Chrysler marine engines and at the very back of the boat another seat for two people. It was a beautiful boat, mahogany with red leather seats.

We docked at Scott's boat livery. Scotty, who was a heavy-set man with white hair and well in command of his small empire, would smile broadly and greet my grandfather, "Well, hello Sam," and they would enter into a brief discussion about the weather, how many five-gallon cans of gas we needed for the outboards, problems with the *Scram,* and whether Scotty could ask Hitchy (Mitchell) to come by the Island since we had a water pump that wasn't working right.

Sambo would then get the car from the lot—or, once I was sixteen and had my license, I would get it—and off we would go. There was a regular route: Waggs' laundry to drop off laundry from the Island and pick up what had been brought there the week before; Campbell's drug store for medicines, newspapers (no phone, no radio at the Island in those early days), and (for me) a Canadian comic book with washed-out colors; several other stores as needed; and then lunch at the Georgian Bay Creamery with its small neat restaurant, where we would also buy milk for them to put in a large box with ice to keep it cold.

After lunch we would go on to the A&P, and that was really special. I would walk next to Sambo as he did the aisles, checking things off his shopping list, and then, with that finished, we'd go to the meat counter. The head of the meat section would say "Hi Sam, you want to go into the cooler?" Sambo would say yes, and we would all go into the cold room. There he would pick out twenty to forty pounds of various kinds of meats, all the while teaching me how to pick out marbled meat for steaks and other lore, stuff he had learned in his mother's grocery store. Leaving the A&P, we would pick up the milk from the Georgian Bay Creamery and return to Scott's. We'd be back at the Island by the late afternoon.

In all that time I'm not sure that Sambo uttered more than a hundred and fifty words, but his presence was powerful. Years later, long after he and all his children had died, a group of the grandchildren, my cousins and I, were up at the Island in a kind of reunion. Of course, we had to go to the A&P to get food for our stay. Two of my cousins and I did the shopping together. We suddenly realized that we were all following the same route through the aisles together, looking for the same things (Dad's oatmeal cookies, for example), and were shocked to realize, although we ranged over a ten-year gamut in age, we had all gone shopping there with Sambo and had all picked up his habits.

Another routine I shared with Sambo was fixing the boardwalk together. We talked very little. I remember this from when he was pretty old. We'd go to the boat house to get the tools— crowbar, hand saw, pencil, hammer, nails, and pine boards, ten feet long, six inches wide, one inch thick. Then we'd go to the boardwalk and find the places he had noticed rotting boards. We'd pry one up, mark its length on the long pine board, saw the new board, and nail it to where the old one had been. Then we'd go on to the next and the next until we had done all the ones that needed to be replaced.

And I think he was proud of me. That summer when I built the dock for "Nanny's Island," it was not a trivial job—a lot of work, in fact. When I was finished, I wanted to paint the top of it, and

Sambo said he would pay for the paint. So, I got green and white paint and created a swirl effect. I had a green and white swirl dock. I don't think I've ever seen another like it.

Sambo paid a lot of attention to detail. At dinner time, for example, a bell, a real ship's bell, would signal a fifteen-minute warning. At the sound of the second bell, we would all gather at the tables. Sambo would come in from the kitchen, where he had been helping with the cooking over the huge wood stove, the food would be served, and we would start to eat. Sambo sat at the head of one of the tables, and I often sat two or three people down the bench from him. He might say, "Johnny, don't eat all of one thing before you go on to another. Take a little of potato, then some peas, then some meat." I would say "OK" and go through one cycle as he ordered before returning to my previous pattern of eating all of each in turn. He wouldn't say anything. I guess our relationship was a little like that. We really liked each other, but neither of us was too flexible. At home our wonderful housekeeper Martha, who lived with us and was pretty much like a substitute mother for me, would get really upset with me and say, "Sometimes you would just drive a man to drink!" She was probably right.

But I'm getting ahead of myself with Martha. I have one more thing to say here about Sambo and the Island. Perhaps it will be no surprise to hear that he could be aggravatingly severe. When I was seventeen my parents asked me to drive him up to the Island. He drove himself as usual from Cleveland to Erie and stayed overnight at our house. Then I joined him and took over the driving. The final stretch of the road, the fifty miles from Gravenhurst to Parry Sound, was still a dirt road at that time. Half way we got a flat. When Sambo was going to the Island, his car, both the trunk and the back seat, was always jammed with stuff he was taking up there—plates, tools, food, blankets, pillows, whatever—so I knew this was going to be a mess. I pulled over to the side of the road and we got out. He was pretty old at that point and suffered from some congestive heart failure from a rheumatic heart-valve problem he got when he was a kid. That meant I did all the work of emptying that heap of stuff from the trunk, getting the spare and the tools out, jacking up the car, removing the tire, putting on the new tire, putting all the stuff back in the trunk. It was a hot day, and by the time I was finished I was a mess. He looked at me and said, "Now look at how dirty you've gotten." That was all. There was a lot more I could have said, but I held my tongue.

BACK TO CLEVELAND

The Island was, and still is, a part of me, and I will have much more to say about it. But it was also very much being with "The Family," just in another venue, not Cleveland. In Cleveland, after the early years of staying at Sambo and Nanny's house, I used to stay with Ruth, my Mom's sister, and Eddie Markus. Eddie, Jr., my oldest cousin, was four years younger than me, and I would sleep in one of the twin beds in his room. I got to feel pretty comfortable there. In fact, the Markuses' telephone number is one of the few I remember. Eddie's younger brother Bobby kept it after their parents died and has it to this day, Longacre 1 XXXX.

I was probably a bad influence on Eddie, Jr. Usually we behaved, but one time we put pennies on the "rapid" (fast street car) tracks to see them being crushed flat. It was an old trick but a dangerous one, partly because the penny could shoot out as a flying missile. In our case, we were told that Uncle Art (actually my grandmother's half-brother), who had a wooden leg, had lost his real leg when he was run over by a streetcar. We didn't do that anymore.

Mom's other sister, Ethel, a fine pianist who taught piano, had a car with a rumble seat. She would take Susan and me for rides, and the two of us would sit in that seat. You may not even know what a rumble seat is. At the back of a car, a lid opened to reveal not a trunk but a seat for two people, out in the open air. Really neat! Probably also dangerous, but of course we loved it.

One way and another I spent a lot of time in Cleveland over the years. For a couple of winters I also stayed with parts of the Family in Miami Beach, where we lived free for a month or so because the owner of the motel-like place owed Sambo money. And, of course, being at the Island was also being with the Family. The last time I was in Cleveland for a longish period was after graduating from Swarthmore. Yale Medical School had the requirement that you had to have taken a course in English composition. I had never done this at Swarthmore, and I was not smart enough (am usually still not) to question such things so enrolled in a summer session in Cleveland at Western Reserve University. I stayed with my uncle, Herb, who was very serious and very competent and I loved that. He was wonderful to me, let me borrow his car to go out on dates, and was kind in every way. I learned somehow halfway through the session that since I had been in the honors program at Swarthmore, where we wrote a paper every week, I didn't need to take that course. When I stopped going, Herb sat me down and asked me why I had quit, concerned that I might be doing what my mother had done when she had dropped out of college. No, I said, I had learned that I didn't need it and of course I had graduated from college and was now going to be starting medical school. He understood.

While I was staying at Herb's I learned you could keep bread longer by putting it in the refrigerator and I took courses in Solfège and Piano at the Cleveland Conservatory. It was an interesting time for me and a very different world. I went out with a couple girls from the Big City. They came from fairly wealthy Jewish Cleveland families and were not like the girls at Swarthmore. Herb died unexpectedly many years later after coronary-artery surgery. He developed hiccoughs afterwards and for some reason couldn't be saved. I went to his funeral and was fine until after they buried him. While returning to the car, I broke down suddenly in sobs.

A year or so ago I attended a family reunion in Cleveland. I hadn't been back there since my father's funeral twenty-three years earlier, in 1995. Mom and Dad had moved back to Cleveland when he retired, aged about sixty-five. It was pretty much too late for Mom. Eventually they lived in a retirement complex, where one time they got a room for me when I was in town to give to give some lectures at the Western Reserve Psychiatry Department. They came to those lectures. Dad told me that Mom blurted out in the middle of one, "This is the worst thing I ever heard." She was pretty senile by then. Maybe she was right, but I hope not.

A few months before Dad's death there had been another reunion. Dad and my kids, Jeff and Sarah, and Jeff's little daughter Sophie (now twenty-six) were there. Mom had died earlier the same year, but, unlike Dad, she had been senile for at least two years. As I began to say a few words about Dad, he interrupted to read a story he'd written for the reunion. It was about Elmer the Whale. When we were little, Dad had told stories about Elmer the Whale to me and Susan and, as the years passed, to all my cousins when we were up at the Island. Now he was having troubles with his hearing and his eyesight and his friends were dying. Did I know Bernie someone, he asked when I visited him. No, I said. "Well, he died," said Dad. And he himself would die of a brain tumor a few months later. At his funeral I quoted his saying that "This was a very unusual family. Not a stinker in the crowd."

The recent reunion was wonderful and very emotional for me. It was beautifully organized. The first evening brought all of us together, and practically all the currently living members of the extended family were there, gathered from Colorado, Florida, California, Connecticut (me), and of course Cleveland, where the majority still live. Three generations in all and, of course, memories of the two generations no longer with us. We still have many things in common. I have known some of these people for years. My cousin David picked me up at the airport—at eight o'clock in the morning—and took me to breakfast. As we ate he told me how wonderful my mother had been to him and his sister when their mother, my aunt Ethel, had died so young from breast cancer.

The rest of the reunion was pretty much like that too. I talked with people of my own generation and the next one down and saw their kids. It was really terrific, very moving. My life has moved on into a very different world, but Cleveland is a page that has been torn out to save and reread—revisit. Just as David and his sister found a support in my mother, I and my sister were sustained by the Family through many difficult years. And the Island, which I have continued to visit throughout my life and to which I will return in this narrative, has been a rock of stability.

Just a few more words about the Family: As I have worked on this book my editor has occasionally suggested things that make me realize or understand things in a new way. For example, in introducing my grandfather, I had originally said something to the effect of "We never called him anything but Sambo. "We" who's we? She changed that to "Only the family called him Sambo." And, yes, "we" was the Family. But it was a simple connection I hadn't made. I knew it all along, just as I know that grass is green or the sky is blue. No one ever told me, I just knew it. That's how the world was, we called him Sambo. But when my editor put in that sentence, I was shocked that I had never thought about it, had never put it into words, although somewhere inside me I knew it—like I knew the grass is green, more than that even.

So what's the big whoop? I had a patient once who was born and raised on Nantucket. I was amused one day when she recounted something to me and called people who were not from Nantucket, "off-islanders." So she identified with a group of a couple of thousand people on Nantucket (which for her was more or less the world), and the other several billion or so people in the rest of the world were so shadowy that she thought of them only as the "others," those who were not "islanders."

The name "Sambo" for my grandfather showed the same thing. "We" belonged, everyone else in the world didn't. There was this tight little boundary around "us" that gave us an identity, connections to each other, a meaning, and all you other people out there, you're OK, but you're not "us." Oh, my god, yes, it's true. That's how I felt and I never noticed it. That's what writing an autobiography is like.

A CHANGE IN
OUR LIVES

Not a bad life, right? Except. . . . When I was about twelve or thirteen—neither Susan nor I can remember the exact time—all hell
began to descend on our family. Up at the Island the previous summer I remember seeing my aunt Ethel, my mother's youngest and
especially lovely and musical sister, with a wide bandage around
her chest. Sometime the next year she died, and then my grandmother did too, also of breast cancer. I have described how close
these people were to me. My father's parents had died when he was
nineteen. Dad had a very nice younger brother, Raymond (whose
middle initial was N which he said stood for "Nertz"), who lived
in Cleveland and who sold fine linens for "Uncle Max," who lived
in New York and whom I met only once. But "the Family" was my
mother's family, and the deaths of these close relatives were terrible losses. And some time not long after Ethel and Nanny had died,
at least by my recollection, I was sitting at our dining-room table
and two men in a black car came to the house and took Mom away
to a hospital in New York.

I don't remember when I learned it, but it was to a psychiatric hospital, part of New York Hospital—Cornell. She had been to a "diagnostician" in Cleveland and then taken to New York. Maybe someone explained things to Susan and me, but as I said before, that whole period was all pretty much a blank to both of us and remains so. There was no real discussion about it, no counselor to help us work things out, as might happen now. It is wonderful now what people sometimes do. We were a German Jewish family, and there was a lot of stuff we didn't talk about. In a way that works well, and in a way it's terrible.

And something else happened about the same time. We had a friend, Walter Strauss, a much beloved young German refugee who had come to Erie with two others as a result of an affadavit that my father and some friends filed. Walter decided he should pay the country back and joined the army, which the other two did not. Before he left to go overseas Walter gave me his little table radio, which I kept at my bedside, and his sergeant's stripes. Then we got word that he had been killed on a French beach the day after D Day. As the woman in *Grandes Illusions* said of a German victory in the First World War, "They said that battle was a grand victory. My husband was killed in it." The Normandy invasion was, of course, a victory, but we lost our Walter.

While Mom was still in New York we moved to a house on the east side of Erie, the second row of houses from the lake. It was a nice though not fancy place, but it was miles away from the neighborhood I had known. We knew no one. Mom had always bought us the best kids books, the Oz books, and for me, the Burgess books about Jimmy Skunk and the rest, and somehow during the move these all got lost. I had just started junior high at Academy High School with all my buddies from Glenwood School. Dad was a member of the Erie School Board at that time but thought he should not use his influence to have me stay at Academy, so I switched to East Junior High.

As I mentioned, no one ever explained to us what mental illness was. Nor did any one counsel Dad about having his life turned upside down, on how to deal with the kids, or much else. We all managed, but it was not fun. I remember sitting in class one day in eighth grade when the teacher was telling us about an assignment. She looked in my direction and said in a kindly voice, "It's OK, John, we know about your mother." I felt acknowledged and soothed but then realized that she wasn't talking to me but to John Salvatore, who sat right behind me. In those years I developed a kind of sinusitis and was blowing my nose all the time. I took two big handkerchiefs to school and filled them up with gunk. Nobody ever teased me, but it must have been pretty disgusting. It finally occurred to me a few years ago that maybe it was my way of crying without crying. Anyway, it cleared up by itself after a couple of years.

MARTHA

But thank heavens, there were some very important good things. A major one was that Dad hired a maid or housekeeper (Dad always insisted on the latter label) called Martha, who lived with us and was a godsend for me. I'm not sure exactly when Martha came to us. It was either just before or just after we moved. The point is, she was there around the time of the latest of many moves—this time to the other end of the earth, so it seemed, or from the west side to the east side of Erie. Mother was not there; she had gone to the hospital in New York a little before. It was Susan and me, Dad and Martha.

Martha Shroeder was from a German farm family that lived outside of Erie. (Erie is surrounded by small farms and little towns, and Dad would take us annually to the Wattsburg Fair, which we all loved. It reminded him of the Loudonville Fair, which was held where he grew up. He took Susan and me to the Loudonville Fair once. It was great—even had a balloon ascension.) Beyond the fact that Martha had been raised on a farm and never married, I knew almost nothing about her—except how good a person she was. Although I didn't realize it at the time, I think she became like a second mother to me. I was very lucky!

Martha didn't talk much but she was always a warm presence. She woke me up in the morning to get ready for school. She was there fixing the meal or cleaning the kitchen while I ate breakfast and listened to classical music from CJBC from across the lake in Canada. She said goodbye to me when I went to get my bike out of the garage (a Raleigh "skinny tire" bike that some of the kids made fun of, not like a rugged Rollfast American bike). She was there when I rode my bike home from East and later the three miles plus from Academy High, to which I transferred back after my one year "to try it" at East.

She made me an after-school peanut-butter-and-jelly sandwich and poured me a big glass of milk. I ate and drank these in the breakfast nook that was part of the kitchen and exchanged a few words and comments with Martha as she worked at the sink.

Is a physical presence a thing? When it is a lovely caring person in the room with you day after day, you bet it is. Martha would sometimes tell me what was going on at the Wright's house next door, which she could see into from our window over the sink. Or she might mention that one of the huge ore boats that traverse the Great Lakes was passing across the sliver of lake you could see between the two houses across the street. She was there—quietly, reliably, competently there in her plain Mother Hubbard cotton dresses, with her curly hair, her wire-rimmed glasses, her plain face with its rather large hooked nose, and her undistinguished bodily frame.

I never knew, and probably never asked, much about the farm just outside Waterford where she grew up. I didn't know what her family was like. I did know, because of her name, that her family originally came from Germany, and she went to the Lutheran church some Sundays, as did many people in Erie who weren't Polish or Italian. Otherwise, I neither knew nor asked where she went on her day off. I don't know if she had dated or almost married, what she thought of school, or if she read anything. She sometimes used local ways of speaking and incorrect grammar, though nothing like "ain't," which Sambo did. She liked to say, "You'd drive a man to drink" when she got mad at my stubbornness, and I'd reply, "Good thing you're not a man." But we would get over it pretty quickly and be friends again.

Martha's presence—that warmth, that quiet dependability, that kindness—may have saved my life. Susan, after all, was soon gone at college. Dad was at work all day—and a man. Martha was always present, always there. All that being together, so few words. I think she got some of the anger I felt from being "deserted" by my mother. I also believe she knew how much I cared for her, but I never told her, and while I was away at my second year of college she died. My parents didn't tell me until well after the funeral. I would so have wanted to go at least to that. I'm not sure but I think my mother was jealous of Martha, with whom I connected so much better than with her. Down deep I was unable to forgive my mother until many years later. Of course, it was not her fault, but since I didn't know I was angry and no one was around to help us, that is one of the things that can happen when you have no guidance and everyone just does the best they can.

VALUABLE LESSONS

East Junior High was pretty much a catastrophe educationally. It served the poorer section of town, and the teachers, except Mrs. Sourwine, who was good, were pretty much happy to get through the day. Tekla O'Neil, I recall, would put the day's assignment up on the blackboard and read movie magazines during the class. But I made friends. Chuck Griewahn lived three blocks from me. His father was an engineer, a real engineer, the kind who drove steam engines, and knew how to fix everything. My father was a wonderful piano player, which I didn't appreciate until I was fifteen, but he didn't know how to fix or make anything.

About my dad and the piano and me: My bedroom was the sunroom off the living room, which was fine with me—tons of windows and light. However, every night after dinner when he didn't have a meeting, Dad played Chopin, Brahms, or Shubert at the baby grand piano in the living room. (Although we lived humbly in many respects, we had some pretty fancy furniture—Mom's influence, of course. For example, we had all our regular meals at a dining room table of beautiful maple, matched by a sideboard. Actually, Mom and Dad both loved fine things—fine food, fine silver, fine furniture, fine literature, fine art, fine music.) When Dad played that baby grand in the evening, it intruded on my treasured space and I would go quietly crazy. For some years it was just invasive noise. But then all of a sudden it wasn't. It was beautiful, and I would sit on the living room couch and listen to Dad sight-read Beethoven, Brahms, Bach, and Gilbert and Sullivan, to which he sang along. In a way his skill at the keyboard also drove me nuts because I was and am a multiple-try failure at the piano, especially in comparison to him. But when Dad was playing, say Chopin, he might turn to me and say, "Now listen to this, Johnny. He changes just one little note and the whole feeling changes." And he would play it over, a part where a ballade changes from minor to major. And he was right, the whole thing changed with one little note. Amazing! Wonderful!

Some evenings Fritz Mahler would come over for dinner. Fritz, the nephew of Gustav, was a fine musician and conductor of the Erie Philharmonic, which was not as bad as you might think. He loved Martha's prune whip and told her it was a symphony. After dinner Fritz and Dad would play Beethoven and other music four hands. To this very day I have an old piano. I still can't play, but once in a while a friend who can comes over and sits down at it. Live piano music in the house again. It fills me with joy.

Chuck Griewahn and I would do all kinds of stuff. We discovered with my chemistry set that if you mix two acids together in a test tube the liquid bubbles and steams and breaks through the test tube and leaves a large brown spot on Chuck's driveway that is impossible to clean off. (I realized many years later that our mixture was the notoriously corrosive aqua regia.) Chuck and I also learned that if a rowboat washes up on the lakeshore near your house after a storm, you can cut down a young tree for a mast, get a sheet for a sail, and a board for a rudder, and with a good offshore breeze head out into the lake. We further discovered that when dinnertime is approaching and you want to head back to shore, you can turn the boat around but that offshore breeze continues to blow you toward the open lake. (Lake Erie is twenty miles across and shallow so known for its sudden rough water in storms—something else I learned later.) On this occasion, Chuck and I rowed like crazy back toward the shore and managed to arrive totally exhausted in time for dinner at our respective houses. I'm not sure either of us told our parents about our afternoon. "What did you do this afternoon?" "Oh, not much, just fussed around." Yet another piece of knowledge acquired later: We had needed a keel or center board. But our adventure taught me at the time an even more important lesson: Bodies of water are really a big deal. They could even kill you if you don't know what you're doing.

My scientific experiments continued. I ascertained that you could make gun powder from ingredients bought at certain drug stores and that you could put the gun powder into a cannon made from lead pipe and sealed at one end with lead solder leaving only a hole for a fuse. The final discovery in this case was that when you exploded the gun powder it could rip the pipe open and make enough noise to get neighbors to call your mother. The explosion might also have the power to kill you if you didn't run away fast and far enough after you lit the fuse. This was something else I only tried once. It's amazing that kids live long enough to become adults.

My year at East taught me some other lessons about life. The school was in the middle of the poorer section of Erie, and there were some rough people around. I literally bumped into Ray Grieves once in the hall, and he turned on me. Everyone knew he was the toughest kid in the class and you didn't cross him. He started to clobber me, and I started to try to defend myself, a hopeless task, but then a friend of his said, "Aw Ray, let him go." He did, actually smiling at me pleasantly as he turned away. Was I ever relieved!

There were many Russians among the dock workers who lived

in the area, and I became friends with Chouka Orloff. (We had a friend, Filmore Biletnikoff, whose cousin was "Bamby" Biletnikoff, the wide receiver for the San Francisco 49ers and one of the most graceful football players ever.) One day Chouka invited me over to his house. I had never seen such a place. Spotlessly clean, with pictures of family members adorning the walls and the mantlepiece, and chock full of furniture, including overstuffed chairs upholstered in black velvet, each with its little lace antimacassar on top of the back. Chouka's grandmother had made cream rolls that day—they were among the finest things I had ever tasted.

I think that was also the year Frank Fox had become our Sunday School teacher. (Remember: I explained about our Jewish Sunday School earlier.) My friend Bob and I were in the same class, and we had a series of not very great teachers who were doing it just from trying to be helpful. Then one day, a new teacher! Frank Fox. Frank worked as a salesman at a cheap jewelry store on lower State Street, but his true calling was teaching. That first day he said, "OK, we're not going to pay too much attention to the textbook [something called *When the Jewish People was Young*], but we're going to talk about many things." So he started teaching us about Spinoza and Montaigne and communism and Buddhism and morality. He had been in the army and, he said, the problem with someone in the barracks who steals is not so much that guys lose stuff but that everyone becomes suspicious and feels they can't count on the other guys. The problem is the loss of trust. Frank became like god to Bob and me. We sometimes went over to his house and sat around and talked. I bought second-hand copies of Spinoza and Montaigne. Oh, my heavens, there are people like that who have really thought!

Unlike the situation with Martha, whom I never told how important she was to me, I did have the opportunity with Frank.

When I was 51, just divorced and living in a tiny apartment in someone's house, I heard from Dad that Frank Fox was dying of cancer. He gave me Frank's phone number, and I called him. Frank was bedridden, and his voice was very weak. I told him that he had been one of the most important people in my life and how much I had gotten from knowing him. I also told him I was a professor now at Yale Medical School. Some Erie folk were very worldly and not impressed by anything, but many others were small-town people for whom teaching at Yale was a big deal. Frank was a small-town person who also happened to be brilliant. He was clearly very grateful for the call, and it was a great gift to me that I could do it.

After that one year at East, Dad used his School Board clout to get me back to Academy even though we didn't live in its area. I had to ride my bike three or four miles, most of it up a steep hill, to get there. Did I really then spend the day at school smelling of sweat? Yes. But with my old friends and new ones I settled in happily. Well, the first year was still pretty tough. I remember reading my copy of Spinoza's *Ethics* as I walked from class to class. It's amazing, but the kids didn't tease me about that. Actually, come to think of it, Spinoza helped get me through that first year back. Imagine this guy from seventeenth century Holland reaching all that way across time to Erie, Pennsylvania, just to help this kid whose family situation had gotten all screwed up!

Being back at Academy got better and better. I had friends and joined the swimming and water polo teams, a fairly big deal there. In fact, I was captain of the swimming team when we won the Pennsylvania state championships my senior year. This was not because of me particularly. I was pretty good, but our star was a tall wonderful swimmer named Johnny Sampson, who was really great. I did well in classes, learned to drive, and went out with some really nice girls. Dinner for two at the Den, a nice but not fancy restaurant, cost $5.50—is that possible?—and was really not bad! My first date after I got my driver's license was with Marilyn Larson, a pretty and very nice cheerleader. I was so anxious I developed a nervous cough and pretty much ruined the occasion.

My friend Bob and I also joined the debating team. We did well at several regional tournament, even the one where I mistakenly left half of the notes for my speech on my chair in the audience and in the middle of speaking had to leave the podium to retrieve them and then return to continue the speech. We were two of the four students who gave talks at commencement. Mine was on what the individual needed to do to find his way between big labor and big business. Sambo came down from Cleveland especially to hear me and be at the graduation even though he was pretty old. I really liked that. We have a photo of him and me together there.

All the school activities helped me a lot. Dad was good but overwhelmed. Susan managed. Mom came back from the hospital but for some periods spent most of her time in her room while at other times she did quite well, I think. But, as I have said, so far as I can recall we never, never talked about that whole situation. And I recognize even now that I am talking very little about my mother.

In the last two years of high school I listened to a lot to recordings of classical music. I especially loved the music of Brahms, Prokofiev, and Puccini, although I liked the works of many other composers as well. One particular favorite of mine was Khachaturian's piano concerto. I heard it again recently for the first time in many years. I had not realized until now how much the anger and anguish that I heard especially in the first and third movements reflected what were certainly my feelings about my mother and our situation in those years. Back then I played my recording of that concerto at peak volume again and again. So far as I know those were the only moments when I connected with those feelings in myself. If my account of those years seems to lack discussion of my feelings, it is because my memories of that period, apart from some anxieties now and then, are just of normal vicissitudes with no particularly noticed feelings about my mother at all.

Working on this autobiography has been accompanied by a lot of feelings, strong but not really identifiable regarding what they connected to or even what they were. One recent dream, though, may help. My mother and I were in a large parking area with grass and trees and many cars. It was about five miles from town. There were no other people there. I was fourteen. We were looking for the two cars that were ours among all the others. We located one but could not locate the other, a Peugeot. My mother helped me look for the second car for about two minutes but then got into the car we had found and drove off. I was alone. I kept looking for the Peugeot and couldn't find it. Why couldn't I find it? Was I incompetent? Should I just keep on looking and looking? Shouldn't she have stayed and helped? Finally, I gave up, got on my skateboard, and rode it on a nearby highway that headed into town. It started raining, and I put either a sweatshirt or waterproof jacket over my head as I skated on the highway. Soon I was soaking wet. After about twenty minutes the rain stopped and the sun came out. It was okay then. The dream ended there, but a few hours after I woke up, I remembered the sinusitis that I had for a couple of years when I was thirteen or fourteen.

* * * * *

So I grew up in Erie, a small city of a hundred and thirty thousand people of very mixed ethnic origins. I went to private then public grade schools, had my own Red Ryder BB gun, and in the winter went ice skating on the bay with my parents and older sister. In high school I rode my bike the three and a half miles to get there. My route took me up State Street, past the Koehler Brewery (Old Dobbin Ale) where a fine spray of beer covered me and my bike. I fell in love with Rose Trimble in seventh grade and went out with Suzanne Carlson in eleventh grade, went to proms, and was captain of the high school swimming team. I was also on the debating team with my friend Bob. When he went off to Cornell after our senior year at high school, I stood on the curb and thought, "Life will never be the same again." And, of course, it wasn't.

But although I went away to college then too and pretty much left Erie behind, in some ways I remain very much an Erie boy. When I go back even now, seventy or so years later, I still know its core. I can sit on the front porch of the B&B that now occupies one of the big old houses on Sixth Street and watch the cars go by. I think of Alexa Collins, a "girlfriend" in second grade, who lived about six blocks away down Sixth Street and of the nearby Church of the Covenant, the Presbyterian church attended by all the people who really counted in Erie and to which many of my young friends belonged. It was like the castle on the hill, which you accepted because that was just how things were and how the world worked. But not too far away, on Eighth Street, was where Frank Fox lived. He of course taught me about another world, the world of ideas and meaning.

State Street was the main street, site of the Warner Theater, the fanciest movie theater. The Warner had a big organ that a man called Tony Conty played to open up particularly spectacular movies. A little farther up, across the street, was Polakos' ice cream and sandwich emporium—neat and simple but central to life in Erie—where Bob and I would have hot fudge sundaes or on very special occasions banana splits after a movie. And at the corner of Tenth and State, the Planters Peanut store. I have always loved peanuts. One winter, Susan and I arrived back from a visit to Sambo and Nanny in the middle of a snowstorm. From the train station Susan called Dad and Mom, who made a reservation for us at the Lawrence Hotel (on Tenth Street, half a block off State and just next to Shea's Theater) and were relieved to hear that Susan had enough money to buy us something to eat. I chose for my dinner to buy a pound of peanuts in the shell and finished them all. On recent visits to Erie with my daughter, Sarah (who is doing a film about my life and work), we have stopped at "The Peanut Store," as it is now called. The woman who works there—an older woman, though much younger than I am, who talks with a Viennese accent and has been at the store for years—says many people come by when they return to Erie to talk about the old times.

Farther south (away from the lake) on State Street was the Western Auto Store, where I bought my catcher's mitt and my hockey stick and puck, and farther still, up the hill, Koehlers Brewery and finally, at Twenty-eighth Street, Academy. There I did all the things that kids do, went to the pep rallies on Fridays during the fall to cheer for the Blue and Gold, was on the swimming and water polo teams, started going to dances in seventh grade when none of us knew what we were doing, then dating, learning to drive, and going steady when none of us still knew what we were doing.

And, of course, my memories encompass so much more. At the post office we bought three-cent stamps. At the library on Perry Square, when I was little, my mother would take me to the children's section to "pick out three books" and then check them out with the kind lady librarian who stamped them. I rode the Peach and Cherry bus to high school when there was too much snow to ride my bike. I took shy, lovely, smart Rose Trimble to the seventh-grade prom. She was so beautiful with her smooth blond hair and the light blue lacey formal with the gardenia that I had given her pinned to it.

On one of our visits together, Sarah and I had dinner at the Maennerchor (a German singing club, also on State Street) with Donna Marie, another girlfriend from seventh grade, and her husband Jim, also in our class. I know these people. They are part of me and I am part of them. That is my relationship to a place where I still feel a belonging in spite of the changes that have gone on in both of us. If a plant that takes in the water by its roots and the minerals from the soil in which it grows is in a sense part of that place, in the same sense I am a part of Erie. It is a place I still love even though I would never want to go back and live there. Living in New Haven with Yale and its wonderful young people and facilities has spoiled me completely. But Erie is a place I know in a way I only know one other place, Paris. Now that is strange, isn't it?

THE ISLAND AGAIN

I'm off to college soon, but before I go, I want to return you to the Island for another look at what it has meant to me. I have described the place and told you how the Canadian Shield grounded me. But the things I did there and the knowledge I gained there have also anchored my life. Now I would like to tell you more about them.

If it isn't already obvious, the Island was the most stable part of my early life. While we were moving from house to house every four years or so in Erie and with the comings and goings of my mother to the hospital in New York, going up to the Island every summer with its wonderful distinctiveness and amazing constancy, even though it was only for three to seven weeks at a time, well, it was always there—those rocks, the sun, the seagulls, the Clubhouse. Even the names: "the Open," "Cap Wheatley," "Scott's," "the A&P," "Sans Souci," "the drink," "the boat," "Riley's," "the Supply Boat," "Two Mile Narrows," "Five Mile Narrows," "the Gut," "Johnny Bay", "Moore's," "Hitchy," and many, many more— they were always there and everyone knew what they meant, an incredible stability!

When I was little, Dad would sometimes take Susan and me for a picnic lunch. We would walk through the woods, across the big island to the side that fronted on the narrow strip of water we called "the Gut." There, we would spread out our blanket and take out our picnic lunch—some sandwiches, fruit, and great Canadian oatmeal cookies —and Dad would read to us from *The Earth for Sam,* a geology book for kids. Surrounded by island, water, and pines with their wonderful smell, it was just the three of us. There was no one else anywhere around.

The Island was where I learned to swim. Even though we went up there every summer I was afraid to swim for a long time. This was a problem and dangerous, with all that water around. But the incident where I almost drowned, which I described earlier, left me with a great fear. I can still see the bubbles coming up in front of my face and feel the total helplessness. But one summer when I was about ten, my parents went into town with Sambo on the *Scram,* leaving Susan and me on the Island with our family friends, the Gottliebs—Lenore, Bernard, and their son Danny—and the other people who were up there at the time. Lenore said to me, "Johnny, how about learning to swim?" Somehow I really trusted her. I said, "OK," and we got into the water and in a few minutes I was swimming. By the time my parents got back hours later, there I was paddling around, no problem.

My heavens, do all things have continuities? I went on to swim a lot and, as I have described, captained the high school swimming team the year we won the Pennsylvania state championships. When I was seventeen, I also won the Georgian Bay Creamery Cup at the annual swimming meet held in Parry Sound. I was a bit of a ringer because of my high school swimming career so I don't know if it was really fair, but I still have the trophy on my mantlepiece—a rather small silver-colored statuette, bruised and with arms missing because my son, Jeff, used to play with it when he was little.

As I had gotten older I had become more independent, of course. When I was sixteen I bought a used canoe in Parry Sound. The outside was green canvas and the inside varnished wood, probably pine. I had learned to handle a canoe many years earlier and was pretty proficient at bowing and prying when sitting at the front and steering when in the back without changing the paddle from one side to the other. I also knew how to "gunwale," or "gunnel," which means standing at the stern with one foot on top of each side (gunwale) of the canoe, bouncing up and down to drive the canoe forward, and steering by putting more pressure on one side or the other. (The word *gunwale* comes from the old British warships where the upper sides were reinforced by planks called *wales* to support the guns.) And I learned to paddle without taking the paddle out of the water so as to be completely silent.

A while after I bought the canoe I also purchased some equipment I found somewhere that included lee boards, keels of a sort, one on each side of the canoe, a mast, and a gaff-rigged sail. The last is a four-sided sail that has a spar at the top (the gaff) attached to the mast, providing a greater sail area when the mast is short. Later on I also had a small sail boat, a Sunfish, which Dad gave me as a present.

I loved my canoe. It was wonderful to paddle among the islands in calm or stormy weather, so different from each other. When it was really windy, I needed all my strength and skill to go in the direction I wanted. I could take the canoe all over, or rather it took me all over, through the shallowest marshes, over rocks that had only an inch or two of water cover, through narrow passages between islands that left only an inch or two between the canoe and the rocks on each side. I could go anywhere, quietly, and so see a beaver diving into the water, a fish jumping, a raccoon eating by a tree on the shore, a porcupine leaving a trail of quills in the water as it swam from one island to another, or a snake making its rippling course through the water. And, of course, there were birds, seagulls and crows to see and, in the evening, a whippoorwill to hear calling from a pine tree on a distant island. Which brings me to being in a canoe on the lake at night.

The summer I was sixteen I learned somehow that there was a girl my age staying at Rileys'. The Rileys' island was about a half a mile from us. In those days there still were many of the islands that no one owned, but the Rileys were one of the few families that had been up there before us. Peggy Riley, the matriarch, was kind but tough and ran the island with an iron hand. She had a son or possibly a brother, Ralph, who had "a drinking problem" and who had been a pilot in the Royal Canadian Air Force during the Second World War. After the war he bought his own float plane and once in a great while would fly it up to the island. You could hear its unique sound as it came close to the water and then landed, likewise the roar when it took off, even if it was a mile away and you couldn't see it through the intervening islands. "Ralph must have come up for the weekend," we would know.

Riley's was a bigger island than ours and the house fancier and more furnished (not very fancy but more so than ours). It also had a large, easily accessible dock, and probably this is why the Supply Boat stopped at Riley's dock rather than ours on its weekly trip to help island people replenish their supplies of milk, vegetables, gasoline, and Cracker Jack. (I love Cracker Jack to this day. Do they still put in little prizes?) As the Supply Boat approached Riley's, it gave two blasts on its low-toned whistle. When I was little, that signal ended our naptime and gave us enough time to get over there along with other people from islands in the area. And speaking of sounds across the water, I should mention that during those years there were few enough people up there that when you heard a boat in the distance—and you could hear half a mile, three-quarters of a mile away—you knew whose boat it was from the sound of the engine.

The summer I am talking about—the summer I was sixteen and heard about the girl staying at Riley's—I seized on the excuse of the Supply Boat whistle to leap into my canoe and paddle over there. There, among the people gathered on the dock, was Emily Sue (Émue), from St Catherine's (Ontario). She was lovely, kind, sweet, and fun, so how could I not arrange to paddle over after dinner when we would see each other again? I did, and I did again, and again, and again. We would sit out on a rock she had chosen and talk, and as it got dark we would watch the stars. There was nothing particularly sexual about it. We would talk, I would put my arm around her, we would lie back on the rock together and watch shooting stars, and we would talk some more.

What did we talk about? Damned if I know. About life in Erie, about life in St Catherine's, about what happened "in the islands" last year or "when I was little." We became very close. Several weeks passed, and Émue was preparing to return to St Catherine's. I had just been reading *Peter Ibbetson*, a novel by George du Maurier, and I told her about the story. Ibbetson and a woman had fallen very much in love, but he was about to be sent off to prison. They worked out a system by which they would meet in their dreams, which they did, for the rest of their lives, and maybe afterwards. A couple weeks later, Émue left as planned. We wrote letters to each other for a while, but we have never seen each other again.

Yes, about a canoe on the lake at night. When I took my canoe to go and see Émue, it was in the evening. After dinner at our island I might take some people who didn't know their way around out fishing in an outboard motorboat. We'd go to Ruth's Rock, my aunt Ruth's favorite spot to fish. After coming back to the Island, we would put away the rods and reels so they wouldn't get wet with dew at night and return the worms to the worm box, and I would hang out in the Clubhouse for a bit, talking with the people and watching some card games while my father read *Lee's Lieutenants* by Douglas Southall Freeman. I would help to light the coal-oil lamps with "mantles" so fragile that they turned into powder if you touched them. Then I would get up to leave, Dad would ask where I was going (not to be intrusive but to know where to look if I didn't come back—a routine question), and I would say "Riley's." I'd get my sweatshirt, go down to the dock, untie my canoe, get in, pick up the paddle, and I'd be on our way.

There would still be a little light. Off to the left, the sky would be a beautiful grey, with a hint of red-yellow way out in the open, beyond even the Umbrellas. Other than the whippoorwill calling, probably in the Pines, it would be totally quiet. I have already mentioned my ability to paddle silently, with only the slightest ripple coming off the bow on both sides and an even smaller ripple coming off the paddle. I would cross our small channel, past Gull Rock, into the bay ahead. In the growing darkness it looked as though the bay was a dead end. You couldn't see the little slit that turned what looked like one big island into two. But of course, I knew it was there, so I would turn right, go the short distance and turn left through that crack to head for the Riley's dock. And there, waiting, was Émue.

After a few hours, Émue's older sister would come looking for her. It was time for her to go in. Émue would take me down to the dock, and I would head home in my canoe. I felt so alone there in the black. But it was also beautiful, each individual star clear in the sky and, with the wind now died down, reflected in the mirrorlike surface of the water. But unless there was a big moon, it was really dark and easy to get lost, even if you really knew your way around. You couldn't distinguish one island from another. They merged together into one black mass. The whippoorwill was now asleep with no other birds to take its place. Total silence. Have you ever been in total silence? Even with my paddle never pulled out of the water you could hear just the slightest ripple of it easing the water aside. But, of course, I could stop paddling entirely—and did from time to time, to look around and up and take in the wonder of it all. I also thought about Émue soon to be leaving. And then before too long, me too.

One final, wonderful thing about the Island. We had several people working for us there, sometimes local Canadian whites but many times Indians, Ojibways. I enjoyed the Ojibways more than the white folk, family, guests, or help. I have already mentioned Joe Pegamagabo, with whom I became quite friendly. I had tremendous admiration for him and his skills. One day we were walking together through the woods of an island. He suddenly disappeared, and hearing a noise above me, I realized he had climbed a tree beside me. Then there was a thud by my foot as a raccoon landed there, and Joe was back beside me, ripping off his belt and looping it around the animal's hind foot while it was still stunned from its fall. Joe also drove the *Scram* fast, faster than anyone else. There were all these shoals in the water and many rocks that you couldn't see. But Joe knew where they were and drove at top speed among them. He had magical powers.

There was also Winnie, a young woman who worked for us and with whom I would sometimes go out in my canoe after she finished in the kitchen. One evening as we were canoeing, she said, "Turn around." I had learned by then that the Ojibways had skills in the outdoors I could never equal and immediately did what she said. "Why did we do that?" I asked. "There was a bear out there in the water," she replied. As I've mentioned, Winnie taught me some Ojibway language and gave me an Indian name, Kiash Koonz, "little seagull."

Wellington "Cap" Wheatley drove boats for Scott's Boat Livery. Cap, half Ojibway and half white, was like a god to many of us. One of the greatest thrills you could have was to sit next to Cap as he drove us out to the Island. Like Joe, he was almost magical in his knowledge of the water and the channels. He wasn't much for talking, but every once in a while, in reply to a question, he would give you a comment that was clearly wisdom from the ages. I wish I could remember an example for you, but you'll just have to trust me.

Speaking of Native American wisdom, I recall a story from a large blue book I had when I was about seven. The book had a kind of padded pebbled binding. I think the title was "Stories from Around the World," or something like that, but the only the story from it that I remember was one supposedly of Native American origin. Across the top of the story's page was an illustration maybe an inch and a half high showing the sun and the north wind (personified in faces) on the left and to the right, but seemingly far below, a small man with a blanket on his shoulder walking on the plains. In the story the Sun and the North Wind have an argument about which is stronger. Finally, they agree to have a contest to decide. The goal is to get the blanket off the man's shoulders. The North Wind goes first. He blows and blows and the harder he blows the tighter the man wraps the blanket around his shoulders. Finally, exhausted, the North Wind gives up and it's the Sun's turn. The Sun comes out and warms the man who takes the blanket off by himself.

This may be my favorite story, and it has stuck with me all these years. Just recently I told it to a young psychology intern when we were talking about how to work with a man who had delusions, the idea, of course, being how to help the man to help himself.

Can you tell? The Island and my Indian friends there helped instill in me a deep love of being out in nature. Perhaps this is related to a desire I've always had to go to Africa. People have asked me how I settled on a career in psychiatry. Do you think I know? The last time I had a plan for a career was in eighth grade. My civics teacher asked me what I wanted to be when I grew up, and I said "a big game hunter." She thought I was fooling, but I wasn't, and she let me write it up.

Those were the days when they had short subjects at the movies. One of those introduced me to Osa Johnson and her husband, whose name (Martin) I never remember because she was the famous one. They were photographers and filmmakers who became quite famous for their adventures in Africa. Then I read about Henry Morton Stanley, who explored the Congo River and a lot of other places and who found David Livingstone ("Dr. Livingstone, I presume?") after Livingstone disappeared in the bush for six years. Later I became a big fan of Isak Dinesen, who wrote about her life in Kenya in *Out of Africa*. (I recommend the movie version too, which includes music by Mozart.)

Thinking about it now, I realize that I didn't want to be a hunter, I didn't want to kill animals. And I didn't particularly want to take pictures either. What I wanted was to be in Africa, Kenya or Uganda, to be in the vast spaces and under the big skies, amid the wildness, the uncertainty, the unknowns, the majesty, the beauty. Maybe I could lead safaris, know my way around those places and things and show them to people, teach them to love them as I did. Just as the Ojibways did for me on the Island.

On one of my last stays at the Island, when I was in my late seventies, I was sitting with my kids, Sarah and Jeff, after breakfast on my birthday when a beautiful float plane landed on the small bay in front of us. I just love float planes. When they take off and land they are among the most graceful things in the world. Jeff said, "That's for us." The kids had reserved it for a flight on my birthday. I had only once been on one, many years earlier, when I flew from Portland or maybe Seattle or Vancouver to a nearby island. Now, at the Island, we took a small boat out to the plane, and Jeff and I climbed in (Sarah preferred not). We took off, the motor roaring with power, the water trying to hold on to us, but with the help of the step on the bottom of the pontoons (I had studied these things) we broke free. Flying over the islands that I had known for seventy years, I realized that what I had always believed was mostly water was really mostly land. I had always before seen it from a boat traveling the channels of water between the islands. Now I got a wonderful new perspective over that beautiful, amazing place. And from a real float plane!

COLLEGE YEARS

Weird for a psychiatrist, maybe, but I have and have always had poor insight into myself. I have almost no understanding of why I do most things. Oh, I know I do them because of the choices directly available to me, but beyond that, not much. I chose to go to Swarthmore because the people seemed friendly, didn't wear ties, sat on the lawn talking and having fun in small groups, sometimes with dogs playing alongside, and because there were broad fields and woods—nature again. I went to medical school because it seemed interesting, fascinating even. I had no clue that I would become involved in research and love the uncertainty, the asking of important questions often with other seekers, the exploration and discovery of new important things, following a path and not even knowing it was a path or where it would lead. Wow, what could be more exciting than that?

LOOKING AT COLLEGES WITH MY DAD

My father took me on a tour of colleges during my application process. It was one of the most beautiful times we had together. Our relationship had always been a complicated one. I don't think I was aware of it until relatively recently, but one difficulty in that relationship was his capacity to be overwhelming. Dad said he hated his father, whom he called a shouting German. Dad never shouted nor was physically aggressive, but he had a way of talking that could push people aside. It wasn't mean but just didn't leave you much room. My mother was angry at him for that quality. For example, she said she had always liked eating fish, but Dad didn't and would make comments about it that had her soon never eating fish again. A related but more positive aspect of his forcefulness was that when Dad was serious you paid attention. In seventh grade I got a C minus in arithmetic. This was at the time of family chaos when my mother had recently been hospitalized in New York and we had just moved to an entirely different part of Erie. Yet he asked, "How did this happen?" It wasn't threatening, just serious. I said something like, "I wasn't paying enough attention." He said maybe he should talk to Mrs. Stump my teacher. I told him that wasn't necessary, I'd do better. And I did. Or he would check the lawn after I mowed, find a space that I missed, and point it out. I'd take care of it, and it wouldn't happen again. He was nice but firm.

And then there were times when being with him was absolutely wonderful. Our college trip was like that. We left Erie by car, just the two of us, and that first night we stopped at Skaneateles. The town is lovely, on the edge of one of the New York State Finger Lakes. We stayed in a nice hotel just across the street from a park by the lake. After dinner in the spiffy dining room, I said I wanted to go out to the park. Dad was fine with that. I crossed the street and sat down under a tree and looked at the peaceful lake. A young couple, maybe college students, walked across the grass and put down their blanket near another tree. It was getting dark. They had a portable radio tuned to music. I could see them sitting next to each other, he with his arm around her and talking. The radio played the "September Song," one of my very favorites. I paid no attention to the meaning of the words at that time but only to their longing quality and that of the melody, "For it's a long long time from May to September." Damn I love that song! Its mood caught my own, a sense that I was leaving something—Erie, high school, Bob, swimming team, taking a girl to the Academy football game or a movie—and going on to something new, unknown, and exciting. But I was already missing the old stuff.

When I came back to our hotel room, Dad was getting ready for bed. I started to do the same and pulled out a book on falconry I had gotten from the library. Why falconry? Well, it's just kind of wild and fascinating. Dad saw the book, and asked if he could see it. I was flattered that we were both interested in the same weird thing and said, "Sure." He read it for a bit while I looked at another book I had brought, and then we turned off the lights and went to sleep. The whole trip was like that—we were together, doing what we wanted, things we both enjoyed. I think it was one of the best trips of my life.

After that first night—or perhaps before, I don't recall—we visited Cornell. I loved its beautiful wooded campus, but I don't recall much more perhaps because Cornell was the last of my four college choices. On the whole I was pretty confident. After all, I had done well at high school. I had gotten all A's, been captain of the swimming team, voted all city guard on our water polo team by coaches and sports writers, and had been a successful debater on our debating team. But I had my anxious moments. Just before the results of the college applications were to come out, I was afraid that I wouldn't get in anywhere. I remember Dad saying, "They have to take someone!" which was only slightly reassuring.

Dad and I went on to Harvard. After he had been one year at

Oberlin and then drafted into the army toward the end of the First World War, Dad had transferred to Harvard. However, in the middle of his first year there his mother died from what was perhaps a botched gallbladder operation by a famous surgeon at the Cleveland Clinic and Dad's father went into the hospital. Although a family in Loudonville offered to support him at Harvard Dad decided to quit school and move to Cleveland to work in the steel mills. I am sure Dad now hoped that I would go to Harvard, but he never said anything about his preferences for me. There was a lot to like about Harvard, of course, but people wore ties and seemed stiff so it didn't feel all that good to me.

But being in Boston with Dad was wonderful. He clearly loved and cherished it. He took us to the Durgin-Park restaurant, where I had the traditional roast beef and Indian pudding. I liked that, and I liked the checkered tablecloth and cheeky waitress.

We went from Boston to Cape Cod, where we stayed overnight. I loved sailing and had done a certain amount in Erie—a few times with Lee, a school friend who had a small sloop that we raced, and once before with Chuck, that time we had trouble getting back to shore in our converted rowboat, an incident Dad did not know about. On the Cape, Dad rented a small sailboat, and I went out in it for a couple of hours with its college-student "captain." I loved it. Afterwards, Dad and I went to a small restaurant by the water for lunch. "Don't look now," Dad said after we had ordered, "but over there is Lillian Gish." "Who's that?" I asked, never having heard of her. Dad looked thunderstruck and then bemused. "She was a very famous movie star," he paused, "I guess that was years ago."

Yale was our next stop. They had someone from the swimming team there show us around. I think those were still the days when the famous Bob Kiputh was the swimming coach at Yale and the team was a real power. I'll bet I couldn't have even made waterboy, or whatever the swim team equivalent is. At Yale they wore ties just like the people at Harvard although they didn't seem so self-important and were more friendly. Yale was not going to be my first choice either.

Swarthmore was the last college we visited, and I fell in love. Kids sitting on the grass, as I mentioned, with someone playing a guitar and singing a folk song. (My two favorite singers at the time were Pete Seeger and Edith Piaf, and I had records of both.) And no ties. (My obsession with ties or the lack thereof reminds me of a song from Kurt Weill's *Three Penny Opera* about the attractiveness of a man whose collar isn't clean even on a Sunday.) Dan Singer, who I later learned was a big student on campus, took us around. I saw the rather basic men's dorm, the piano in the sitting room just inside the entrance of the main building, kids everywhere talking together, sometimes about what they had just read or about a class, and, of course, right next to the campus—actually a part of the campus—were the woods and the stream that ran through them. And, yet again, none of the boys wore ties. I mean, what's not to love.

We drove back to Erie. Harvard and Swarthmore were my main choices, and I was accepted at both. But I couldn't decide where to go—until I got a nudge. During spring vacation I was working out in the pool at the Y for an upcoming swimming meet. One day I had just come in the front door when the assistant director came out of his office. We knew each other a little because I was on the city swimming team, and he asked me if I knew where I would be going to college. I told him I was having trouble choosing between Harvard and Swarthmore, about my dad having been to Harvard, and, it being Erie, about everyone knowing about Harvard but not having heard of Swarthmore ("Isn't that a girls' school?"). And the man said, "Well, I had a friend who went to Swarthmore and he really liked it." That was what I needed. It would be okay to go to Swarthmore. And so I did.

That was a beautiful trip, certainly one of the most outstanding of many rewarding times with my father. Since his death more than twenty years ago I have thought of him often. Yes, I have remembered the difficult times, of which there were many, but since his death I have had a few dreams in which he and I were together and could talk for a while. It was wonderful being with him again. One of the things he would say when I was worried about a test or something else was, "Well, just do the best you can." And he really meant it. I loved that, it helped a lot.

BEING AT SWARTHMORE

My four years at Swarthmore were fine. I joined the swimming team but got tired after two more years of swimming back and forth from one end of the pool to the other and went out for wrestling and cross country instead. Coach Macadoo of the swimming team was a lovely guy and sorry that I left—in that league I was pretty good—but no one gave me a hard time. There was an openness to people doing what they wanted, maybe part of the liberal side of the Quaker tradition, and I actually competed as part of the two other teams and wasn't too bad. In fact, wrestling became a passion. Did you ever wrestle in competition? Nine minutes of total effort, mental, psychological, physical. If you let up for a few seconds you lose. A combination of speed, strength, knowledge, and stamina, nine minutes of being totally there! Above all, though, I loved running through the Crum Creek woods, along the path by the creek. Often I felt like I was flying, beautiful!

The classes were good—and I will have more to say about the psychology classes in particular—but I know that I was to some degree on automatic pilot. It was like, so what are you going to take next year? Well, I think I'll go into honors in psychology. And I'll take these seminars—you took two at a time. And then I'll minor in philosophy and in English. And then the seminar has a reading list. And you're writing papers every other week for each seminar.

But the more I think about it the more I realize that I did not take full advantage of my classes. In this regard, I realized a few years ago (at the age of 83!) that I had made one terrible mistake. In my first year at Swarthmore I took the one further year of language requirement that I needed, Hilda Cohen's second year of basic German. We read Heine and Hesse and Schiller, and Miss Cohen was very kind and very patient with us. I did fine, getting two A's, I think, but I never arranged to go to Miss Cohen's office to talk with her. How sad that is! I loved the Heine and Hesse's book *Knulp*. In fact, sixty years or so later, I bought *Knulp* in Paris and read it in French. I still loved this story about a wanderer who comes to believe that in refusing to be tied down he has wasted his life but is told by God as he lies dying in a snow that he has brought "a little homesickness for freedom" into the lives of others. When I got back to the United States I tried to reach Miss Cohen through Swarthmore. I hoped to thank her and tell her how much of an impact her teaching had on me. But she had died two years earlier. It saddens me that I never got to know her, to ask her how she picked those wonderful books, and learn what she saw in them. And it's sad that I was not able to relax enough when I was in school to talk to her then. I guess I was just hanging on, more tense than perhaps I realized at the time.

As this suggests, I was okay at Swarthmore but probably missed a lot. I did well, had friends. One friend in particular was my roommate, Ralph Brown. He was bright and fun, went into history, and knew so many things. He was my old Yankee friend, and I was kind of his Jew.

Besides school stuff, I took flute lessons from Mrs. Roberts in Philadelphia, who lived in a beautiful old row house, very colonial. I went in weekly and practiced daily, working on some Handel and Bach pieces. But, as with my classes, I was not completely engaged. I wanted to be, but sometimes I have this way of trying to do something and resisting at the same time, which is rather sad. I did what was necessary but without a full heart. The full heart was there for some things: for one girl I dated and then another with whom I fell in love, for running in the woods, for spending time with friends, for hitchhiking across the country one summer and going to Paris and hitchhiking in Europe the next summer, and even for wrestling.

Falling in love, did I say falling in love? Oh boy, yes. I'll mention her later on, but I'll introduce her now. This girl—her name was Ann—was two years behind me at Swarthmore. She was tall and slender and beautiful—aquiline nose, high cheek bones, and almond-shaped eyes. She was also very smart. We felt so close, so intimate with each other. Yet, there were times of agonizing, horrible tension that pulled us apart. That was to be the story of our relationship.

Only now, as I write this, have I realized that my sense of being alive during those four years at Swarthmore had relatively little to do with the classes I was taking. In my second year I actually made plans that would have taken me away from the college for a while. I got the idea that I wanted to spend a year in India. Why? Over several years I had read about Buddhism, yoga, and some philosophical ideas to be found in India. Also, I had seen the movie *The Razor's Edge,* based on a novel by Somerset Maugham. This was the original version starring Tyrone Power. One of a bunch of

Americans in Paris in the '20s, he goes off to India to find himself. It's obviously a silly story—though perhaps not entirely—but it's very romantic, and to some extent, that's kind of my thing. Anyway, I went so far as to get information from some universities and almost booked tickets on a P&O (Peninsular and Oriental) liner that would have taken me from London to India. But the people at Swarthmore and my parents were not enthusiastic. It was one of the few times in my life that I wanted to do something out of the ordinary and allowed people to dissuade me. I was disappointed, but I think they were right. It would probably have been too much a break from the more ordinary stuff that was probably good for me.

I should say that I did finally get to India about twenty years later. I went for just two weeks to do some work for the World Health Organization (WHO). I arrived two days before the meeting so I could have a least a little time there by myself. While I was with WHO we traveled all over but were in meetings all the time and didn't get much sense of being anywhere unusual. So I landed in Delhi and I stayed at the Oberoi, a fairly fancy hotel with modern architecture and a central open area not unlike Yale's British Art Center. When I woke in the morning and saw monkeys in palm trees in that open area, I knew I was not in the United States anymore. At a restaurant for lunch I told the waiter that if another customer wanted to join me I would like that. He soon brought over an elderly man and within minutes we were talking about god. I don't think I have ever talked with anyone in a restaurant about god, before or since. He told me that for many Indian religions there were no leaders, like priests or rabbis, who directed things. That sounded good to me and in fact brought to mind a place across the creek in the Swarthmore woods where there was a Quaker meeting that I sometime attended. The idea that we attendees shared our experiences and thoughts without anyone telling us how or when to do it worked just fine for me.

Swarthmore was a Quaker school, of course, but not oppressively Quaker. The place across Crum Creek was a Quaker retreat center called Pendle Hill, which hosted people from the American Friends Service Committee as they prepared to go off and work in India or Africa or wherever. One summer, I think it was, I stayed there for a week. I loved it. The Quakers can be a pretty fantastic group. I hate the word community, but at Pendle Hill there was that kind of togetherness. We ate together and then everybody helped in cleaning up. It wasn't planned, It just happened. It was the Quakerly thing to do. There was a young South Asian woman there, a little older than I was, who was from Dhaka. She wore a sari and had a red spot on her forehead. Her name was Gouri Bose. She was wonderful. We would talk for hours.

My friend Tom Styron has asked me if there are things in my life I might have done differently in hindsight. For example, what if I had taken that year out of college and gone to India? Am I really sorry I didn't? Of course, I have no idea of what would have happened if I had gone. Would I have died of cholera? Would I have fallen in with a group of mindless fanatics, followers of some guru? (Unlikely, I think.) Would I have been overwhelmed by the severe poverty and bureaucratic morass? Would I have met a young woman like Gouri Bose? Of course, I don't have a clue. That was a door I did not open, and I have no way of knowing what might have awaited me on the other side. And that would have to be the answer to Tom's question in most if not all cases. I feel okay with the decisions I've made, but how would I really know?

SWARTHMORE SUMMERS

Looking back, it seems to me that the summers during college may define that period of my life more than the times spent at school. During the college year, I studied, spent time with friends, was part of the swimming team and then the wrestling team, had girlfriends, and enjoyed music and French movies. That stuff was good, sometimes difficult, but in some way predictable and ordinary. It was the summers that were so striking.

I barely remember the summer after my first year at school, but I was back in Erie and, I think, a lifeguard on the Peninsula, a job I had had before. Frank Petinato, our swimming coach at Academy, was also head of the lifeguards at Presque Isle State Park, so it was not hard for those of us on the Academy swimming team to get a lifeguard job there. Being a lifeguard was fun, though sometimes boring. You met some nice people. There were Corky and Babe, for example, a young couple who came up for a week; I think he worked in a small store in Pittsburgh. The job could also be dirty. At the beginning of the day we were supposed to clean out the two changing cabins, and the one for girls often contained used sanitary napkins. The stereotypical lifeguard meets a lot of girls, but I didn't. On cool days or rainy days there was almost no one at the beach and I spent my time reading a book or skipping stones

My Hitchhiking Trip Out West

Being a lifeguard that summer I lived at home, and it was a good way to reconnect to my past after a first year away from Erie. The following summer was very different. I set out on a three-month hitchhiking trip around the country. I don't really know where the idea came from. I didn't know anyone else who had done it, nor had

I read about such trip. The general idea wasn't totally foreign—I had, after all, read John Steinbeck and Jack London—but Kerouac didn't publish his account of his road trip until 1957, a full five years later, so he was not my inspiration. Remember, though, that I had just been dissuaded from going to India for a year. Maybe I thought, if I can't do that, I'll do this.

For whatever reason, I wanted to do it and did. When I got home from college that year in late May, I must have talked it over with my parents. I don't really remember, but I have the strong feeling that Mom was not very enthusiastic. Dad, though, was okay with it. The way he dealt with me when I wanted to do something special was something special in itself. He was never enthusiastic but also never tried to hold me back. In some way he may have glowed a tiny bit, giving me the feeling it was really all right for me to do it. And that was all I needed. Actually it was great. He was quietly showing me that he had confidence in me, that what I proposed was natural, and that people needed to do things like that.

A week or so before I was to leave I took down my old army surplus knapsack and sleeping bag (Second World War vintage) and started piling up things I'd take. I don't remember much of what that was. Of course, you can't get a hell of a lot of stuff for a three-month trip into a knapsack. I suppose I took a change of clothes, a razor, a toothbrush, and so on. I know I took my jackknife, a jar of peanut butter, a harmonica, and maybe a dull hunting knife I'd bought somewhere years before. I know what I didn't take, though. Other than the sleeping bag, I had none of the gear you might need for camping—no tent, no ground sheet, that sort of thing. As I finished however, Dad, who was a great photographer, gave me his prized Leica camera to take pictures during my trip.

The trip began with Dad driving me out route 5 to the western edge of Erie. We had agreed that I would call home (collect) every Sunday morning to let them know I was okay, and that was about it. I'm sure Dad and I looked at each other as I got out of the car. He did a U-turn to head back home and I, wearing a Penn State tee shirt I'd bought during our high school state swimming championships (I didn't think many people would have heard of Swarthmore), put out my thumb.

The memories come in pieces. I had never been west of Cleveland before, but by early afternoon that first day I was in Indiana. A guy picked me up in an old car, a nice guy. As we went through one small town we stopped at a tavern and he bought me lunch and a beer. He was naturally kind and—dare I say it—"real people." It felt like "well, of course." By that evening, I had reached Hannibal, Missouri. I knew Mark Twain came from there, but it probably never occurred to me to do any museum stuff. When you're hitch-hiking you go where your rides take you, and I was on the edge of town. (It's good to stay near the main roads—very few super highways in those days.) Very tired, I found an open field next to a house and prepared to bed down. I probably had some peanut butter for dinner and maybe some bread I'd taken from home. As it got dark, I thought it might be better to tell the people in the house that I would be sleeping in the field. I did that and then put my sleeping bag out on the ground and soon was asleep. I woke in the middle of the night and looked up at the stars. It occurred to me that not a soul in the world who knew me knew where I was. Of course, in those days, no cell phones. Strange now, to think of that. When I see people in the locker room of the Yale gym talking on their phones, I can't help but reflect (which they probably never do) that they never get away, are always half with someone else— but only half, because the other person isn't even really with them. Out there in that field in Hannibal I was definitely by myself. It was part scary, part just amazing. And I fell back to sleep.

I awoke as the sun was coming up which was kind of lovely and someone was coming out of the house toward me. He invited me to come in and have some breakfast, which I did. Those first days were so powerful for me. The people I met were so kind and friendly, straightforward, utterly without pretense. Not all of them, of course, but actually throughout the whole three months and 9,000 miles I had only two problematic rides. A man from New York who picked me up in Nebraska said he expected me to pay for the gas—the only time that happened. And a guy outside of Chicago, toward the end of my trip, propositioned me. I didn't know what it meant when he told me he was gay (the term was not widely used in those days), but I soon figured it out and told him I was not; he let me out of the car. Generally, however, people were really kind, and they didn't need to be.

The idea that hitchhiking was dangerous was beginning to gain traction, and in some places, it was against the law—or so someone told me in Wyoming. When I was out there and saw a state police car on the road I would take down my thumb and just walk along. But I never ran into any situation that was particularly dangerous—unless you count the time when I was with two old guys who passed a gin bottle back and forth between them in the front seat, all the while asking if I wanted some, as we sped along the narrow Silverton (Colorado) mountain road with a sharp drop off on our right. As a way of judging human nature, I have to admit that hitchhiking is a very biased sampling method because only the nice people stop; the not nice ones can't be bothered. I will observe that in all my travels that summer, never did a wealthy person pick me up, never. This makes me think of what John Steinbeck said in *The Grapes of Wrath* about the common people being the ones you could count on. When I was little, a man named Andy worked for my dad—I mentioned him earlier. Andy had a cart with two huge wheels and a big bag hanging from a square frame between the wheels into which he would put the trash from the apartments. I remember Dad saying at some point, "It's important to respect Andy. He works hard and does a good job." On the road, I met a lot of good, hard-working people—almost all with more money than Andy and at least some with more learning, but good, kind people.

Early on the trip I hitched across Nebraska, soaking in those wonderful long vistas of space where you can see forever! The small towns all seemed to have grassy parks in the center and a swimming pool, where you could hear the kids splashing around and laughing. In one such town, I think it was Belleville, I found a small drugstore on the western edge. There weren't all that many cars out there in those days, and sometimes I would have to wait two or three hours. This could be a bit daunting, and on this occasion I went into the store to buy an ice cream cone to brace me before I looked for a ride. A young girl fixed one for me, and I asked her how much it was. "A nickel." Many years later I wrote a little story about "The last nickel ice cream cone in the world." For me it was.

Bordering on Nebraska was Wyoming. I reached Cheyenne near the end of that first week and got a job working for the carnival at the Frontier Days rodeo. But while I was helping set up the Ferris wheel a huge steel gear wheel fell on my finger and opened it to the bone (the first time I ever saw that). It hurt like hell for several days, and I was scared. I still have the scar. But I was lucky in that it was only the end of my finger. They took me to a doctor, who washed and bandaged the finger. He didn't give me any pain killers, though, and it never occurred to me ask. They switched me to a job selling hotdogs at the rodeo. I walked around the grounds and the stands with a tray of hot dogs in front of me supported by a strap around my neck, and I had lots of business because the manager forgot to hire anyone else to do the job along with me. Within a few days, I had earned $50, which was enough money to carry me through the whole three months of my trip. At the end of the first day when I returned to the hot dog stand and was counting my money, a woman who worked there warned me not to do that in the open. Another helpful person looking out for my interests. Also a reminder that though I hadn't run into nasty people, they were out there.

And there was one time when I might have had a problem. On the last day of the rodeo, I was sitting in the stands, watching the events, and then walking around. (By then I had as much money as I needed and had stopped selling hotdogs.) I don't remember why—maybe I was wearing my Penn State tee shirt—but a young fellow sitting on a fence started to pick a fight with me. I showed him my hugely bandaged finger, his girlfriend looked at him, and he said, "Oh, okay"—and that was the end of it.

Another memory of Cheyenne: One day I was sitting at the counter of a Hot Shoppes eating breakfast (hell, my finger still hurt, but I had made all that money so why not treat myself) when I noticed that the guy next to me, a man in his 40's, was reading the *Saturday Review of Literature*. I was surprised—after all this was Cheyenne, not exactly *Saturday Review* country, I thought—and he noticed. After we'd talked a bit, he smiled at me and said, "Yes, people out here read this kind of thing too."

And, of course, I met other educated people. At the Grand Canyon, I started talking to an older man set up beside me in the camping area. Turned out he was a geologist, and the next day we walked part way down into the canyon together and he explained to me what all the layers and formations were. Outside Gallup, New Mexico, when I was on my way home, a couple with the names, Jim and Cinny Stephenson picked me up. After I'd settled into the back seat, I noticed a book by Jung on the seat next to me. I learned that Jim had just finished his internship in San Francisco and Cinny was a nurse, and they were headed back to New York. We became friends. When a week later I got back to Erie, I told my dad about Jim and that his father was a professor. Dad said, "I wonder if his father is the famous history professor at Cornell." I visited Jim and Cinny several times, first in their apartment in New York and then, after I was married, at their house in Old Greenwich, Connecticut, so was able to ask Jim if his father was that person. He was.

That house they had in Old Greenwich? A big old rambly one. But once when I stayed there with them they told me a sadder truth. Jim had been a bombardier during the second world war which they had told me before. His plane, a Flying Fortress B17 had been shot down over Germany. Jim had parachuted to safety, well, more or less safety. He had hidden in a culvert under a street but then had been found by a gang of kids and some dogs and been taken to a prisoner of war camp where he had stayed until the peace. Now, over ten years later in their big house, they had realized that they could hear a distant train when it came by. At night Jim would wake with a start when he heard a train pass and couldn't get back to sleep. So he ended up just sleeping in the basement of the house. I guess it recalled to him those nights in the prisoner of war camp and the allied planes coming over every night to bomb the city. PTSD, of course that didn't exist then, but that's what blighted the rest of his life though he never complained. A couple of years ago, having lost contact with him, I called Cornell Medical School where he had been a student since his old phone number no longer worked. They told me Jim had died. I guess that happens.

There was no way of contacting Cinny. Maybe she was dead too.

Thinking of that, I recall the man I met on Highway 101 along the California coast. He was driving a long black car, and as we drove south, he said, "Don't look in the back." I asked why not, and he said, "Because there's a dead man back there." I was in a hearse, and the driver was taking a man's corpse to the cemetery in a town down the coast. He asked me what I was doing, and I explained that I was hitchhiking around the country on my summer vacation from college. He asked me about school and, after a while, said matter-of-factly—or was it sadly—that he had wanted to go to college but that his family didn't have any money (it was during the Depression) so he had to go to work and was never able to continue his education. I began this chapter talking about how my life had been shaped by immediate circumstances. My companion's life was another example of a life also been marked by a "decision" heavily influenced by environmental conditions.

I saw many glorious sights on this western trip. Vivid memories include waking up one morning in the field where I had slept and for the first time in my life seeing through the haze the towering peaks of the Rocky Mountains. Also, after I was dropped off in Glacier National Park, I walked up a path, past mountain goats, to a small, glistening blue-green glacier lake. I put my sleeping bag down by its shore, had my peanut-butter sandwich, and went to sleep. Early in the morning as the sun was just beginning to rise, I awoke and to see a lovely doe drinking from the lake nearby. And a sight of a different kind: On my way home a guy—I think he was a steelworker—picked me up in Indiana and asked me if I'd ever heard of Cal City. I said, "No," and he said, "Well, I'll take you there." He drove me to bar where the famous stripper Sally Rand was appearing. We sat at the bar in front of the stage and had a beer. While we waited for the show to begin, a couple of "lightly clad" girls came over to us, but my new friend, Jim, sent them away. Sally Rand did indeed play a central role in the show that followed. Afterwards Jim and I left, and I took of a picture of him that I still have. A few years later I was watching television when my famous stripper came on. There on television was a woman (clothed now) that I had seen almost naked!

I keep coming back to the people I met, and I have one more experience to describe. After one long ride I ended up in Provo, Utah, at night. When you're hitchhiking It's bad to arrive after dark, because when they let you out you don't know where you are or what to do or how to get organized. I was in a residential area, and the lights were out in all the houses. But I did see one big building with lights on, and I walked towards it. It was a bus repair barn or something of the sort and in it was a guy working. I coughed so as not to surprise him and asked him if he knew of a park or somewhere around where I could sleep. He said yeah, told me about a small park a couple blocks away, and showed me how to get there. As I turned to go he called me back. "Just a minute," he said, "Take this," and handed me a $5 bill. I still felt rich from my earnings in Cheyenne, which I had left less than a week earlier, so I thanked him and told him I really didn't need it. "No," he said, "You take it. When I was doing what you're doing, someone gave it to me. I'm just passing it on." I have never forgotten him or his words. He showed something about the linkage among us ordinary people, something almost poetic. At this point in my life I can say that I believe that the links, the commonalities, the connections that are possible among humans are even more important than the decisions you might or might not have made.

You know what, and maybe you won't believe this, but on my whole three-month long trip I only slept inside five or so nights. I spent two or three nights at the house of a Swarthmore friend in Spokane, one night in a huge sort of dollhouse in the backyard of a woman in Oregon, and one night in a hotel in San Francisco before I began my journey home. Yes, I was on the road for three months, and it never even rained! Just as well, perhaps, since it had never occurred to me that I might need rain gear. So I was lucky, very lucky, but—and perhaps this was luck too—I was also the beneficiary of a lot of goodness.

On my way home it took me only five days to cross from west to east. I'd had enough and was eager to get home. When I was still about a hundred miles out, I called Dad in Erie and he said he would drive to Cleveland to pick me up there. He did. It was wonderful seeing him. I think he liked it too. We drove back to Erie together. And that was the end of my trip.

* * * * *

You may well be asking the question, "How could your father have let you take that trip?" Yes, I have often wondered myself. Would I have let my nineteen-year-old son hitchhike for three months across the country? Would I have driven him to the edge of town to start, as my dad did? Well, not now certainly. The world has become a more dangerous, less predictable place—so no, not now. How about in 1952? Well, probably not then either, at least not so easily. But here's another question: What if I was not sure I could stop him? I hear my father reasoning: I did after all go to Cleveland to pick him up as he was coming back three months later. I talked with my wife about it. She was very hesitant, but maybe because of her mental illness she did not put up much of a fight. And he did promise to call us every Sunday to let us know how he was.

Although I, the son, have asked the question, I have always been very grateful that he did not stand in my way. Always. I saw it as a sign of his confidence in me. Also I think it was sort of as his view of the world—and what a growing boy should do in it—that a youth should set out to brave the world, to see it, to get to know it.

In spite of the uncertainties, of the dangers even, that is how life should be lived. You shouldn't avoid it. In some ways sooner or later, you can't avoid it.

And I went. I can't really tell you why. I didn't have a "reason" for it. I just needed to. Maybe he knew that too.

To tell you the truth, I think he also let me go because it was for him too. His life had been more afraid, also more difficult. Remember his parents had died when he was eighteen. He was the older brother who needed to take care of his brother. I don't know if he felt alone, scared, out of place—there are so many things I never asked him, never thought to ask him, maybe, in trying to avoid my own feelings about life, never dared to ask him.

He had quit school, gone to work in the steel mills, married— he told me once—to have a family, and married my mother's family. And they were very musical, which was important to him. But marriage and having kids brought the obligations of being a family man, and at a difficult time economically. Not just that, though. I think he was kind of afraid to take risks and regretted that. So when I said I wanted to go off on my trip around the country, he never stood in my way, I don't recall that he even questioned me. I think I did it a little for him—mostly for me but a little for him too.

Years later when I got separated on the way to divorce, Dad asked me why I was doing that. I said I was dying in the marriage, suffocating. I couldn't make it clearer than that because at the time I didn't understand it myself. Again and again, he asked why, and I thought he was being critical of me so I would repeat the same reason. Sometime after he died twelve years later, I began to think he wasn't being critical, or at least only partly. None of us had been brought up to think we might ever get divorced, and his own marriage had become so very difficult for him and horribly unsatisfying that it must have been hard to him to think that escape was possible.

Maybe he even had the slightest tinge of a thought that maybe he should have gotten divorced too. I never asked him. Never thought to. And he never said.

I recently came across an NPR segment in which the Russian-American writer Gary Shteyngart discusses his favorite novel, Turgenev's *Fathers and Sons*. He speaks of the relationship between Arkady and his loving father: "I've fallen behind, he's gone ahead," the father says, which could be the lament of any sensitive father whose kid has just come home from his first year at Swarthmore. Wrong year, but there it is! I think that's why he let me go on that trip—and do other things too, like take a year out of medical school to go to Europe. He never even questioned me about the latter choice even though his friends had told him I'd never go back to med school. I know how lucky I am to have had such a father. I wish I had told him so. When he was ninety-four and couldn't see or maneuver too well, I cleaned his refrigerator for him. He thanked me. At least I did that for him, and he didn't even have to ask.

At Long Last, Paris

I have several times talked about my love of Paris. It has been one of the anchors of my life, like Erie/Cleveland, like the Island. I went there for the first time at the end of my third year at Swarthmore, in 1953, sailing aboard the *Queen Elizabeth* from New York.

When I decided to go to Europe for the long vacation, I asked my brother-in-law, Mike, to help me get a third-class ticket on an ocean liner. Tickets were difficult to obtain, but he knew a guy who could get me one, and he did. Three months later I found myself on the top deck of the *Queen Elizabeth* with two close college friends, Sara Lee Moltz and Lisa Steiner, who had come to see me off. Ocean liners are huge, really huge, and the *Queen Elizabeth* was the largest of the day—slightly larger than its sister ship of the Cunard line, the *Queen Mary*. From the top deck of that black sleek monster of a ship we looked down, way down, to the small people and cars on the dock below.

It was nice of Sara Lee and Lisa to have come. At that moment I think I knew deep down that I was embarking on something big (and not just the boat). We talked—you know the kind of conversation that doesn't say much about anything but covers over a lot more at such times. The horn or whistle blew, and the loud speaker told visitors that it was time to leave the boat. They did, and now I was alone on the top deck without them. I went down to check, and perhaps stow, my gear in my tiny, shared cabin in the bowels of the ship. Then I returned to the deck to wave to my tiny friends way down on the dock. The tugs pulled the ship slowly from the security of the pier and turned us around to head down along Manhattan. Under her own steam, the ship then sailed out to sea, with the New York skyline and America falling farther and farther away. Oh, my goodness! How exciting, how amazing!

Why had I decided to go to Europe? Once again, I felt I "needed" to go. I did it pretty much by instinct rather than by any thought-out reason, just as I do most important things in my life. But now, in writing this all these years later, I think it was actually, at least in part, to get away from Erie, from Swarthmore, and from my life as I knew it—about which more later.

I loved the boat trip, which took five days. Each day you set your watch ahead one hour. At meals, at the table to which I had been assigned, I met Lisa Billig, Elena Ottolegni—a lovely girl half Italian and half American, kind and warm and gentle—and some other people more or less my age. Toward the end of the five days at sea I felt a little like Columbus: After seeing nothing but water over that time, you begin first to see birds, then bits of branches and things, then a thin line on the horizon, and several hours later you are coming to land—in our case, at Le Havre.

The smells were different, from the exhaust fumes of the cars and the cigarettes the workers were smoking as they began to unload the ship. The colors were different! The workers wore blue smocks, and the roofs of the houses were orange. And when we left the ship, the cars of the "boat train" to Paris were different too. They had only four wheels, were smaller than American train cars, and had a corridor on one side, giving off to compartments on the other. As we traveled to Paris, small villages, orange-roofed houses, farm fields, and small cars parked and in motion went by, and then we arrived at the *Gare Saint-Lazare,* with its enormous, high-arched, glass roof—just like in the movies!

Aboard ship I had become friends with a young Israeli, and we decided to find a hotel together. It's still there after all these years, L'Hôtel des Etrangers, on the corner of the rue Racine and boulevard Saint-Michel, though it has a different name. My roommate left after a couple days, and I had planned to travel on to Perugia to study Italian. But it was too late. I had fallen in love with Paris. So I wrote the school in Perugia to cancel, found a pension, and started studying French at the Alliance Française. At the pension, on the rue Madame, a young boy aged about nine, who lived with his aunt, helped me with my language studies. He laughed when I told him I had bought a croissant at the bakery. When I asked why, he explained that I pronounced "patisserie" (bakery) like "petit souris" (little mouse). That's how I began to learn French.

I didn't have much connection with other Americans while I was in Paris. I did go to the American Express office, on the rue Scribe near the Opéra, to pick up my mail at the poste restante there. I also went with Lisa Billig and her father to the Fourth of July celebration hosted by the American Embassy. Sometimes, though, I hung out with some French boys my age whom I met perhaps at the pension. We would get together in the evening to have a glass of wine at a café. Have a glass of wine?! Yes, that was entirely new for me. I never drank any alcohol when I was in Erie, and very little at college. I doubt that I realized it then in Paris, but I think now that in the United States and especially in Erie I felt as though I always had to have my wits about me. Because of tensions in my family? Unspoken tensions? Yes, I think so. But, whatever the case, I think the glass of wine in the evening in Paris was the sign that at last in my life I could really relax. And you wonder why I love Paris?

Like one of Konrad Lorenz's ducklings imprinting themselves on him, the first thing they saw as they emerged from their eggs, as if he were their mother, I had attached myself to Paris on first sight. I had fallen hopelessly in love not just with Paris but with the French language and literature, art, and culture.

I took this, my first trip to Paris in 1953. My next one came in 1956, when I took a year out from med school to study with Jean Piaget in Geneva. It is important to try to grasp how things are different in different contexts, contexts that include not just place but time—time both in the sense of era and of the stage in my life. I never really "recovered" from these trips to Paris any more than I did from my hitchhiking trip out West in 1952. These relatively brief periods opened up something about life, its possibilities, its dangers, its beauties, its fearfulness, that have become a basic part of me.

* * * * *

The summer after my fourth and final year at Swarthmore was when I went to Cleveland to live with my uncle Herb for two months. As I recounted earlier, I thought I had to take a course in English composition in preparation for medical school. So I spent the summer in Shaker Heights and found it a strange place, both more like Erie and more foreign than Europe. After that I was ready to begin medical school, pushing off, like the *Queen Elizabeth* itself, from home soil to a new and distant life.

PSYCHOLOGY STUDIES, MEDICAL SHOOL, AND PIAGET

Why psychology?

I have always been interested in pretty much everything. In high school—and college, as I have described—I liked languages. I took German and tried to learn some Russian. I recall taking courses in chemistry and biology, but they were not special and I was always one of the last kids to finish the laboratory work. On the other hand, I really liked reading in science—I remember I had a college book on beginning chemistry and read things on evolution. And I read a lot of other stuff, including communist classics like Karl Marx and John Reed's *Ten Days that Shook the World*, for example. In college, though, I think I felt the appeal of psychology from the beginning. My friends tended to be psychologists. Of course, I had some friends in other areas, history, mathematics, physics, and other subjects, but the psychologists, they were more my people. I think one appeal of psychology is that, for me, it is a discipline in which everything is relevant. Also, for me, my mother's severe psychiatric illness was an inescapable fact, although I wasn't particularly aware consciously of how much that influenced my life.

A major issue in those days was that if you didn't stay in school you were drafted into the army. I wasn't sure I wanted to go to medical school, nevertheless I took all the basic pre-med courses—chemistry, biology, physics, comparative anatomy, organic chemistry—just in case. But I came—almost mechanically, as I described earlier, yet also inevitably—to the decision that I would major in psychology and the humanities with a minor in English and philosophy.

THE GESTALT INFLUENCE

My first psychology course at Swarthmore was taught by Henry Gleitman. He was a lot of fun and very smart but, to my knowledge, never did all that much creative research himself. However, the department was a hotbed of Gestalt psychology, and I was taught by three of the giants—Wolfgang Kohler, Hans Wallach, and Solomon Asch.

I had a learning seminar with Kohler, who was one of the earliest and most important of the Gestalt psychologists. However, he discussed very little beyond his own work. That was to be true of Jean Piaget as well. Neither seemed to have much interest in other things. Kohler talked about his work in the field of insight and creative thinking, to me a terrifically important area that is, I'm sad to say, often neglected. He described his studies with the chimpanzee Sultan, who would pile one box on top of another to get a banana. He also discussed the old *umweg* problem, which involves solving a problem by taking a detour or indirect action. It is presented in the form of a dog who is across a fence from some meat. To get to it, the dog must leave the meat, go to the end of the fence, and come back on the other side. The Gestalt people saw that—and I think it seems right—as screwing up the simple stimulus-response paradigms and the more mechanistic views of intelligence. Beginning with Max Wertheimer, they were very interested in the whole idea of insight. To me that was to become really crucial. I don't think I realized that at the time, but the Gestalt ideas were an important introduction.

Wallach was the psychology professor for perception. He was, in my view, by far the best scientist of the pioneer Gestalt psychologists at Swarthmore. Perception is a wonderful area for Gestalt folks because there they can do controlled experiments while retaining the same focus on total experience and complex phenomena. In those days a basic concept was "good form," the overall structure of a perception or a behavior. The Gestalt people had a lot of trouble in defining good form, but a basic part of it was the idea that the human being is acting on, contributing to, the structure of the situation. It's a much more Kantian idea than the more simplistic "organisms merely respond to simple stimulus" concepts that were dominant in American psychology of that era. In Gestalt psychology there is an interaction between what's going on with the person organically and psychologically and what's going on with the outside stimulus, and it's those two things together that construct the psychological experience. That view makes much more sense to me than seeing the person as a rather limited simplistic responder to the environment.

Solomon Asch gave a seminar called "The Individual in Society," a wonderful name. Actually, I only recently realized how good a name it is, specifying both the individual and the context. Perhaps the concept is only obvious in retrospect, bringing together as it does the psychological and social. In fact, this juxtaposition is extremely difficult to manage in theory and practice, and the field has still barely started to try to deal with it.

So I received my initial psychological training in a Gestalt-oriented department, imbibing a much more complex view of the individual in the world than that offered by many other approaches to psychology. Its philosophical roots, as I have said, are primarily in the philosophical works of Kant.

MEDICAL SCHOOL

The First Two Years

Have you ever touched a dead human body? Have you ever cut into a dead human body? Well that's how you start medical school. The first day! Or at least that's how we did it. "You're in the Marines now" was a bit how it felt. "Don't question, we'll take care of that. Just do what the assignment tells you to do." I have to admit, I kind of like that sense of "This is serious. It's important. So here's what needs to be done." It's not only "serious and important", it's "You're a big boy now," and then, "You can do it, you need to do it."

So there I was. I graduated from Swarthmore in 1954 and that fall started medical school at Yale. I had gotten into both Harvard and Yale but chose Yale. Harvard was more prestigious—one Yale professor said incredulously, "You came here rather than Harvard?"—but for me Yale had more freedom and a sense of autonomy. The Yale program treated you like an adult. There were no exams except at the end of the second and fourth years, whereas Harvard seemed to have them every couple of weeks. Yale required a thesis, which Harvard did not. Throughout the program you had the sense that you were an adult now. The professors would help you and give you guidance about the things that needed to be done, but you had the responsibility and power to do them in a way that worked for you. The "thesis," for example, could be a minor piece based on the literature or it could describe Nobel-level research. It was up to you. "We will not approve of work that does not meet our standards for what is required to be a good doctor, but how you meet the standards and how far you take it is up to you." The program just reeked of that, and I loved it.

At the same time I wanted to keep a foot in the general world. I rented a room near the university campus, which was a couple miles from the medical center—in other words, not right near it. In fact, the two other people living in the same building were drama students, very reassuring.

Med school was a lot of work for me. I had taken the minimum of pre-med courses, and I was now presented with a lot of new things, which was great but hard. Actually, I've always had to work pretty hard at school, unlike some—for example, a medical student who was in one of my writing groups a few years ago and who never went to class but did beautifully.

I spent many hours poring over my anatomy books and others. Days were in labs and classes, doing exotic new things like cutting open the body of a dead person or experimenting on cats and dogs to test various physiological processes. The latter involved putting catheters in their necks and so on. They were anesthetized and so did not suffer in that way, but it was clear that they would be killed (I hate the word "euthanized") afterwards. I love animals and felt really bad about what we did, but I believed that it was a necessary preparation for the kinds of procedures we would soon be doing with people. In fact, I have not followed the debates about such issues in medical education recently, but I see no substitute so far for a graded progression that will help a doctor to get used to the idea of putting a needle in a living person, cutting that person to start an operation, handling their internal organs, and sewing or stapling the person up—or more generally, to get used to all the things that physicians need to do that go way beyond the usual experiences of life. For that matter, I also believe that doctors in training must become accustomed to working very long hours if necessary or getting awakened in the middle of the night to make major decisions. Those "Marine Corps" aspects are an essential part of medicine, and you damn well better learn how to deal with them if you are going to be a physician. And I am not just talking about cognitive and physiological learning. You must figure out who you are, how you are going to spend hours or years work-ing with a sick person only to see them die, how you are going to deal with the sadness, and with the guilt that is so often there— "Isn't there something I could have done that I forgot, didn't know about, didn't realize?" I'm not sure there is any sanitized way to go through medical learning. I am delighted that Yale, at least, has now added some training in how to talk to patients and bring bad news— "The tests are back, and they show that you have a wide-spread cancer." We never got any help with that kind of thing, even at Yale at the time. On the other hand, once you were working on the wards in your third and fourth years, the interns and residents were often very helpful about everything you needed to know and be able to deal with.

But I digress. In the first year we studied human anatomy and physiology—and was there ever a lot to learn! Just the sheer amount of new vocabulary was overwhelming. (In anatomy, I had two "cadaver partners," one of whom, like me, had majored in psy-chology and the other in anthropology. We were the "social sci-ence cadaver", and we invented terms of our own for nonexistent entities such as the "so-called space of Traub." The second year was devoted to illnesses, various disease systems, and areas like blood dyscrasias (yet another of those thousands of new words).

I liked what we were learning, anatomy and physiology and pathology. These subjects are not exciting the way literature is exciting, but they are exciting because this is stuff that's all around you and in you that you didn't know. And some of what you're doing is just bizarre, which brings me back to dissecting human cadavers. The bodies were all wrapped up in formaldehyde gauze, and the first thing you did was unwrap the gauze. Then you started—with the shoulder, I seem to remember, which is very complicated. But you ended with the face and the hands, and these had much more impact because they are the seat of humanity. And you knew, of course, that one day you would be doing this for real, on real live people.

Toward the end of the second year, though, I was getting pretty filled up with all this biology and decided to see if I could go somewhere else for a year to "work on my medical school thesis." One of the great things about Yale was its flexibility in matters such as this. When I went to Associate Dean Forbes, who was a lovely person, and asked for permission to go to Geneva to study with Jean Piaget, his only question was "How is your French?" I said it was okay (I knew only a couple of hundred words but figured I could learn it quickly), and he said, "Fine." Of course, I had already talked with my parents about this. They accepted my idea but made it clear that they couldn't pay for a year out like that, which seemed reasonable to me. They had paid without question for my college and medical school, a fact that I appreciated but also pretty much took for granted. Oh, those wonderful days! I feel bad for kids these days who have to work as they go through school and often incur huge debts. I'm not sure I could have made it through my schoolwork if I had needed to do that. I know, of course, that there were kids in my day who had those obligations, but at least it was more unusual then.

In choosing Piaget and Geneva, several things were involved. I wanted to go to a place that was not a medical school. Also I thought it would be good to work in another language, and since I had fallen in love with the French language (as well as with Paris) during my earlier summer in Europe, a French-speaking place seemed a natural choice. And at Swarthmore I had read several of Piaget's books and discussed his ideas with student friends. But I think my main goal after two years of med school was really to get away and to breathe more freely for a bit.

I wrote to Piaget—and heard nothing. Then I sent him a telegram, and he sent me a telegram back: "Yes, it's all right for you to come." (I still have it. My daughter prompted me to look for it, and I rediscovered it recently, a treasure.) So I made my ocean liner reservations, figured how much money I had saved over the years I would be able to spend on a weekly basis to get through the year, and was all set.

Except for the exams. At Swarthmore I had been in the honors program, which involved taking two seminars a semester and writing lots of papers but only having exams, sent in by outside professors, after two years. I had been incredibly anxious when the time came for those exams—not a unique experience among students taking similar programs—but had made it through the written portion (typing at breakneck speed for three hours) for each of the various seminars and then the orals, conducted by those external professors. I remember my history of modern philosophy examiner questioning me at length regarding theories of free will, to which I responded citing all the evidence that free will did not exist. Then he asked, "And what do you believe?" And I replied that I believed in it. I graduated with high honors anyway.

Yale was somewhat similar. We didn't have any required exams during the first two years, though there were periodic voluntary exams that you could take anonymously to gauge your progress (you put a number rather than a name on your exam booklet so the professor wouldn't know whose it was). At the end of the two years, however, we took the national board examinations—I seem to remember a three-hour exam for each of the courses taken over the two years. As at Swarthmore, I was consumed by anxiety and prepared extremely hard. I got through them. They consisted of multiple-choice questions. Some were easy enough, but with others I didn't even know what half the questions were about and checked boxes almost at random. A really awful experience. Was my future really hanging on random check marks? I got the results about six weeks later when I was already in Europe and picking up my mail at the American Express office in Paris. I recognized the envelope and opened it fearfully. Eighty-six. I had passed.

The Story of Ann

I was with Ann when I picked up that letter. We spent that summer together, some of the time in Paris, some of it hitchhiking around the continent. As always, being with her was a tumultuous experience. One moment we were intensely and wonderfully in love and the next, lightning was crackling between us. We never fought, but the tension could be almost unbearable. And that summer more or less brought an end to our relationship.

I share a birthday with a friend named Jaak, and we celebrate with a joint birthday dinner. During the most recent dinner, as three hours sped by, I told him this story. The past is so present!

I think it's Aristophanes who said it. When a person is born, half splits off and becomes another person and you go through your whole life trying to find the other half of yourself and to reunite with it. I was a senior in college when I first thought I had sighted my other half. Swarthmore was a small enough school that you knew a large percentage of people who were within a year or two of you. Ann was two years behind me. I thought she was ravishingly beautiful. She had been going with a guy but then apparently had broken up, and I began to fall in love with her. Of course, I had been involved with girls before, thinking I was in love with them too, but this was different. Pretty soon we were studying with each other. On Sunday mornings we would meet in a classroom in Trotter Hall. I would bring my phonograph, a weighty twenty-pound thing, and some LPs of music such as Prokofiev's violin concerto, tearingly beautiful and romantic. The spring sunshine came through the windows along with the clear, soft fresh air and the scent of flowering trees. I know I was in love, and I think she was too.

She was from New Rochelle, up a little way from New York City. During vacations I would come to New York. In the winter I wore galoshes—I was from Erie, remember—and she didn't much like that, my being such a bumpkin in her big beautiful city. She visited my house in Erie, and my father thought she was terrific. Well, she was—smart, funny, and sophisticated, but not overly sophisticated. In the summer she worked at the *New York Times*; I still have her letters on the NYT stationery. After I went on to medical school, she would come up for weekends. When she was at home on vacation, I would ride my first motorcycle, a tiny 125cc BSA, down the Merritt Parkway at my maximum speed of 45 mph to visit her. One night I arrived late and threw pebbles at Ann's window. She didn't wake up, but her mother did and let me in. I felt terrible to have awakened her. She had cancer, and I think she was having some test or operation the next day.

That incident was a good example of the way the relationship between Ann and me seemed to go. Our hearts were in the right place, but so often things went wrong. It wasn't always that way. There were many times when it felt that the Aristophanes problem had been solved—we were together and in harmony. I felt that if I were to lose her, I would never be whole again. It continued like that for more than two years, swinging between deep togetherness that was beyond beautiful and a sense of agonized incompatible distance from each other that felt like Alaska in the winter without heat.

That summer of 1956 in Paris, before she headed off for a year at Cambridge after graduating from Swarthmore and I, of course, would be going to Geneva, it was the same thing—either kissing in front of the Café Danton before I went to French class or quietly fuming at each other for not connecting. One time, after an awful day with her, I was unable to sleep in my hotel room in the 6th arrondissement. I finally got up in the early hours of the morning and took myself to Les Halles, the central market in Paris for food produce. After a night watching the bustle and activity of that place, I realized that life was bigger than the sad struggles that Ann and I had. I also realized in the course of that summer that our relationship had to end. In September I went with her to the Gare de Lyon, where she would board her train to London. She walked away from me with her suitcase down the long *quai* under that high arched glass ceiling. I couldn't follow because I didn't have a ticket to get through the gate. Standing there and watching her, it was like a French movie. My heart was breaking. I thought, we will never be together again in the same way, perhaps I will never see her again.

I did, though. She came to Geneva trying to reconnect before we parted for good. I held my ground but just barely. The following summer she again came to see me, this time in Paris, at the Hotel du Luxembourg, rue Vaugirard. She sat on my bed, cross-legged, facing me. She said she was becoming involved with another man, in fact the guy was to become her husband, but perhaps we could try again. It was horrible. I had to struggle to find the resolve, but I managed to say no.

Later I read that she was in graduate school and then that she had married. Twenty-five years on, I had been married and was now divorced and heard she was too. I called her. She was living in Washington, D.C., at the time. She had always loved government; "There's so much organizing," she would say. I was visiting Washington several times a year for the NIMH grant review committee. I called her. Could we have dinner together? Yes. A month later we did. She was still beautiful to me, but our conversation did not bring us close. When we were in college Ann had a long red scarf that she wore in winter. When we walked together, she would throw it around her neck and always hit me with it, as though I weren't there. I hated that. When we left the restaurant in Washington all those years later, Ann was wearing such a scarf. She tossed it around her neck and would have hit me had I not held my hand up. I guess in some ways I still didn't exist for her.

But what was that Aristophanes thing between us? Why didn't it work? I can, of course, develop all kinds of psychoanalyticoid explanations. But somehow, they just don't fit. Jaak and I have discussed quantum mechanics, and it's my contention that one of the things so impressive about the theory is that although its laws are true, they are impossible to understand really. I think Ann's and my relationship was like that. It just was what it was— terribly beautiful, and impossible.

Geneva and Piaget

When I arrived in Geneva in October of 1956, after that tumultuous summer with Ann, I found a place to live at a pension. The woman who ran it was Finnish, a Mrs. Pilverman. She served dinner at her apartment every night, but her people lived at various places around Geneva. She happened to assign me to a house owned by an old and much revered Geneva family, who let her use the room in return for some favor she had once done them. I never learned what that was. So I lived in a small room in the Reverdins', a medieval, maybe Renaissance, building that was like a small palace or castle in the middle of the old city. It stood on the edge of the precipice above the University of Geneva. The family's great-great-uncle or some such ancestor appeared on horseback as a statue in front of the main university buildings below (and also on the twenty-franc bill, I think).

After getting the room I went to the university and signed up as a special student. With that status, I was able to get my papers at the police station and to enroll in all three courses that Piaget gave. The first day of school I went down the cliff—well, around it—to the bottom and attended my first lecture by Piaget. There were about a hundred and forty students there. He entered the room and began his lecture in a pretty pro forma way, beginning to talk about what he saw was the problem of psychology and how to go about understanding the field. From my distant seat way up in the lecture hall I could see a man who wasn't very tall but who seemed totally sure of what he knew and what we needed to learn. As with the Gestalt people at Swarthmore and the psychoanalytic psychiatry professors at medical school, he was not much interested in ways of thinking that were not his own. Some students seemed attentive and others not. I learned in succeeding months that a lot of students felt that having to take this course was a nuisance since it was not helpful for giving the tests they would be using in their subsequent work as psychologists.

I, on the other hand, was enthralled. First, I was overjoyed that I could understand the words and sentences Piaget was using. After all, although I had picked up some vocabulary on my first trip to Paris, I had really just started learning French this past summer. Fortunately, Piaget was Swiss, and the Swiss tend to speak French in distinct, separated words rather than a line of sound as tends to be true of the French—the separated words being much easier to understand. I was also enthralled that here I was hearing the ideas and procedures of the very man who had written so impressively.

Each day after he gave the general lecture, Piaget gave a smaller class for about sixty students. There he would mostly lecture in more detail about the problems of psychology and how and why he had used particular approaches to understand and solve them. This was a "discussion" session in that it was all right to ask questions, which he would then answer at length. It was very interesting.

And twice a week—I think that was the timing—he gave a seminar on genetic epistemology. There were only about six people in this class and we could all really talk together. I am ashamed to say that I learned only recently what the term "genetic epistemology" really refers to, but I found those sessions mind blowing and wonderful. Since there were so few students, Piaget learned our names. I was, of course, "Monsieur Strauss."

In the Oz books of Frank Baum there is a character called Bungle, a glass cat. Since it is glass, you can see through it, except for its brain. When it is thinking, you can see the wheels in the brain turning and its levers moving. Those sessions on genetic epistemology were like that. Piaget would explain in great detail his thought processes about, for example, how a child seeing water poured from a broad beaker to a narrow glass would say that there was more water in the latter (because the level was higher)—what that meant for a structural theory of the child's acquisition of knowledge and how you could vary the experience and pose questions to clarify more exactly the basis for the child's evolving thinking.

On some afternoons I crossed the Rhône, which feeds Lake Geneva, and went to the Palais Wilson, a huge structure on the waterfront that was formerly the headquarters of the League of Nations and is now occupied by the Office of the United Nations High Commissioner for Human Rights. (Yes, it was named after Woodrow Wilson.) We used it as a gathering place from which we would break into small groups and then go to Geneva elementary schools to use Piaget's tests on kids.

And there were days when Piaget's research group of young faculty members and graduate students would meet to discuss with him their ongoing research projects. That's where I saw him at his least formal. In the three different teaching settings in which I observed him he became less the stern European professor the smaller the group of students, but he seemed most at ease with the research group. For example, on one occasion someone asked how we knew there were three stages in the evolution of a child's knowledge in a particular task, and another replied that with Piaget there were always three stages in levels of thinking. Piaget smiled along with the rest of us and did not seem at all annoyed. Piaget also talked about what he called the "American Question," his perception that Americans were always interested in how to make development happen faster.

Piaget reminded me of my grandfather, just a little shorter and a little more round. There was something about him that above all demanded respect but also accepted and even admired gentle humorous chiding. But there were limits to the informality and sharing of ideas. I came back through Geneva six years later, having written my medical school thesis using Piaget's tests on adults who had schizophrenia to see what we could learn about mental processes in people with severe psychiatric disorder. I had sent Piaget a copy of my thesis but never heard back. Now, visiting Geneva, I called him and told him about the thesis again. All he had to say was something like "Schizophrenia, I don't know anything about that," and that was the end of our conversation. I learned a couple years later that apparently his mother had a severe mental illness and he did not like to talk about the topic.

While I was at the University of Geneva I took French and some courses that were more classical and literary, stuff like Plato and Kafka. That was like taking a drink of cool water after a long drought in medical school. I read a lot—most of Piaget's books and some Camus. Sometimes I was lonely and felt adrift, but often life was good. On weekends in the winter and for a whole week over Christmas the university organized trips to the various ski areas surrounding Geneva. I became quite a good skier, able to go easily and fast down the expert slopes.

But Geneva is rather dull, especially compared to Paris. The university had a long and a short semester. I was there for the long autumn semester, maybe six months long, but I didn't go back for the second semester. Instead I bought a lovely 250cc BSA motorcycle and went back to Paris. I had decided I did not need to work on my thesis until fourth year of medical school (which worked out fine) and mostly don't remember much of what I did for the next couple of months except savor being in Paris. I made some French friends, got to spend time with an American girl who had come to Paris to write, spoke beautiful French, and whom I really liked (we were "just friends"). In that life I felt very much as if I belonged. I stayed, as always in those days in the 6ᵗʰ arrondissement, at hotels between the Café Danton (metro Odeon) and the Luxembourg

Gardens. I had a student card and could get special rates at some events and eat at student restaurants. I lived on and supported my motorcycle on the equivalent of about $21.00 a week. Needless to say, there was nothing fancy about this life. One of the hotels I stayed in gave me a small room with a door but no windows except for an opening in my wall giving off onto the corridor with wooden bars on the "window." But it was cheap!

During this period I arranged to take a "stage" (a period of time, usually about six weeks, that a medical student can spend learning on a particular hospital service) in a Paris hospital, Hôpital Broussais. The *chef de service*, a really big deal, was Pasteur Valery Radot, an expert on the kidneys. I think he also had been importantly involved in the French Resistance against the Nazis. But he wasn't just a kidney specialist, or even just a doctor, but also an expert on the composer Debussy (whose music I love). I didn't know that when I started my "stage" but learned it along the way. It was a fascinating experience, mostly because, as with Piaget and my mostly German refugee Gestalt professors at Swarthmore, Kohler, Wallach, and Asch, these were people who each had a range and depth of knowledge and diversity of involvement. I am not saying they were better than Americans—I don't think they were—but they were different at least from many Americans. And I think that without recognizing it, maybe until this very moment, I loved that.

I spent my last month staying at the Hotel du Luxembourg. I have a photograph taken from my window there on the fifth floor, looking down to the street with my beloved "moto" waiting for me at the curb. I must have realized that shortly I would be packing up my things, putting them on the back of the seat, and heading out to the coast to take the *France* back to the States. When the ship docked in New York I had to wait for my motorcycle to be unloaded. Then I went to meet my parents, who had kindly come to New York to meet me. They had reserved a table at a fine restaurant the "French Shack," where we met. It was very good to see them but strange to be back in America. The restaurant served food portions that were too big, which limited the number of courses. I was acutely aware that I wasn't in France anymore.

* * * * *

Here's a comment I recently noticed on Youtube following a recording of works by Erik Satie:

"So many years after and still in love. Those long, long ago days gone by. Extensive walks in the fog impregnated Jardin de Plantes, drop into the exotic smell of oriental fruit and blossoms in the botanic exhibitions, a cup of coffee lasting a whole morning in the Quartier Latin, enjoying the river at the Vert Galant."

I guess I'm not alone.

Finishing Up Med School

I returned to my third year of medical school, sharing an upstairs apartment on Howard Avenue with my friend Ray Turner, who had been in my original medical school class. (He was a fourth-year student, but I had started out with him in the same class. As he said, I had been "left back." Always a tease, he never explained that it was because I had taken a year off to study with Piaget.) I subscribed to the airmail edition of *Le Monde,* but somehow I couldn't hold on to France. After a few weeks someone backed into my motorcycle, knocking it over—something that had never happened in Paris. I ended up selling it, didn't renew my *Le Monde* subscription, knew that Ann and I had finally broken up, and sank back into medical school.

That sounds sad, and it was, very. I didn't realize until years later how much that year in Europe had influenced my life. Through several weird twists of fate, the year with Piaget would be the foundation of my future career involvement with psychiatric research, and that year of immersion in French would lead thirty years later to my involvement in French psychiatry and life.

Despite the feeling of loss, however, I was almost immediately deep into my medical studies. The third year is the most intense of all four med school years. You are now on the wards, working often from early morning until late at night, having one new and involving experience after another. There is little time for much else. It is hard, and often it is magnificent.

In general, the house staff (interns and residents) were very good—smart and really invested in patients and patient care. Moreover, many went out of their way to help us students learn our profession. On the wards in general there was real attention to doing the right thing, something I saw throughout my work as a student and later as an intern and resident. You felt as though you were a part of a serious, "no kidding" thing. What you sometimes hear about medical humor did take place occasionally, but I rarely remember it being mean. Most often, it was just in fun or to relieve the tension of taking care of really sick people, some dying, whom you got to know and often care about. That was especially true in pediatrics. Seeing and taking care of a kid who is seriously sick is very tough.

My first rotation was in psychiatry, which was nice because it was easier than surgery or medicine. We worked with patients at the Veterans' Administration Hospital. But it was also weird, and I will have more to say about it. One good thing: We had a psychiatric study group. One student, Thomas Lennon Lincoln, had studied with Jung. I had studied with Piaget. And there were others, David Carlson who later became a leading psychoanalyst and another student, Ernie Hartman, who was the son of Heinz Hartman. There were others too. So, we had quite a group. It was terrific.

Then I moved to surgery. What a contrast! On my first day they assigned me my "cases" and the resident told me that one of them was to be presented at grand rounds the next day, a Mrs. R., who had been in the hospital for two months and who had a complex problem with her blood chemistries, which were evaluated every couple of days. And by the way, I was the person who would "present" her—that is, describe the circumstances of her coming to the hospital and the course of her hospital stay—and this had to be done from memory, without having any of the hospital records in front of me. I'm sure I was pissed off and felt hard done by, but I did it, even though I had to stay up all night to memorize the major parts of her two charts, each about four inches thick. Surgery was highly structured. You did what they told you and generally they would show you how to do it. When a patient came in, you worked them up. You started by interviewing them: "Hi, I'm John Strauss, I'm a medical student and I'm here to find out what's been the problem." It's like being in the Green Berets or something like that. And you're not supposed to complain. You just do it. That was surgery, and I really enjoyed it!

Medicine came next—the queen of the fields in medical school. Actually, I don't remember much about that rotation except that I thought the head of medicine, whom people still revere, was a very cold person. Apparently other people did not or didn't notice. Then I did pediatrics. An intern on the ward where I worked, Joyce Grabowski, used to say "hi" when she saw you. I thought that was such a great thing, and I picked up the practice. It was important to me, that humanity in the middle of all the stress and sadness of very sick kids. In some ways, though it ran counter to the some of the implicit ideology at Yale. There, it's sometimes regarded as peculiar to be friendly, a New England or Ivy League thing, I guess. At the gym, for example, I say "hi" to people I encounter in the locker room, including people I don't know. And I get different responses. Some say "hi" back and seem delighted that you can connect with someone. Others are just disconcerted that you are speaking to them and may like it or not. Some don't even hear it. Sometimes I do it for fun, just to see the reaction, but I really like the connection when it's possible.

Another memory of the pediatrics rotation. I caught chicken pox, I think while I was on call in the pediatric emergency room. Chicken pox as an adult is no fun, much worse than as a child, but I was recovering well enough. My doctor wanted to see me one more time and had called to set up an appointment. He came to my apartment, can you imagine? When my doorbell rang, I went to answer it. There he was, smiling and friendly as always—until he looked down at my feet. Severely, "You don't have any slippers or socks on. You shouldn't go around like that when you're sick." Chastened, I went to my room and put on my slippers. I loved him for that and loved the fact that he made a house call, to see a chicken pox patient. My goodness!

And this story reminds me of another occasion, twenty-one years later, when I too made a house call. By now, I was a professor of psychiatry at Yale. However, unable to get grant support for my growing interest in subjectivity, I had taken on an impossible clinical-administrative role as "medical back-up" for two hundred and fifty psychotic patients. I had been informed by leadership that it "was a half-time job that will leave you half-time for your research. Tenured professor or no, you have to earn your salary, and no, of course you can't earn it by teaching, we don't pay anyone to teach." I couldn't believe they really meant that, but they did.

One of my 250 patients was having a lot of problems. A woman troubled by psychosis, she refused to come in to get follow-up care and her medications. We were concerned that she might be getting into serious difficulty so we scheduled with her to make a home visit, a house call. The nurse and I arrived at the front door of her apartment, an apartment actually only about six blocks from where I had lived years earlier as a medical student in the same kind of duplex house. When we arrived, a policeman was waiting on the porch. I think we had organized his presence ahead of time just in case our patient was going to be violent. We rang the doorbell, climbed the stairs to her apartment, and found her waiting at her open door. She was clearly agitated, however, moving restlessly and with a troubled expression. We entered the apartment, and I quietly explained that we had been concerned by her not coming into the Center and wanted to make sure she was all right. This did not help to calm her. Neither did my further explanations or attempts at small talk. When the nurse started to talk about their previous contacts our patient became even more agitated.

We had pretty much given up when the policeman stepped in. I have no idea what he said now. I only remember how calm and natural he seemed, so unchallenging—like the ideal neighborhood cop you might see on television. And of course, he reached her. As the two of them talked, I wondered how the hell it was that a cop could be so terrific with a psychiatric patient when I, a board-certified professor of psychiatry, and a very competent psychiatric nurse had been such losers. I still wonder that. Our house call was a total success, but only because of that policeman.

Rotations in psychiatry, surgery, internal medicine, pediatrics. Each field, and the characteristics of the doctors and house staff in them, is so different from the others. (The surgeons were deadly serious; the medical people were calm; the pediatricians loved kids and, most of them, showed their caring; and the neuro-surgeons, as I learned doing that subspecialty in my fourth year, were a bit wild.) Although you became progressively more competent in how to be a doctor, in each rotation the differences in required knowledge were so great that in some ways you felt as though you were starting all over again. So much to learn: how to evaluate a patient, even just to talk to them; how to behave, how to deal with different kinds of people and problems as well as with family members, attending physicians, nurses, house staff. It was very exciting, sometimes almost overwhelming. And there's nothing like the experience, repeated again and again, of feeling, OK, I think this is what's going on, and then finding out you were wrong, but increasingly you were only half wrong and sometimes even right. Learning, learning, learning. The hours were long, from 6:00 or 7:00 in morning till midnight or later. Sometimes walking home from the wards late at night or early in the morning, I would go by way of the old Jewish section of New Haven on Legion Avenue. Passing a bakery where the workers were busy baking for the next day, I would go in and buy a still-warm loaf of rye bread. I relished the smell of it as I continued my quiet walk home at the end of a day that had left me with so much to ponder or even just to get over. Third year was tough, but I loved it.

Fourth year was more relaxed. For one thing, I knew a lot more. Also, we were in subspecialties like dermatology, which in some sense were not so serious as the basic third-year rotations. What I remember chiefly is working on my thesis. It involved collecting data on patients with schizophrenia at the Veterans' Administration Hospital using some of Piaget's tests. My thesis advisor was Norman Cameron, a terrific psychiatrist and an expert in paranoia and paranoid thinking. However, he was having a lot of personal problems apparently so I saw him only two or three times.

A wonderful and very kind psychologist, George Mahl, taught me how to do chi square tests on a calculating machine. So I put the data together and wrote it up in about a hundred and thirty pages.

Two years later, when I was a medical resident, I submitted my paper to *Psychological Monographs*. It was accepted! I remember the editor, Norman Munn, calling me out of the diabetes clinic where I was working to tell me so. I was overjoyed, of course. Two months later, though, I got a letter from the journal saying they had changed their mind and would not be publishing it. Four years later, when I was in my first year at the National Institute of Mental Health, a fine psychologist, Julian Silverman, worked intensively with me and helped me knock it down to a hundred pages, to seventy-five, to forty-five, and finally to fifteen pages. I sent it off to the journal *Psychiatry,* which actually did publish it. My first publication!

About twenty years later I started to get some idea of what that paper was about. It wasn't apparent to me when I was working on it because at the time I wrote mostly about concreteness of thinking. Now I believe it was really about how environmental factors interact with a person's mental processes to influence what the person experiences, a very Kantian idea I now know, having come to almost worship that wonderful philosopher. The paper reflects how that interaction between person and life context affects the way people, including people with mental illness, understand each other. Now I bring a very Kantian perspective to bear on my thinking, focusing on the interaction between what is out there that we observe and our own mental processes, including "psychotic" as well as "normal" thought. I had no more than a vague clue about all this at the time I wrote the paper. I have more to say about this in talking about Piaget at the end of this chapter.

The tests I conducted at the VA assessed certain kinds of

cognition, but they also allowed me really to talk with the people I was testing. I remember very clearly some of the stories these vets told me about their service experiences in the Second World War. One said of his infantry duty during the fighting in Germany, "You know I was never brought up to kill people." Another told me about a time he heard a noise in the bushes and raised his gun to shoot, but a little boy walked out; the veteran said he realized how close he had been to killing a child.

I have one other key memory of working at the VA hospital, though this was as part of my psychiatry rotation at the beginning of my third year. They told me there that I was to work with Mr. W. I still remember him a little bit, his name and what he looked like. I was just to get to know him, and I don't think there was any more detail about how to go about it. Mr. W. and I would meet and go to the cafeteria at the VA, have coffee together, and talk. I had learned all this physiology and science, and now I was talking with this guy without knowing why or what I was supposed to be finding out, if anything! It felt weird and not very psychiatric but somehow worthwhile. I wasn't treating him, I wasn't diagnosing him.

How to deal with all the things I was learning and the welter of theoretical orientations with which I had been in contact? I recently realized, after talking with a wonderful second-grade teacher at another family reunion, what a great opening it would have been if rather than starting with a particular theoretical orientation, I could have been putting the person at the center of our understanding and then seeing how various ideologies did or didn't help. But, of course, with Mr. W. and so many teaching experiences since, the faculty didn't know how to carry out or follow up with such a loosely structured approach on the opening given to you when you start working with a psychiatric patient. The ward chief told me that Mr. W. was schizophrenic. When I asked how they had arrived at that diagnosis, he said because he's in this hospital. I was just starting to learn so that didn't seem so strange an explanation at the time, but I never forgot it. A few years later when I got involved in research I realized how inadequate that reasoning was.

SOME MORE THOUGHTS ABOUT PIAGET

I never saw or communicated with Piaget after the brief conversation that time I had revisited Geneva when he said he wasn't interested in mental illness. About twenty years after that trip, my wife commented on how much his thinking had influenced my own. Only then did I realize that he had. Piaget's concepts about the evolution of how we think and how we deal with reality are, I believe, extremely important. I don't mean that his particular structural theories about stages are necessarily always correct, but his efforts at considering changing patterns in how we integrate experiences into our understanding of the world provide a model for how we might think about, for example, the development of and recovery from delusions.

Let me take a couple minutes here to give a quick and dirty statement about Piaget's views. Best to start with some basic philosophers, again to do this in the briefest of ways. I warn you in advance, I will not do any of the following people justice in regard to the beauty and subtlety of their ideas. John Locke in the eighteenth century stated that a person's mind at birth was a blank slate (*tabula rasa*). According to him, their experiences then wrote on that slate so that their minds became an accumulation of those experiences. Immanuel Kant some years later added that the mind itself had major ways of processing those experiences that generated more complex ideas and beliefs. I tend to be a Kantian, and Piaget was too.

Concerning Piaget's research, it would not be too wild to say that he only did one thing during his entire life. (Of course, one could probably say that also about Mozart or Brahms.) In his student days, Piaget studied the interactions of snails and their environment on the bottom of Lake Geneva. During the rest of his life he did the same with humans, although of course not on the bottom of Lake Geneva. By looking at how human beings of various ages conceptualize environmental phenomena (so, as with Kant, how our minds act on our experience to give us our ideas about reality), Piaget, along with such collaborators as Bärbel Inhelder, developed series of "tests" that could be given to children of different ages to understand how, as they got older, they made sense of what they saw. An example is the test I have already mentioned in which the "experimenter" pours colored liquid from a wide container into a narrower one. Of course, the level of liquid is higher in the narrow container. When the experimenter asks a child what happened, a young one will say, "There's more water," while an older child will simply look at you as if to ask "Why are you asking such a dumb question?" Asked to explain their answers, the younger child will say, "Because the water's higher now," and the older child will say something like, "It's higher, but it's in a narrower glass" or "All you did was pour it." Thus, the children doing this simple test will have demonstrated how, as we grow up, we develop ideas about conservation of materials, the older child combining attention to two dimensions while the younger child notes only one. In this particular example, Piaget states that the child goes from a preoperational way of thinking to an operational way. And in fact, over the course of a wide range of tests, Piaget and his collaborators developed an impressive example of a structural theory of the development of mental functioning. In a sense, they used empirical means to develop Kant's notion of how mental processes structure our experiences into ideas and beliefs.

So what? For one thing, somewhat unkindly, I am saying that mental health professions have tended to be like the younger child in how we have understood what we call mental illness. In many ways we, too, have been "preoperational" in our thinking. We have gone from believing that mental illness is biological, to that it is psychological, then that it is social, and now back again to believing it to be biological, without ever really integrating what is happening in the various domains.

One further note in this truncated explanation of Piaget's thinking: In observing many of the tests it is apparent how the changes that take place are visually riveting and thus deceptive. The sight of the liquid rising higher in the narrower bottle is really impressive. That does not, in my view, mitigate the importance of the experiences but merely emphasizes how the tests often take Locke's ideas of experience to show the increasing power of the mind in shaping these experiences into more adequate and complex concepts such as "volume" and "conservation of matter," as suggested by Kant.

Some may argue with the outline of Piaget's thinking that I have provided—and, of course, much has happened in understanding human reasoning since his time—but I personally find his ideas, together with what he called the "clinical method" (described elsewhere in this book) that he used in his research, to be wonderful pillars for understanding human mental function and for learning more.

CHAPTER 5

INTERNSHIP AND RESIDENCY

Mr. W was diagnosed as having schizophrenia because he was in a mental hospital. That was truly strange, and not at all scientific. While I liked talking with him, I didn't feel as though I was practicing medicine. And I liked science, I liked medicine. I wasn't ready to leave medicine behind. In fact, I chose to do my internship in internal medicine.

MEDICAL INTERSHIP AND RESIDENCY

Having survived the board exams at the end of my fourth med school year (again a major source of anxiety), on July 1, 1959, I began my internship at the New England Center Hospital in Boston. In those days, you could do a mixed internship, with some medicine, some surgery, and some third thing. Or you could do a straight internship in medicine or surgery or something else. And I did a straight medicine internship. I don't really know why. I do know that I was fascinated by the seemingly endless complexity of medicine, the fact that there could be a subspecialty of something as esoteric as blood dyscrasias within the subspecialty of hematology within the specialty of internal medicine. Maybe I went into medicine because it seemed that there was so much to learn there.

It felt on that first day of internship as if I knew nothing, a disquieting sensation after spending four years busting your tail learning about medicine. But the amazing thing was that you actually did have the underpinnings of knowledge, and you caught on quite quickly. And you had to. As an intern, you are now a doctor. You wear a white coat and have a stethoscope around your neck. People recognize you as a physician. And you have certain responsibilities for the patients. You do the evaluation of the patient, the history and physical exam. You order the tests, make a provisional diagnosis and a differential diagnosis, which is a list of other possibilities. This was a high-powered internship so there were always a lot of expert doctors around. But you still had more responsibility certainly than you ever had before. People would say, what are the potassium levels? And you were supposed to know that. As a medical student, you were supposed to know it too, but now having that knowledge was central for the care of the patient.

We had a very helpful and benign nursing staff, and of course, they were the ones who really taught us to be doctors. Above all, I had Miss Kelly, the head nurse for the first ward I served on. A former army nurse, tough but kind, she would say, "Dr. Strauss, would you like to order some Seconal for this person to sleep, like 100 milligrams, at night?" And I'd say, "Thank you, Miss Kelly, I think that's a really good idea." Miss Kelly's assistant head nurse was another lovely person, as was Ms. Andress on the floor above. We also had wonderful nurses at Boston City, where I did my residency the following year. We had a lot of very sick patients on the ward, and the nurses were terribly busy, but if they had any time at all, they would give patients backrubs. One hears about platoon solidarity in the army. I can't speak for the army experience, but on a medical ward you definitely have that feeling when it's working well. If you have good people, you really depend on each other. A nurse may say, "John, Mr. X is looking like he's in trouble." Because you're off busy doing something else with Mr. Y or Mr. Z, it's really important that the nurse lets you know what's going on and it's important that you pay attention to what they say. We mostly had really good, knowledgeable working groups.

Our attending physicians were good too. We learned rapidly about some of the complexities of illnesses, how to make various diagnoses, how to prescribe treatments, and of course about the human beings who were our patients. Many of them, along with their families, were incredibly brave and patient, some were less so, but only very rarely was one difficult. The hours were long, but not as bad as in many internships. When the winter came, on our weekends off, we would finish work around noon on Saturday and have lunch at the Hofbrau House a few blocks away, then leave early enough Sunday morning, usually around six or seven, to be up at Canon Mountain or Wildcat when the tows opened, ski all day, and be home in time to go to bed and to start work early Monday morning.

New England Center Hospital was sort of a tertiary hospital in the sense that it was where patients were sent when other doctors couldn't make a diagnosis. The hospital had all these specialists who would consult with us: a great infectious disease specialist, a great neurologist, a great hematologist (the head of hematology was one of the leaders of the field in Boston, which is saying something because Boston is a great medical town), a not so great psychiatrist. I loved the experience. If I really liked those last two years of medical school, I found that year of internship to be one of the finest in my entire life.

I loved it so much that although I had thought I would probably go from my internship directly to a psychiatry residency, I decided I wasn't so sure and took a year of medical residency at Boston City Hospital instead. It was another great year. I knew more now, but you never know enough, though sometimes you do (how good that feels!), and again the nurses and physicians I worked with were wonderful. Do I seem too positive about all this? Of course, there were one or two people at each hospital who were not exactly great, but the majority were very impressive, hardworking, caring, intelligent people! Two terrific years!

As a resident (unlike an intern), you are really it. At Boston City, the attendings and senior residents were outstanding, but I had considerable independence and responsibility. Our ward had maybe thirty-five or forty patients. And everybody was really sick. You couldn't get inpatient care at Boston City unless you were really in very bad shape. We saw, I think, seven cases of scurvy during my year there. It was fascinating, and it was very exciting. And some of the people on the house staff were amazing. We had a senior resident who could draw a three-dimensional section of the brain, any section—and, believe me, the structure of the brain is complicated as hell. He was Australian, Steve Mistilis.

So I learned a lot, and considering the difficulties of internal medicine, I was pretty good. But although our patients there were very sick, someone warned me that year that practicing internal medicine was not always like this. If I were to go into private practice or work in many other hospitals, I would have to get used to treating a lot of people who weren't really sick.

And if I went into research, I would be doing things like chasing thyroid molecules. Neither of those prospects appealed to me, and that turned me back toward psychiatry.

As I mentioned, I had earlier been planning to go straight from my internship into a psychiatric residency. I have described why I detoured into the medical residency. It is harder to explain my decision to go back to psychiatry. Based on what I say above, Sarah Kamens suggests, "It's almost as if psychiatry was the medical field that was closest to general medicine in terms of what you were doing on an everyday basis. And you wanted to stay doing what you were doing. In order to do so you chose psychiatry." She may be right, I don't know. It did seem to me that if I were dealing with people who were not really sick, I wouldn't use all that I had learned. In psychiatry on the other hand—and I'm not sure whether this is just my feeling now or was then too—you don't really know as much as in medicine. You are always learning, and there is always the possibility of learning more. Besides, you can get into subjects that you've got no business doing, like history and literature as well as biology—the stuff that I have been interested in forever.

I made another fateful decision at this time. At the end of my first year of residency my options for military deferral under something called the Berry Plan were going to run out. If I wanted to do a complete residency, I was required to enlist now for military service after I finished that residency. I was planning to sign up with the air force. Three days before I sent in my papers a friend told me about some possibilities at the National Institute of Mental Health (NIMH). NIMH was considered an alternative to military service. Moreover, I was told that there was a guy at NIMH running a program that might be interesting for me. I found out more about it and applied. It turned out that the "guy" in question was interested in cognitive functioning in schizophrenia. Since my medical school thesis was based on what I had learned about cognition from Piaget and applying it to people with schizophrenia, I was chosen to become a "clinical associate" there. In those days the applications for the NIMH program were very competitive since many people wanted to join the "yellow berets" to avoid going to Vietnam. Anyway, my course was set. When I finished my psychiatry residency, we (I was married by then and we had a wonderful son) moved to Washington, D.C., where little by little I got into research—and, of course, I became immersed in schizophrenia studies.

PSYCHIATRIC RESIDENCY

Before that, however, was my psychiatry residency, which I did at McLean Hospital in Belmont. As I begin this, I realize that it is a particularly difficult section to write. What makes it difficult is that the more I think about it, the more I am torn between the recognition, on the one hand, of how much the residency has shaped my current thinking about how to understand and think about treating psychiatric disorder and, on the other, of how much my thinking has changed and to try to figure out now, whether I want to or not, how much I would do things differently especially in providing a greater variety of interventions such as work or hobby-like activities and particularly in not seeing the patient solely as victim of a disease but also someone whose desires, choices, and activities are a basic part of the whole process of improvement. In this way, I now see psychiatric disorders as somewhat different from many basic medical diseases and somewhere between them and everyday human life with many factors involved, biological, psychological, and social and including the active struggles and choices of the person.

At the beginning of the residency, without realizing or thinking about it, we used what we had learned in medical school to deal with illness. We would ask the basic questions that had been so central from our earliest clinical encounters in the late second and the third years of medical school: What brings this person to the hospital (symptoms and signs)? When did it start? Was something going on that might have caused it? What makes it better, what makes it worse? Then, we'd use answers to those questions to begin to consider diagnosis (the medical label of what is wrong) and what is needed to make it better. We had learned to take a "history" way back then, and now we needed to alter it a bit to focus more on psychiatric issues. Considering it that way makes it all sound pretty simple. The only problem for me now is that the basic explanations people have considered for psychiatric problems have changed so often and so radically over the years that I think we need to broaden greatly our perspective beyond any single one of the biological, psychological and social triumvirate.

To start with something concrete and easy, I will describe the structure of the residency. You went to the psychiatric hospital, received a couple hours of orientation, and went to the psychiatric inpatient ward where you would be working. Your work initially involved being put in charge of half the patients (about ten) on the ward and writing orders about their "privileges" (could they go off the ward if it is locked, could they leave the hospital grounds, and so on), their therapies (individual psychotherapy, group psychotherapy, etc.), their medications, and any special observations they required (suicide precautions, violence issues, etc.). Of course, to do all that you needed to familiarize yourself with all that stuff from basic medicine (symptoms, signs, behavioral problems, what helps) and, of course, the patients' histories. While serving on the inpatient units we would also admit new patients and serve periodically as on-call doctors for the entire hospital on evenings, nights, and weekends.

At McLean, we called that work "being an administrator" and that's what we did during the first few months of the residency. Then we also started to take on patients to do psychotherapy. For these patients we had no direct responsibility for writing their orders and making the living setting decisions but used the time with the patient, usually three times a week for an hour at a time, to talk with them in depth about their problems and their backgrounds, their feelings, and their thoughts. We were then the "therapist" for that patient. This structure provided what we called the "therapist/administrator split," which left the therapist free to talk with the patient without the role of taking responsibility for treatment decisions. We worked like that for the first two years, changing wards every six months, and then the third and final year of residency we went to an outpatient setting where we saw patients who were not in the hospital and in most cases never had been.

During the period of my residency, psychiatry was heavily Freudian. We learned a lot of new vocabulary: the basic *ego, id,* and *super ego,* of course, and then fancier things like *cathexis, counter-cathexis,* and many more. These concepts and the various developmental and pathology theories around them were taught as truth, as part of medicine. McLean was more liberated psychoanalytically than was common in Boston because a lot of the psychiatrists at McLean were from Washington. (Washington had a very progressive psychoanalytic society, which I was told was often threatened to be kicked out of the American Psychoanalytic Society periodically because they were interested in less orthodox approaches to knowing people and were more innovative.)

When I was a first-year resident, we were doing individual therapy with patients no matter what their diagnosis, three times a week for an hour at a time. We also had group therapy. South Bellnap One (SB1), the ward that I was on first, was big on milieu and group stuff. Some of the supervision was really good. I had a supervisor for group therapy who said, listen to the person with schizophrenia, they often know more what's going on in the group than anybody else. And I think that's often true. So, we never had the idea that you couldn't understand people with schizophrenia. I never learned to not take people with schizophrenia seriously.

Although the people at McLean were relatively open-minded, the Boston religiosity touched us anyway. There was little attention to an alternative way of thinking. Let me explain: In medicine there are areas like radiology that seem magical. Reading an X-ray is tough, and you need some magician, a radiologist, to tell you what you are looking at. When I was an intern, the head of radiology was the magical Alice Ettinger. At McLean we also had magicians, sorcerers, gods and goddesses, to tell us what things were and explain the meaning of, for example, *counter-cathexis* (a term I particularly hate). The nice thing about X-rays, however, is that any reading of them can be confirmed or disconfirmed by surgery or whatever. Not so with psychoanalysis. The gods and goddesses teach you psychoanalytic concepts to define reality, they tell you what to think and use these big words, but you really have no good way to confirm if they are right or not. The only confirmation comes from people farther up in the hierarchy.

At the top of our hierarachy was Elizabeth Zetzel, who was a very big shot in Boston psychoanalysis at the time. When I was in my outpatient year, I had as a supervisor a very famous woman who had, I think, been psychoanalyzed by Freud. One of my patients was a young woman who had trouble having an orgasm except

121

when she was on top, and I and the supervisor spent time trying to figure out psychoanalytically how that might be explained. Years later, I asked myself, "What were we doing? How could we assume the problem was psychological? " It was a very strange world. More bizarre in a way than the current medication world in psychiatry, although that can be pretty bizarre as well.

One of the good people at McLean was a psychiatrist named Steve Washburn, who ran the day hospital—maybe it was called the day care center—at McLean. Steve looked like Abraham Lincoln, and he acted a little bit the way one imagines Abraham Lincoln might have done if he were a psychiatrist. At the day hospital, we had patients who were assigned to us but lived off the hospital grounds somewhere. We saw them in a small house, and we would have lunch together there. I don't remember who fixed the lunch, but I know the psychiatrists and the patients cleaned up together, which was very unusual. I would see somebody in psychotherapy, and forty minutes later we would be washing dishes together. Steve started that, and I really liked it because you had two different views of the person. You had the one from the psychotherapy and the other from doing something practical together. There was not so much hierarchy. Honestly, I don't know what it meant to the patient—perhaps just getting the dishes washed—but it was significant to me. Much later, when I was a consultant at a halfway house in Washington, we had the same thing. I wasn't treating patients there, but I would come for dinner. We'd all eat together, and then we'd all clean up. It reminded me of Pendle Hill.

If I sound critical of the Freudian dominance now, I mostly was not critical then. You know what they say about fish and water? Fish don't know that water exists because it's all around them and it's all they know. My residency was good because there was much to like. The supervision for doing psychotherapy was often very good, and I've mentioned washing dishes with the patients. Also, if psychotherapy with a patient involved certain kinds of basic verbal communication problems, you could walk around the McLean grounds while you were talking together.

McLean had some patients who had been there fifteen years or longer, but SB1, my first ward, was for acute patients. I don't know if they were all psychotic, but they had pretty severe problems. Yet, when I first went on the ward, I thought, my god, these people are just like me. Remember, up till then my experience had been medical except for a couple of psychiatric rotations. In the medical context, the patients were different from me because I was a healthy young man. Also I wore a white jacket or coat—in those days we started wearing little white jackets as third-year medical students, graduating to longer jackets or coats when we became interns—and I had my stethoscope and ophthalmoscope and other tools of the trade. And the patients, they wore hospital gowns. In psychiatry, on the other hand, at McLean, the patients dressed like everybody else. They didn't wear uniforms and, so far as I remember, neither did the doctors. I had one patient later on who used to tease me because I wore keys on my belt, my keys for the hospital. She said, "You're wearing your keys out where everybody can see them because otherwise you wouldn't be so sure you were a psychiatrist." And she was absolutely right.

That patient—I think she had schizophrenia—went right to the heart of the matter. What was the difference between me and these psychiatric patients? They were locked in—it was a locked ward—and obviously having troubles. Supposedly, they were very troubled psychiatrically, while I was a competent, totally normal person. Yet, they seemed pretty much like me. It was a scary realization, perhaps because it seemed to mean that I could end up in their place or perhaps because of a broader sense of vulnerability.

As I think about it, I realize I might have had the same feeling as a doctor, a real doctor. But in that case my white coat and all the stuff I had learned, the job I had to do, made it weird to think that as a physician I could put myself in the place of the patient. When I started as a medical intern, I felt as though I didn't know anything, but I soon realized that I did, and eventually I knew I was the expert in the room. This was not always so clear on the psychiatric ward.

How do you learn to be a psychiatrist? You begin to interview patients. And you just learn as you go, and your knowledge expands. You become more comfortable on the ward, getting to know the nurses and learning how to act. As you become more expert, your feelings of vulnerability and not knowing what you're doing are less overwhelming. There are things you have to do, meetings and so on, that not only serve utilitarian purposes but give you a schedule different from that of the patients. Years later, I wrote a paper with Martha Staeheli and Dave Sells called "Becoming Expert." Part of our argument was that people teach you how to be an expert, and you begin to feel more confident because you have all these things to do—and because you have the keys. Which means also that you become more distant from the patient. In other words, it's a delicate balance. To be too distant is to be cold and unfeeling, too close means losing perspective. And how close or how distant at best depends on particular patients and particular professionals.

Yet in the most profound sense, you still don't know all that much. You are just more comfortable with that fact. For me the excitement of psychiatry lies in the uncertainty. I have discussed this with my close friend the psychologist Larry Davidson, who has done outstanding work with people who have severe mental illness. I think I said to him something like "I don't know why people have delusions," and he said, "Well, that's really discouraging." "No," I told him, "It's really wonderful because clearly we don't have the answers, but there is more we can learn." Something that he saw as a failing or a block, I saw as a potential. I still feel that way. The psychologist Fred Wertz, who is an expert in phenomenology, the understanding of human experience, was the first one to provide me with a conceptual framework for this. As with Larry, I was saying that I didn't understand something in mental health, but he responded that in phenomenology it's clearly accepted that you never understand everything. "You mean, it's all right?" I asked, and he said, "Not only is it all right, it's just the way it is." I thought that was fantastic. If I had the sense that I knew everything about something and yet couldn't make things better, I would hate that. I also wouldn't believe it. There must always be the possibility of learning more or seeing something in a different way.

Another observation about my time at McLean: After a month or two I received my first patient for intensive psychotherapy, Mrs. S. I don't think I realized it at the time—probably didn't until years later—but she reminded me of my mother, which didn't make it easy. I saw her three times a week, an hour at a time. This is the kind of thing that makes being a mental health professional complicated. The "coincidence" of finding that the person you are working with reminds you of someone you are close to or even of yourself happens often and can be really difficult to manage. It needs your attention and sometimes guidance from an outside consultant.

LIVING ON LITTLE MONEY

At the time of my internship I started going out with a fine woman, Jane, and we married during the first year of my psychiatric residency. We lived first in a small apartment and later moved into one half of a small duplex house in Cambridge owned by the famous restauranteur and chef Joyce Chen. My earnings after leaving medical school were $1,000 a year plus room (tiny) and board during my internship, $2,000 a year without room and board during my year of medical residency, $2,400 a year during my first year of psychiatry residency, $3,000 the second year, and $3,600 the third year. Jane and I lived on what I earned until my second year of psychiatric residency when I started a pre-psychoanalytic psychoanalysis as part of my training. The IRS audited my tax returns that year, asking how I could spend $5,500 for my psychoanalysis plus support my family on a $3,000 salary. The answer was simple, borrow money.

During the second and third years I also worked one weekend in four at a state hospital, which gave us a little more money. The experience also prompted me to learn how to breathe through my mouth as I passed through the wards to get to the staff cafeteria. It was a horribly sad place and only slightly because of the smell. Far worse were the severe limits for the patients on the treatments and the environment and the limited knowledge shown by the doctors trained in other countries who served as regular staff. I had perhaps not noticed it before, mostly because the staff positions in my other work settings were filled by university graduates from Boston, but my experiences at the state hospital showed me the abysmal level of mental health care for poor people in those days.

Our finances were tight, but we were in the company of the other medical trainees in the area who were living the same way, and life was really pretty good. We even got to see Joan Baez in one of her early performances at a small concert at the Golden Vanity. Our son, Jeff (Jeffrey Walter, the Walter in memory of Walter Strauss, killed on Omaha Beach) was born in 1962. He was very fussy when we tried to put him to bed (we were probably too rigid) but superb otherwise. In the morning when I brought him downstairs and put him on the floor, he would crawl right over to the old television set on the floor and pull off the knobs. This scene was recreated in the opening sequence of the HBO series *Dream On,* for which Jeff was a writer many years later.

MY WORK

People ask me about my career, my work. I never really thought about having a career. Certainly, I knew there were things that I liked: trying to understand people, for example, history and adventure. And there were things that I didn't like, including the idea of making lots of money or working in an office. In other words, I never wanted to grow up particularly to be a businessman, a politician, a lawyer, or even a scientist. A doctor maybe, but that was certainly never a longstanding goal. It always seemed more like: Well, this is a time you need to make a choice. Here are the various possibilities, here are the things you like and care about, which direction will I take?

And about work, I'm perverse about that too. Stupid or, worse, effete as this may sound, I don't "work." I do this thing, I have always done this thing, I'm not even sure it has a name. My "work" at the Cheyenne Frontier Days or during summers as a life guard, carrying packages of windows at the lumber mill, or digging ditches with a pick and shovel with a crew fixing gas-pipe leaks wasn't really work. I got money for it, of course, but it was just part of life. "Work" was a job I got one summer (through my dad's pull) driving a sit-down power mower for the school board. I quit after one day. Why would anyone want to do a job like that? You don't get any exercise, you don't meet anybody. My career has not consisted of work.

If there has been one consistent life goal, it probably was for freedom, for indulging a wide range of interests, for understanding things, for hands-on stuff, and, I hope, for doing good, for bene-fitting people. And I imagine, deep down, though I do not have a direct awareness of it, for understanding my mother and for help-ing her. In any case, my "career" has worked out well for me. I love being a physician and a psychiatrist, occupations that have allowed me to be involved with the concrete and the theoretical and with the wide range of interests—biology, psychology, philosophy, the-ories of science, methodology, and the humanities, all of which are directly relevant to being a physician, a psychiatrist.

And, of course, I have been extraordinarily lucky not only in the various opportunities that have opened up for me, coming it has seemed pretty much from nowhere, but because I more or less fell into a kind of research that has always involved talking with patients. I have really loved that, just as I have also loved "working" with colleagues and students. With these people I have learned more and more, engaged in the never-ending process of learning, using, and creating methodology and in trying to understand, to conceptualize, what this field is all about. In the end, maybe the principle that has been most central for me is a paraphrase of Yogi Berra (the twentieth century Francis Bacon): "You can see a lot by just looking." Learning to "see," learning what questions to ask both of patients and of our concepts, and hopefully having a help-ful impact—these are the goals. Learning where to look and how to see what has been in front of us all the time—that has been the most fun and most exciting.

NIMH

In 1964 I began my work at the National Institute of Mental Health, in Bethesda, Maryland. I was at that time what was called a clinical associate. I was involved with some administration of our small inpatient research ward, where we had about a dozen adolescents diagnosed with schizophrenia. I carried out psychotherapy and medication management with these patients and was also involved with doing family therapy along with a co-therapist. The head of our branch was Lyman Wynne, who was a terrific chief. In conferences and meetings he always seemed to view a situation or a problem from a new and broader perspective and there was never a rehashing of the same old biases, the same old points of view. He taught me the possibility of such an innovative "opening up" approach, which became a goal for me. The staff people were very good, and because of Lyman's work and the powers of NIMH we had a constant flow of national and international experts in the field of family therapy visiting us, discussing their work and occasionally demonstrating how they conducted treatment and treatment interviews. Harold Searles, for example, showed an uncanny ability to grasp people's unconscious thoughts. Sal Minuchin, while conducting an interview with a family, said to the mother, "Here mother, come and sit over here with me." This reflected a kind of homey, friendly, paternally direct way of being—something to do with his Italian heritage?—that contrasted with the approach of our more distant Protestant-leaning group.

So, a lot of caring, discussing, thinking in the context of clinical care. What could be better? Much later, I thought we were doing what we thought was best, but in retrospect I would rethink much of what we considered to be optimal care. Several years after arriving at NIMH my family was on a skiing trip. Our daughter, Sarah, was nine years old at the time and was using skis given to us by my in-laws. She and I were skiing together one morning. In the beginning I stayed with her slowly going down the hill. After several such descents, I said, "Sarah, I'm going to go down ahead. I'll wait for you at the bottom. Take it really slowly." From the base of the small slope I had a clear view of her coming down, going faster and faster. She fell. She broke a leg. It was terrible, a sight firmly embedded in my memory all these years later. If someone had even vaguely suggested that I was at fault (which, of course, I was at least partly), I would have clobbered them. And the experience made me realize that when we were doing family therapy a few years earlier, we had been too insensitive to the guilt and anguish those parents of kids with schizophrenia must have felt. Well, as I've said elsewhere, it is inherent in the position of being a physician that you are not going to be perfect, and the imperfections can be awful.

Overall, those years were good, even spectacularly so. Sunday's sometimes I would play touch football with other "clinical associates," John Davis, Will Carpenter, Jan Fawcett, Dick Wyatt, Loren Mosher, Herb Meltzer, and others. Most of these people, highly diverse in their orientations, were to become leaders in the field.

Family and Extracurricular Activities
And money! I was earning about $10,000 a year so it was possible to pay off the debts from my residency, buy a Plymouth station wagon, sell our old Peugeot, and live like human beings. While we were in Cambridge, I had taken out my saw and hammer and nails and built some simple things, such as a folding portable crib for Jeff that we could put in the car when we traveled. In Bethesda, in those first years, I went one evening a week to classes at a woodworking center for all military personnel. I qualified because I was

technically an employee of the Public Health Service, which is one of the uniformed branches of the military. "John," who did his best to teach the neophytes how to use the various machines, also taught us the phrase, "Cut wood, not meat" (meaning not yourself), a useful safety reminder. During the first couple years in Bethesda I built all kinds of things, a rather complicated sewing table for Jane, a drop-leaf dining room table, and a rocking chair for Jane based on an antique Swedish chair I had seen in the window of a furniture store. For Jeff, I made a "boat bed," a bed in the shape of a boat with a mast to hang clothes on and storage space in the "hold" of the boat, and a rocking boat, which was a set of steps when placed one way up and, when turned over, a kind of teeter-totter boat on which two kids, sitting at opposite ends, could rock. I really liked making those things, starting with just the basic wood, varnish, and so on and ending with something that didn't look too bad and was useful. Several years later, I realized that when I started writing papers, I had without noticing it stopped the woodworking.

We had what today people would call "a traditional marriage." Jane had finished her degree at Simmons School of Social Work while we were still living in Boston. (One of her professors had taught them that it was important when working with poor people to make sure to instruct them to iron their bed sheets. They probably don't teach that any more. Sometimes, fortunately, things do change for the better.) Somehow, without ever discussing it, we settled into the pattern that it was my responsibility to bring in the money, fix things around the house, do the lawn, help a bit with the cleaning up after dinner, and get up with the kids at night if they woke up, while Jane's role was to care for the housekeeping, meals, do the shopping, arrange for doctors' appointments, and things like that. When we moved to Rochester and the kids were getting older and required less time, Jane started doing pottery. She got her own brick kiln, wheel, and other equipment and was very good and creative at it; it also got her in touch with a whole new group of people. The Rochester area is very active in crafts, and as a family we would sometimes all help Jane set up for fairs and various sales. When we moved to New Haven and the kids were even more autonomous, Jane took a full-time job at one of the schools.

When I talk with young people now, I have to explain my view of this: When you have two people in a couple, each can essentially do only one full-time thing. If you have two people doing three full-time things, as in two full-time paid careers and one unpaid career managing a household and raising kids, there will necessarily be some skimping and probably a bunch of running around and feeling inadequate and stressed. The math is really simple and intractable, two people can simply not do three full-time things. I won't attest to its fairness, but the division of work we had when the children were young is very efficient. I feel bad for young people now who so often seem overstressed trying to support two careers, a household, raising kids, and so on. I don't know what the solution is.

But Jane and I also deviated a bit from the "traditional" male and female roles of the time. While we were living in Washington, D. C., she became involved in politics and was a precinct captain for the Democratic Party. This brought us into contact with the fascinating D.C. political world. At parties, we would often hear people say (from having actually been there) things like "The Senator said today. . ." or "In the House we voted on . . . ," and so we felt in almost direct contact with politics even at the national level. I, on the other hand, was "hatched." As a government employee, I was prohibited by the Hatch Act from direct political involvement. Instead, I became president of our local elementary school PTA. That was also a fascinating experience, though the issues I dealt with were things like how to use money that we had been given for art projects and trying to cut off a long discussion about whether people should put their trash bags in the street next to the curb or on the lawn next to the curb. Thus, our "traditional" life brought us a range of new experiences, as a married couple, as parents, and as citizens. It was busy but not crazy impossible.

In general, we lived the usual lives of "young marrieds." The family was enlarged by the arrival of Sarah in 1966. My thought just before she was born was that I would be kind to her but not give up my loyalty and love for my son. As it turned out, within a few minutes of seeing her I discovered something that is now obvious but that even the me-as-child still finds hard to believe: the simple truth that love is not a zero-sum game and that you can love two or more people at the same time. Jeff and I had many wonderful adventures together, such as going to hardware stores, watching model airplane contests, and, when he got older, my favorite, driving him around on early Sunday mornings to help him deliver those massive Sunday papers for his paper route and using the occasion at the end of the deliveries to begin to teach him how to drive. Sarah and I did different things. We had long sessions of playing catch as I watched her become a star athlete in many sports. We also competed in various sit-down games like Battleship, in which we were intractable rivals. Jane frequently had to intervene with an "OK you two, settle down," which we would immediately do, and with relief.

And there were, of course, the great pleasures of reading and story telling to both children before they went to sleep at night. My father had always been a wonderful story teller, which initially inhibited my attempts. But I soon realized that the children didn't know any better and were happy even with my bumbling efforts. Family classics, such as my story of Peep Peep and Nutty (a bird

and a squirrel, of course), were accepted with pleasure and sometimes even wonderment and eager participation. It had become
the practice for me to get up with our kids at night if they were having a problem, and I confess now my secret, that I really enjoyed
doing that. In medical school and subsequently I had learned how
to get along with little sleep and to be called in the middle of the
night. Getting up was not a big deal, and being alone with and able
to help one of my children through a difficult patch was a very great
and heartwarming pleasure for me.

This was the civil rights and anti-Vietnam War era, and I, along
with four other physicians at NIMH, became involved in these
issues. We organized government workers against the war, produced a newsletter, arranged for the very gracious and wonderful Pete Seeger to come down and give a concert in the National
Institutes of Health Clinical Center, and organized a treatment
center on the Mall for participants in the Poor People's March, the
anti-war "Moratorium," and other marches held in Washington in
those years. In the process we met many great people who helped
in such efforts and others who despised them. We also learned how
bureaucracies act to discourage groups they see as threatening by
warning you that you're destroying the program. On the eve of
one of the peace marches, I drove into a central Washington full
of troops, tanks, young kids, and others and stopped by a group
of late teenagers to ask if they needed a place to stay that night.
Five of them did, so they came home with me and stayed overnight. Now, that seems rather naive in many ways, but we enjoyed
meeting them and having them with us. During the marches we set
up on-site treatment centers, and I got used to doing psychiatric
counseling under a tree.

Of course, I'm now describing a time period longer than the two
years for which I originally contracted to work at NIMH. Toward

the end of that period, Lyman had asked me to stay on for another year, which I did with pleasure. In the middle of that third year I began to look for a position elsewhere. I was about to accept a post as assistant professor at the University of Colorado (near to ski country!) when Lyman called me into his office and said he was going to be involved with an international study on schizophrenia sponsored by the World Health Organization (WHO) and would I like to stay and work with that. I asked how much travel it would involve, hoping for some but not so much that I would be significantly away from home. He said a couple times a year, so I talked it over with my wife and we decided to stay. Actually, I was overjoyed, although I had almost no idea of what the project involved.

IPSS

The project was called the International Pilot Study of Schizophrenia (IPSS), and it involved attempting to determine if we could identify people as having schizophrenia in different countries in the world. The definition of schizophrenia at the time was so vague and so varied that it was impossible to compare the efficacy of treatment methods, identify causes, or even identify if this disorder existed in diverse cultures. Our goal was to establish common diagnostic approaches and criteria.

It was a fascinating project in many ways. First of all, there were the people. IPSS was centered at WHO in Geneva with nine participating centers around the globe. I had the opportunity to meet some of the international leaders in psychiatry at our annual meetings. Eric Stromgren stood out. One morning at the hotel where we all stayed during meetings, I came down for breakfast and Professor Stromgren was sitting alone at a table. I asked if I could join him, he said yes, and we started talking. Soon he was telling me about European ideas and the history of the concept of schizophrenia. I knew something about it, of course, but here was a man, thoughtful and reflective, who was really into it. What a gift! And there were people like John Wing from England, wise in the ways of the world. Our meetings brought together maybe thirty people from nine different countries sitting around the table; the discussions could be interminable and often about minor issues. John would sit there quietly, perhaps writing something down, and after an hour or two or three, when people were exhausted, he would say, "Well, here's a possible solution." And everyone would be too tired to argue and just accepted it happily.

In Washington I worked most closely with Will Carpenter, a psychiatrist of wonderful wit and intelligence, and John Bartko, a brilliant biostatistician. Will and I collaborated well together and became close friends, which we remain all these years later. In the early days as we were collecting diagnostic information on patients in our center, Will started talking about papers we might write and publish. Although I had published my Piaget study findings, somehow it had never occurred to me that we were not merely participants in the WHO study but could also use our data as the basis for independent research and communicate our findings. Thus, it was Will who introduced me to the possibility that I might be a researcher! Quite a gift! Will, of course, later became a leader in the field of psychiatry.

We in the Washington center did the reliability studies for IPSS. We had collected a ton of rating scale data including follow-up data on over one hundred and thirty patients with severe mental illness and we began to analyze it. There's just a million different ways of looking at reliability, as I learned at the knee of the kindly and soft-spoken John Bartko. He instilled in me a respect for the fundamentals. When I said something like "Let's try multidimensional scaling" for working on a problem, John would say, "Well, first why don't we just try plotting out the data," in other words, start with the basics of plotting out ratings on a graph rather than getting into some fancy statistical procedure. Plotting out the data gave you a picture of how the results distributed, something of immense value in trying to figure out what was going on and what statistical procedures would be the most useful.

Of course, it went way beyond that. The idea of two or more investigators agreeing, for example, on whether a patient experienced hallucinations is really important—the essence of rating reliability in fact—and ought to be pretty simple. Well, it isn't. Deciding on whether a rating of 1 on a scale to measure if a patient had a hallucination was closer to a 2 or a 0 was an issue, and if one rater gave a 1 and another a 2 for the same patient was that an agreement or a disagreement, were we interested more in presence (1 or 2)/absence (0) or in relative intensity (a linear scale: 0, 1, 2)? It got into the question of giving weights of importance to ratings. It rapidly became clear that as essential as the numbers were, they could not be analyzed without our making many judgments about what we were really interested in and how to collect the right data and analyze it properly. And reliability was one of the simpler issues.

There was the question that is the foundation of all diagnosis, if patient Bob was similar to patient Peter and different from patient Bill. Which if any, could you put in a group together? "These patients have X and those have Y. If Bob and Peter both had hallucinations, and Peter and Bill both had depression but Bob did not, who was more similar to whom? And when you were working with thirty or more symptoms and over a hundred and thirty patients the problem of "similarity" became even more complex. And then if you wanted to add in level of function, age, social class or other variables, what were you going to do with that?

This question of similarity led into this even more difficult question of diagnosis, what categories (or dimensions) were you going to use to put patients into diagnostic groups of "similar" people so you could compare the groups, look at different outcomes, durations of illness, treatment needs, whatever.

So John and I joined the Classification Society, a group originated by biologists that had come to include statisticians, physicists, marketing people (interested in what groups of consumers are likely to respond to which advertisements) and a psychiatrist (me). We studied the amazing complexities of determining how to put similar individuals into groups, the issues of which are still vastly underestimated in psychiatric efforts to work out diagnostic systems. The problems were immense. The keynote speaker at one of our meetings was from Bell Labs, a very sophisticated organization of experts, and he gave a long talk about a new method they had developed to classify individuals. I'll never forget the final words of his talk: "And after all that, our method didn't work."

Starting out on all this, we were nobodies, just data collectors and interviewers, but Will pushed us beyond those identities. We wrote a paper on diagnostic issues in schizophrenia based on our data and submitted it to the annual meeting of the Association for Research on Nervous and Mental Diseases (ARNMD), an important organization in psychiatry. And it was accepted! At the meeting to present the paper, I found myself sitting in the audience among all these older and famous people listening to Malcolm Bowers at the podium. I hadn't even presented our paper yet, but Bowers was talking about the work of Strauss and Carpenter. And he was saying that it was good and important. I will never forget that. Malcolm's kindness really got us started.

Will and I became known partly for our studies of diagnosis. Clarity of labeling types of disorder was particularly important for the growing biological and pharmaceutical field, and there was some interest in our work on prognosis and outcome, both essential pieces of understanding a disorder, any disorder. During this period we also published empirical critiques of Kurt Schneider's diagnostic system, which was becoming increasingly appealing in the United States, and we introduced with empirical support the concepts of positive and negative symptoms based on the work of Hughlings Jackson in England. We published more and more articles. One year I presented five papers at the annual meeting of the American Psychiatric Association.

Our work on scientific and reliable approaches to diagnosis was welcomed more by biologists than by psychoanalysts and many clinicians who tended not to realize the importance of this problem in psychiatry. The latter really demonstrated their blindness in response to our study, based on our patients who participated in the Washington center of the IPSS, showing that people with schizophrenia could improve. When we submitted our report to a major psychiatric journal it was rejected, one reviewer saying only that "We know the thesis that people with schizophrenia can improve isn't true." Our paper was published later in an even more prestigious psychiatric journal, and many studies carried out subsequently by investigators around the world confirmed our findings. This experience with our results and that review confirmed permanently for me the importance of scientific methodology in our field. But when later I became increasingly interested in the importance of subjectivity in trying to understand what is going on in psychiatric disorders, I was confronted with the struggle to value both scientific principles and the subtleties of subjectivity, an issue that is very much in the forefront of my current work. In fact, I learned, with our more open-ended methods described later, just how much a person's determination, for example, to "pull myself together" or the help of "someone who cared" and other even more complex factors could at certain times, for certain people but not others make a major difference for improvement. I came to believe that psychiatric disorders were often influenced by far more factors than was true for many traditional medical disorders and that we needed other concepts to deal with the complexities of many psychiatric problems.

All told, this was a period of great excitement and fun, and we felt we were contributing significantly to the field. Apparently other people thought so too because we won some awards for our work and found it easier to get our articles accepted for publication. At the same time, as preparation for writing the report for the IPSS project started, I was named to the editorial board and went more frequently, three or so times a year, to Geneva for the publication committee. It was strange returning to the place where I had years earlier studied with Piaget and had felt so free. Now and again, a yearning for that freedom wafted over me. There was a young woman still living in Geneva whom I had met when I was a student there, Michelle Maquard, lovely and very bright. No, we didn't start a romantic connection—I think I was too straight arrow for that—but we would have dinner together when I was there, and being with her brought back those earlier, freer times.

ROCHESTER

Jane and I and the kids had been in Washington eight years (1964-1972) when my branch chief, Lyman Wynne, was invited to become chairman of the psychiatry department at the University of Rochester Medical School. NIMH was becoming more and more biological in emphasis and our branch was being narrowed down to largely biological research. Lyman invited me to come to Rochester with him, and our family decided to do that. Washington had been good to us, but the world changes and we had a good opportunity to adapt to those changes.

We continued our life in Rochester, which I loved. During the wonderful summers we had an abundance of fresh fruit, and during the winters we had mountains of snow, piled often six feet high along the roads by the efficient plows. In a small community near the medical center we found a rambling old house with huge trees, a big lawn, and a long driveway. I got a gasoline snow blower for that driveway and loved getting up early in the morning while it was still dark to plow us out. There's something serious and beautiful about doing that, being alone too. Not to mention how good it looks and how useful you feel when you're through! And, of course, it was fun delivering those huge newspapers with Jeff early on Sunday mornings and playing catch with Sarah. I would throw the ball over our high fir trees and watch her catch it or I would play catcher for her impressive pitching. We became good friends with a neighboring family whose children were the same ages as ours and settled in so easily to this new world. The weather, the countryside, and the people all reminded me of Erie, but Rochester was bigger and much more of an intellectual center so did not have the disadvantages of Erie. And although Washington had been fascinating, I think I had never really become an East Coast person.

Working at the university, first as an associate and then a full professor, was good too. There I continued tackling the issue of diagnostic groups. For example, we evaluated all first admissions to the psychiatric inpatient ward from a particular catchment area and then did a follow-up. We did structured interviews and got information on patients' symptom pictures. Then we analyzed the data using a technique called the biplot, which was developed by the biostatistician Ruben Gabriel, in which you plot two things at once on the same graph using principle components analysis. In our case I made up ratings on a bunch of invented "patients" on the symptom interview so they would fit the diagnostic categories for paranoid schizophrenia, depression, bipolar disorder, and other categories. Then we took symptom ratings on real patients that we had seen and plotted the two against each other on the same plot. The patients came out on the plot as little dots and the symptoms came out as vectors or lines. The made-up patients, of course, clustered neatly in the diagnostic categories. But the symptoms of real patients spread them all over the place on the plot, including on a severity dimension from very severe to not very severe at all. There was a certain amount of grouping, validating the traditional concepts to some extent, but the real patients did not form neat little groups as the made-up patients had. We published a bunch of papers from this research. The one I am happiest about was "Do Psychiatric Patients Fit Their Diagnosis?" which we did with Ruben Gabriel.

During this period I was involved in the development of DSM-III, the third edition of the Diagnostic and Statistical Manual of the American Psychiatric Association. In the 1960's, as I have mentioned, attention to the biology of psychiatric disorders had grown along with more effective medications for their control. As a result, the interest in psychiatric diagnosis grew as well. What medications were best for which disorders was a major question. Previously under the dominance of psychoanalysis, diagnoses were used, but it was rare indeed when anyone did something as radical (and perhaps also considered uninteresting) as defining diagnostic criteria or studying diagnostic agreement (by which I mean the degree to which two professionals seeing the same patient would arrive at the same diagnosis).

Because of the growth of biological psychiatry, some of the older diagnostic practices, especially in the United States, where, for example, a person could be considered to have schizophrenia "because she is in this hospital" or "because she has been sick for so long" or "because she has so much trouble relating to people," all differing explanations that I heard during my medical education, became intolerable. If one person calls a cat a dog and the other person doesn't realize that the two of them are talking about two very different things, language becomes meaningless and communication breaks down. This is why I became interested in diagnosis. One thing led to another. American psychiatry began to try to develop more solid diagnostic practices and settled on "operational definitions," which in our case meant the development of reliable criteria, especially focused on defining groups of symptoms that would designate each diagnostic category. The result of this effort was DSM-III, which was published in 1980. DSM-III has been much criticized for a huge range of reasons but was accepted internationally simply because it was the best and clearest that existed. I served on the committee that developed it and because of my research, among other things, suggested that it have a "multiaxial" format. That is to say, because our research had shown how important some characteristics other than symptoms were in determining the prognosis of a disorder and even for influencing medication effectiveness, characteristics such a person's ability to form relationships with other people, there needed to be separate "axes" besides symptom criteria in our diagnostic judgements. That recommendation was accepted by the committee and then by the American Psychiatric Association, and thus became part of DSM-III, which was constructed to have a multiaxial structure.

About the same time as work on DSM-III got underway, NIMH gave me money to do a follow-up study like others for the WHO study but in Taiwan, which had been one of the original participating centers and had been kicked out of the United Nations (and thus the World Health Organization) when communist China came in. I visited Taiwan to consult on that, and Jane went with me. It was the first time we had been to Asia, and the cultural differences were striking. When I visited the excellent psychiatric hospital with all kinds of modern programs, I saw in one patient's room a visitor praying over incense with the patient. It was a striking example of how they managed to blend the traditional culture with the modern, something we in the United States could do much more.

The whole trip was fascinating. We went to Japan first and stayed at an inn in the middle of Kyoto. Here you were in this big bustling city, but when you went through the door of the inn it was suddenly unbelievably quiet. You left the city behind. And then the food we had, flavors that I'd never tasted before. Japan was for us organized and understated, and we noticed that they used a lot of earth colors. Not so in Taiwan. There many of the buildings in Taipei had bright red and gold roofs. When we went into a restaurant, the big windows were dirty. But the food was fantastic even though we seemed to be eating all kinds of weird things. And we went to a Chinese opera, equally fantastic and beautiful—gold and dragons and unusual sounds and people singing in falsetto voices.

We were told by a well-known anthropologist who was there at the time that the Taiwanese were fine hosts, but they didn't show much emotion. Well, we were there for five days and five nights, hosted by the man with whom I was doing the research. Every night we were taken to a different restaurant with a different group of people, the psychiatry residents one night, faculty the next, I don't remember who else. The food, excellent throughout, was extremely varied because Taiwan has a lot of different ethnic groups from Mainland China as well as from Taiwan. On the final night it was our host who took us out, with his wife, his secretary, and his married daughter and her husband. We went to a humble little restaurant. After we finished a delicious dinner, our host rocked back in his chair, closed his eyes, and started singing "Auld Lang Syne" ("Should auld acquaintance be forgot") in Chinese. Then everybody sang it in English. It brought tears to our eyes.

The results of our research were that you could use the methods we had developed to identify people with schizophrenia and evaluate their status at follow-up in Taiwan just as you could in the other countries. However, our report had to be published separately from the WHO material for political reasons. Politics in mental health research! Bah!

Concerning the follow ups to the WHO study, as with all follow-up studies, there was a little problem with perseveration, just doing the same thing because that's all you know how to do. But in each study, especially if you're doing longitudinal studies, there's always tons of stuff you start to realize you don't know, that you haven't asked or you didn't pay attention to at the beginning. For example, in Rochester we did a follow-up study and then edited a whole issue of *Schizophrenia Bulletin* on premorbid adjustment (how well a person functions before the onset of a disorder). For us, although I don't think I was conscious of it, this was a way of taking a next step in understanding the longitudinal aspects of psychiatric disorder, starting with how a person was beforehand, then how the disorder starts, then how it evolves, and then if the person recovers, how that happens.

YALE

After five years in Rochester (1972-1977) I was offered a post at Yale. Jane, who had been brought up in the Boston area, really wanted to get back to New England, but, as I've described, I really liked living in Rochester so moving to New Haven was the hardest decision I've ever made. The kids, too, had a difficult time with it. We all managed, however and found a very nice rambling one-story house with a two-acre lot in a town next to New Haven. The house was great, and there were woods nearby where our dog Barney and I often ran together. I bought a riding mower for the first time in my life, the kids started their new schools, and Jane was back in New England—with her brick kiln, which the psychiatry department had paid to have moved to New Haven.

Over time, coming to Yale proved to have been the right move. For starters it provided me connection to wonderful students and other young people and easy access to outstanding facilities, arts and conferences. There were, however, many complications that I will not detail but that resulted in my divorce from Jane. As divorces go, it was relatively benign, but of course it was incredibly difficult for all of us. A year later I found a small house in New Haven that I really liked and have lived there since. I had the benefit of continuity with my great secretary, Nancy Ryan, who had come with me from Rochester. She was so wonderfully competent that she had easily replaced the group of three secretaries who preceded her. And, of course, my life was enriched by wonderful new friends: Larry Davidson and his family, Jaak Rakfeldt, Sophie Tworkowski, Barbara Shiller, the Grazias, and others.

Yale hired me as a professor and as head of the Yale Psychiatric Institute (YPI). They told me that YPI was a half-time job and that

I could do research in the other half of my time. I realized very quickly that to do the job right I really had to spend more than full time as chief of YPI so I was doing my research from midnight to 4:00 am. It didn't work. You certainly can't do research interviews at two in the morning, and I had papers to give and meetings and conferences, international conferences, to attend. There were a lot of people out there who were not only smarter than I but who were spending full time on their research. How could I keep up? It became clear to me that much as I liked clinical and administrative work, research was my chief love. I think a tipping point was when I found myself sitting on a court house bench for over an hour one day waiting to see if a case in which my hospital was seeking to increase its rates would be heard that day, realizing that once again my research was going to have to be squeezed in after midnight. So, after six months on the job, I resigned from being head of YPI.

It was hard for everybody. Then I got lucky and received a grant, then a couple more, including one for a follow-up study and one as a career investigator. I worked with a group of fine people here to do yet another follow-up study, and we published a lot from that. I also did some work with Courtenay Harding on her great Vermont longitudinal study. But the work we were doing, follow-along research, seeing patients several times periodically rather than only once at "outcome" led us to become increasingly cognizant that we were not dealing merely with diseases in passive patients, but that these patients were real people whose desires and lives at work and in the everyday world were crucial and that we really were dealing with "biopsychosocial" issues. George Engel at Rochester had identified that conception years earlier, and even I had previously written such articles as "The Person with Delusions as a Person." But now I was moving beyond that. I was learning that "subjectivity," what the person wanted, how he or she decided to act, and

148

how that connected with their context was really important, and that maybe we would have to rethink the nature of what we had called "psychiatric disorder" or "mental illness" in ways that would change our ideas about their causes, the factors in a person's getting better, and indeed the entire way of thinking about what we were dealing with as mental illness.

But this is all extraordinarily complicated. And in an era when biological thinking was once again (as it had in the late nineteenth century) dominating the field, focus on that complexity and on the patients' subjective aspects of the process was not highly thought of. Our funding dried up. I was told that tenured professor or not I would have to do something to earn my salary and that teaching didn't count. Once again, I took on what was said to be a half-time job (leaving the other half for my research), which involved serving as "medical backup" for a team of nurses and social workers caring for two hundred and fifty psychotic patients. My friends had said, "You'll see. You can do it." What I saw was really good nurses and social workers doing their best. I also saw many situations like this: When I met with a patient, I would ask "How are things going," and the patient would say something like "I'm taking my medications and I'm still hearing voices, but it's not too bad"; I'd say, "That's good, but I'm really interested in how things are going" and get the same the same response. Usually by my third try the patient would begin to tell me more about his or her life, which, of course, was what I really wanted to know, but that took far longer than the ten minutes allotted for the doctor's visit every six months. Apparently the patients had been trained to be brief and say only what the doctor was interested in. I realized—how do I explain my naivete except to say that I had never before encountered such a system— that the psychiatrist was implicitly expected only to renew or perhaps adjust prescriptions and to have no other function. I fought to change the system and they reduced my case load to one hundred and seventy-five patients for my "half time job," but I knew I could not function that way. The system was struggling (and failing) with the problem of how you really do community mental health care in contrast to some of the old systems, and I was either going to have to commit myself to that or to my research. Of course, I chose research. But only by retiring would I be free to devote myself entirely to that. I worried about that. I had never planned to retire. But Nancy, my frank secretary, said, "You better do it before it's too late." And I was sixty-five, so why not?

"RETIREMENT"

Ah, retirement! Pictures of a lazy afternoon in Florida near the pool. Or a cozy time watching a granddaughter on the swing. Or sheer misery with not enough money and nothing to do. Even worse, no friends, except perhaps that friend who says as he passes, "It's nice that you're keeping busy." (I'm always tempted to reply, "It's nice you're keeping busy too," but I never do.)

I had no idea what it would be like, none whatsoever. But as the time approached, the best advice I got was from the department chairman, who was not all that inclined to give fatherly advice. I asked him what he thought of the offer I had received to become the editor of a well-known psychiatric journal, and he said essentially, "Be careful what commitments you make. Don't rush into anything." Was he ever right! Nancy also steered me straight—again. When I told her that I was thinking of keeping my office in the mental health center, she said, "Why would you want to do that?" So I just jumped off into the void, and it turned out that the "void" was one of the nicest places I have ever been. I remember my father saying when I was young that the British aristocracy had a problem because they didn't have to work and so were really useless and without meaningful goals. I don't think he knew about the French aristocrat, de Toqueville, who didn't have to work either but in the early nineteenth century wrote *Democracy in America*, which became a classic. The fact is, things happened rapidly for me and within a year I wondered how I had ever had time to "work."

As an emeritus professor I continued to have access to all the Yale facilities and conferences in fields like history, sociology, music, and theater, as well as medicine. I broadened my education by taking audio and video courses from *The Great Courses* series produced by the Teaching Company, on literature, art, music, history, philosophy, and even psychology and other sciences. And I started having breakfasts, coffee, and lunches with friends at my new "office," the Atticus Book Store and restaurant.

During the "meetings" at my "office" the discussions often hinged on research we were doing, or our work, and what we were trying to accomplish. Many of those I met with were younger people, often graduate students, post docs, or junior faculty members whom I had come to know through my terrific friend Larry Davidson, who was the head of a growing and very exciting mental health research center, or just by chance encounters occurring at the theater, at the gym, or while having coffee at my "office."

I continued doing one thing that I had started before. I led writing groups for people at any level or in any discipline who worked with psychiatric patients, "Writing creatively about clinical experiences." These still take place, at my house over food. A couple of members have been in them from the beginning, others have joined this past year, and others in between. In these groups the major rule for people commenting on a piece just read is to pay attention to "what works" rather than what people do wrong. With this simple rule, as naive as it may sound, I find that people as writers just continue to grow, to try new things, to write with increasing beauty and power. It is like magic, and I still often can't believe that something can work like that.

And I started writing my own papers in new ways, papers that I read to the group, written exactly as I wanted to. One in particular, on the idea of mental illness, started out with a quotation from Victor Hugo, followed by a fairly brief psychiatric history of a patient, then by the statement that the "patient" was my mother and a description of how her life and problems had appeared to me as her son, and the implications of those two perspectives ("professional" and "son") on a person for understanding mental illness in its association with competence and social context. The paper was entitled "Uncertainty Theory" because it borrowed from ideas of that field widely used in domains such as economics and politics that deal with a wide range of complex interacting variables. My paper was turned down by two major psychiatric journals, one reviewer saying, "Whatever you do, don't write about your mother." But the paper was then accepted by a very good psychiatric journal, accepted without even being sent out for review, the first time in my life that had ever happened to me. The editor also solicited commentaries to be published with the article, another first for me. So, although my previous life had been very good to me, now I was doing exactly exactly what I wanted and was lucky enough not to be rejected.

For several years when invited to give lectures in Europe I would spend a month in Paris, where I improved my French and wrote and published articles in French journals. I made friends, whom I would often meet in one or other of my two "offices" there, the Café Danton and the Café Rostand. I have much to say about my experiences of Paris, my love affair with that city, elsewhere in this volume. Here, however, I have to say that it was Paris over these later years that also brought home to me that my body was beginning to deteriorate. Where once I was able to walk across the entire city from one side to another, now I eventually found that a couple of blocks was all I could manage. That was just one of the signs. I who had almost never needed medicines was eventually taking five different ones a day. Having at one time been able to do three sets of twenty pushups without a problem, I discovered now that I couldn't do even one. My hearing got worse, and I needed hearing aids. Even with those, however, I often miss words and the meaning of what someone is saying. So my body has begun to have problems, and now I have pretty much stopped traveling. I miss Paris and my friends there terribly. Of course, I am lucky—and grateful—that my mind is still in pretty good shape. In fact, I think I have a broader understanding of things, people, events, than I have ever had.

EXCERPTS FROM MY INTERVIEWS WITH SARAH KAMENS, I

As I mentioned in the introduction to this book, the idea of writing an autobiography was planted by my good friend Sarah Kamens when she asked if she might interview me about my life and work. The interviews were incredibly enjoyable, but the transcripts of our conversations were less than spellbinding. Some parts were all right, but in others I was not particularly clear and sometimes barely comprehensible. So I decided to try writing a chronology of my life, with the result, after some editing, that you see here. In addition, however, I wanted to include some excerpts from the interviews that enlarge on—and I hope shed additional light—on what has gone before. They will also give a sense of why I so enjoyed the interviews with her. This is the first of two such chapters, in which the excerpts have been edited for clarity.

CONCERNING DIAGNOSTICS AND PSYCHIATRY

John: When I started in the International Pilot Study of Schizophrenia there were a fair number of relatively high-powered people who were struggling with how you classify patients. It's a big deal. It's one of the many problems in psychiatry, or actually any medical field, since it's the foundation of discovering causes and treatments for each of the various disorders. In fact, diagnosis is central to the whole history of medicine. People don't really realize the complexities of the issues. We in psychiatry tend to be isolated. It's not just let's make these diagnostic categories or let's use dimensions and not categories. One of my papers that I really liked that I wrote a long time ago is called "Diagnostic Models and the Nature of Psychiatric Disorder," which was published in *The Archives*. I think nobody paid any attention to it, but it described the problems and strengths of various diagnostic approaches in psychiatry. Psychiatry as a field doesn't have any idea about these complexities or that there's anything other than deciding which diagnostic categories are best or which criteria are best. We're a very stupid field in a lot of ways because we think we're the universe. And we're not.

In medicine if you have gram-positive infections (shown by a color response on a slide), there's certain medicines you use. If you have a gram-negative infection, there are other medicines that you use. And the medicine for one will not be very helpful for the other. So earlier on, I thought well maybe through numerical taxonomy (also called cluster analysis) or other techniques you could find diagnostic groupings that were really solid.

How you make diagnostic categories in medicine is not trivial. And so I thought maybe that would be true in psychiatry. After we were trying to figure it out for several years, and I got more and more involved in it, it seemed to me that it was not going to work. My feeling was that we didn't know enough about what we were dealing with, that is, the nature of psychiatric disorder, to come up with diagnostic categories that would help you define etiology and prognosis and select the appropriate treatment. I don't think diagnosis in our field is like diagnosing a torn hamstring. It's not like gram-positive or gram-negative infection. It's not that clear. Maybe it's something that's simple once you know the answer or maybe it's complex but maybe we're measuring the wrong things. In NIMH recently they decided to base psychiatric diagnosis on the biological underpinnings. If our field is intricately connected with biological, psychological, and social phenomena as I think it is, focusing only on biology or any one of those areas in isolation doesn't seem to me to be a very good basis for understanding psychiatric problems and hence for building a diagnostic system.

. . . But if we're working with an N dimensional space, a variety of variables all of which are important and which interact, we're dealing with a complex system which cannot naively resolve to a simple diagnostic structure. "Dropsy" is a really interesting idea because it was a diagnostic term used centuries ago to describe any kind of body swelling. It was considered a disease, a category. Over time, they realized that no, it wasn't a disease. There were different ways in which a person could get generalized body swelling. Kidney disease or pulmonary disease, cardiac disease or an endocrine disease, any of those could cause it. So it lost its value as a diagnostic category because it had so little selectivity for knowing cause, prognosis and treatment..

Sarah: It sounds like you started to get interested in issues of classification and general medicine perhaps even before psychiatry. Is that right?

John: It may sound mostly academic, but in fact you have to realize that classification is central for thinking about causes and treatments.

Sarah: You have to?

John: Medicine intellectually is a beautiful system. It's a branching system. I would say to a patient, what brings you to the hospital? And you say well, I have a pain in my chest. Okay, so I'm thinking—and this is what you learn in medical school and forever after because it's really complicated—I'm thinking, okay chest pain, likely to be either lungs or heart or it could be a muscle strain. So already, see I've got it down to three things. If you had said well you have pain in your belly then that would be other things. So, you start making a differential diagnosis.

Sarah: There's a difference between learning about how to make a diagnosis as a trainee in medicine and thinking more conceptually about the kind of meta issues in diagnosis like how are these categories formed historically and conceptually? You don't have to do that, do you?

John: Not in medicine, no, or in any system that's really effective. You just learn these branches. It's a beautiful branching tree system. But in psychiatry there's so much overlapping of symptoms and treatments for the diagnoses we make that we need to question the very conceptual system we're using.

CONCERNING THE IPSS: WHAT IT WAS AND WASN'T

John: Well, if you're going to study schizophrenia, you'd better know how you're going to decide who has it and who doesn't.

Sarah: Wasn't that one of the questions?

John: No, that's a question of validity, does the diagnosis you make actually identify a real specific illness. The question we had was *can* you diagnose it in the different centers, in the nine different centers in similar ways, that is can we actually develop methods for knowing that the various centers are using the word "schizophrenia" to mean the same thing. It's almost like trying to develop a word for a dictionary. The question of whether that word identifies a specific disease is an even more complex question. "Dropsy" was a word with an accepted meaning across various medical traditions, but it turned out not be valid for identifying a specific disease.

Sarah: So you wanted to identify the same meaning for the term "schizophrenia" internationally?

John: Yeah. Yes, can you diagnose it? And to develop a way of doing that which works for all centers.

Sarah: Internationally?

John: Yes. Which is why WHO was involved.

Sarah: And was there any question about cultural differences in deciding who has it and who doesn't? In a different country, it might be different from the United States.

John: We would have meetings, I can't remember if it was once a year or twice a year, where all the investigators from the nine centers would come together. And we'd have some consultants. One was Bill Caudill, who was an anthropologist. We drove actually several consultants fairly crazy at the meetings. Bill, for example, would raise questions about the cultural factors and we would just sort of ignore him. Because the simple problems of reaching a diagnosis were so complicated. There were problems at the most basic levels, for example, symptoms used to make the diagnosis, could we agree on what was an hallucination?

It seems stupid to ignore cultural factors, but logistically I think we were probably right. You can't do everything at once. The thing that was sacrificed was cultural differences. I remember at a meeting in Cali, Colombia, after one of the days of the meeting we were having a dinner and doing some dancing. I was dancing with a woman who was the wife of one of the Cali psychiatrists. And she said, what do you do with patients who have this and this picture? And I said well, I didn't know there were patients like that. So we systematically didn't pay attention.

Sarah: They weren't enrolled.

John: I guess not.

Sarah: Well, tell me something. Okay so in order to simplify the study you had to exclude consideration of these cultural differences. You were trying to figure out how to diagnose schizophrenia. What was the point of doing it in these nine different places, if cultural differences weren't . . .

John: It developed interview methods that could be used across centers. So, the same interview questions could be asked in the nine centers.

Sarah: So you wanted to generalize the method of being able to diagnose, but not to diagnose...

John: To evaluate, even broader than diagnose.

Sarah: So it was more about honing the method of assessment and diagnosis than it was about modifying the diagnosis itself?

John: Yes, I think people now have problems with diagnosis. But in those days the problems were even worse. I think people now don't recognize how awful the system was in the past. That DSMS-I and -II, there was no reliability built into those systems, none. So that you could call somebody schizophrenic and somebody next door could call somebody schizophrenic and you were using the same word, but you had no idea what they were talking about. Not only that, you didn't know you didn't have any idea of what they were talking about. So, you really had a pseudo-language. That was bizarre. So for the International Study the goals were really very humble, but they needed to be because the psychiatric world at the time was so scientifically backward. If somebody from India said, I have a schizophrenic patient should I use Thorazine? You had no way of knowing what they were talking about. Thorazine was still Thorazine all over the world, but in terms of what they were calling schizophrenia, you didn't have a clue.

So, you couldn't do epidemiologic studies. You couldn't do any kind of research. I guess the Bible says something like in the beginning was the word. Words are just terribly important. And if you've got a word that nobody knows what it means, or what the other person is talking about, your word is not very helpful. In fact, it's worse than helpful because if you're using the same word, you think you know what the other person is talking about and you don't really have a clue.

Sarah: It sounds like for you and for many people working on the WHO study the purpose of those studies was to remedy that situation.

John: Yes.

Sarah: Okay.

John: And it was very basic. It was at that level really. Can you identify schizophrenia as more or less the same thing in the nine different centers? That was it.

Sarah: And if you could not, would the reason be because of the assessment methods or because schizophrenia is different in these different places?

John: See, there were people like you we would have kicked out of our project.

Sarah: I was excluded a lot just like the people with the complex diagnostic picture.

John: Yeah, no thinking is allowed. Just don't bother us with that. We can't deal with that. The assumption was that we needed to figure out how to create a method that would allow people to answer your question. We couldn't just jump into answering your question if we didn't have a common basis for diagnosing people.

Sarah: So this finding that you and I have talked about and that many people talk about nowadays, the surprising finding that the prognosis was better in certain places than others. Was that something that you were even intending to look at?

John: No.

Sarah: Okay. So that was just something, kind of, thrown in there.

John: Yes.

Sarah: And in maybe just playing around with the data?

John: I haven't followed those studies in detail. But I do know from having worked with the original study, that people are often much happier to get results than they are to look at whether they're really valid. I know that they've done a lot of studies since then, but because of that fact I just can't judge them.

Sarah: Because of what fact?

John: That people are often much more interested in getting results than they are to make sure that they're meaningful. That's where, for me anyway, for areas that I know something about, it's really important to know who the investigators are. Some are really careful and really want to get truth. And some don't care or don't know how to do it. I know there have been a lot of studies correcting for various problems. Because there were major problems when the original claims came out about people doing better in developing countries. There was no sense of how much the sampling techniques were different in the different centers. I think it was possible, for example, that the people whom we diagnosed in those days as having simple schizophrenia or poor premorbid schizophrenia and were sort of quietly disturbed did not come to the attention of people in the developing centers. They were watching the cows or quietly doing some other job ordinarily given to young children, for example, which was true in one instance I saw in India.

And so we may have had a sampling bias that in some cultures you can get by with a severe but non-dangerous disorder in the culture. The example in India was that there was a man with schizophrenia out in the field in one of the villages we visited who was now working. So, he had improved, right? So, he was working watching the cows. Somebody was smart enough—maybe it was me, but I don't remember—to ask the question, well, is that what adult men ordinarily do? What men do at this age? And they said, no, that's a child's job. But he could have easily gotten the rating of "he's working and living adequately as a regular person."

Sarah: I don't recall what exactly the outcome criteria were? It was working and having functional improvement?

John: I was not involved in any major way with the comparison of outcomes in the different centers and I don't know. I don't remember who did that. They may have done that in the headquarters at Geneva.

Sarah: Did they imagine there was a functional component and a symptom component?

John: We did that in Washington with patients from our center. We developed our outcome scale and tested its reliability. I don't know what other people did. At that point I started to follow it much less because I had gotten involved in other things. I guess it's probably true for most research, it really helps to know who the people are that are doing the study and how they are doing it. It's the reason that people reviewing grants and reviewing papers try to be critical. It helps somewhat making sure that something is done in an adequate way. It's a big question. It gets into the more detailed questions that you were asking that we would have kicked you out of the study for. What does it mean that this man was watching the cows? Is that the same thing, for example, as a person who has a forty hours a week job in the United States?

Sarah: Okay. What about some of these other interpretations that people have offered for those results? Like in developing countries, there are stronger family bonds and social structures and they're not as alienating and individualist cultures as the Western world?

John: I don't know. As I say, I hadn't really followed it closely because it was like the situation with the guy watching the cows. If you don't know what questions to ask, then you won't know what a finding means. There are a lot of studies that have been done on those questions since, but I haven't followed them in detail

Sarah: Have you heard people suggest the interpretation that perhaps it had something to do with the way in which we are treating or offering services to people?

John: Yes, I've heard that as an explanation. I've heard that the developing cultures are better than ours as an explanation, that ours are more demanding and more technologically demanding and more complex. Yeah, I've heard a lot of different...

Sarah: What do you think of those explanations?

John: I don't know. But I'm not a good judge because, as I say, I haven't followed that area. There's a bunch of studies, and maybe some of them are good. I just don't know. There have been subsequent studies where they've collected other data.

You know about the studies of "expressed emotion"? That's another area where I don't have that level of certain detail. But it's an interesting concept, expressed emotion. There were some questions about the research involved, but again, I haven't really followed it. The question was whether so called "expressed emotion" in families was connected in some way with schizophrenia in the offspring. It gets into your question about cultural differences. The studies were done in England and there was some question that if you were English, in those days you didn't express much emotion, so if you do, it has to be abnormal. And in fact, I did have an experience that might be relevant. The Tavistock people were doing these group programs to study group process. They brought that whole thing over to the United States, and the British who were involved with these programs in the United States were starting to have major problems because Americans weren't behaving in the same way the British were. Americans were doing much more extreme emotional things in the groups. And British leaders weren't sure how to deal with that.

So, it's cultural differences. Again, all I can say is that if you don't have sophisticated people who are going to do careful work, you can't count on their results. I left this area that you're talking about pretty early. So, I don't really know about the details of the work that's been done

Sarah: Why did you leave?

John: I got more interested in the processes involved in determining course of disorder rather than just the "outcome" and then in specific aspects of diagnosis, and then in subjectivity.

* * * * *

Sarah: How did you know that schizophrenia was the same in all places? How did the group... I'm curious.

John: You put it in a way which I would not accept. That it's the same in all places.

Sarah: Okay.

John: That it can be diagnosed using the same criteria in all places. I feel that we can do that. Whether the diagnosis means the same thing in basic processes, not just symptoms in the US as in say, India, I'm not sure. There's a psychiatrist named Michael Woodbury who was interested in cultural factors. I remember Michael saying that he had spent time in Lambaréné, which is in West Africa [Gabon]. Albert Schweitzer had gone to Africa to work with the indigenous people. Schweitzer, you know about him?

Sarah: No, tell me about him.

John: He was a very famous organist, Bach organist and he was also a religious figure. And he went to Lambaréné and set up a medical clinic there. Anyway, Michael Woodbury went to visit this clinic, and he said that when somebody said they had experiences of, say, being influenced by ghosts, he couldn't tell whether the experience was delusional or cultural unless he talked with the people there who could tell him.

Sarah: So you're saying that the belief may not have the same implications in all places, but that it could be identified in all places.

John: Yes.

Sarah: Can I play devil's advocate? When you said it could be identified in all places. So, there's something. It's not just about the criteria and being able to diagnose it. It's that it exists in some kind of similar form in all places. Because I could tell, I could train a group of people, and forgive me for this, but I could say that anything that walks on four legs and is smaller than a breadbox is a unicorn. And I could send them out.

John: Yes.

Sarah: To any country. And they would reliably.

John: Diagnose unicorns, okay, yeah.

Sarah: But they wouldn't necessarily believe that these animals are unicorns. But there was a belief there and I'm not saying schizophrenia is a unicorn or that it's false, but there's a belief underlying the idea that we can reliably diagnose this. That there's something similar, in essence, in all of these cases.

John: Well, first of all, we would have kicked you out of the international study.

Sarah: I shouldn't have used that example.

John: No, that's all right you can use it, but then you'd have to leave the study. We would not invite you back to the next meeting.

Sarah: I hope you'll continue to interview with me. That was an extreme example.

John: That's not my feeling. I'm not representing my feeling. I'm telling you about the project. I think what I would have said if I had been the head of the study, is that question is an excellent question, which I think it is. But we can't deal with both questions at the same time. And I think that's probably true. You can't imagine how complicated that study was. And it was complicated at every level: research level, political level, funding level. And you had to get these people from different countries and different backgrounds to relate to each other because people get angry at each other because they're human beings. At our meetings where everybody would get together, people would discuss at great length the most trivial or unimportant things. And what you do as a young person there, which I was, is you learn fascinating stuff about people in meetings. One of the guys I had mixed feelings about was very smart, John Wing who was the head of the English group. He's the person who wrote the original symptom interview, the present state exam, the basis for the interview that we used.

John, I suppose, was more or less typical English in the sense of the sophistication of how you deal with impossible social situations. He would sit back and not say anything during one of these long discussions about various trivia. It's amazing how you can get into different things. He would sit back and after an hour or two or three, people would get really exhausted. And John would say well, I've been thinking about this. And here's what we could do. So, he would have a solution all settled. And by then everybody would be exhausted. And so, we would accept his solution. He did that again and again and again. He was masterful. That was his strategy for helping to get things done. So you have the interpersonal level, the political level, all these levels. For a study like that you really have to keep it as simple as you can. Even at that level it's very complex.

We . . . did the reliability studies. And there's just a million different ways of looking at reliability. John Bartko was terrific with that. Is A the same thing as B? Or is Patient A similar to Patient B? Well, by what criteria? And is A more like B than he is like C? So then, do we call A similar to B? But if you have A prime and A is really more like A prime than B, is B then different from A and so should be put in a different diagnostic group? So you get into all these questions. Or if a person has hallucinations at a level of one, but he has no delusions and the other person has delusions at level two, is one clearly psychotic and the other one not? It's just amazing. So, you have a simple question of do two people agree on a rating? Or is Person A like Person B? You have to keep making judgments of how you are going to judge similarity all the time.

We did a study in Rochester. The First Admissions Study, the same data we used for the biplot. We had three research assistants. They would come to me since I was the principal investigator, and ask me, is person X social class two or three? Social class is a very basic concept and this should be a simple question, but it's not. I knew the criteria, but the decision was difficult because maybe they didn't fit neatly into either group, so feeling like a low-grade Solomon, I would make an arbitrary decision. There was no way of definitively deciding. So at each level from the most minute to the most large and from the least to the most political, there are a lot of problems with a study such as the International Pilot Study, yet in my judgment, even with its shortcomings it was very worth doing. It's a bit like another criterion, which I think is super-basic: Does our study provide more information or better methodology than we had before, and in my view the answer was "Yes." It's far from perfect, but it's much better than we had previously.

CONCERNING RESPONSES TO OUR WORK

Sarah: Do you feel like other people felt the same way as you did or were also noticing these things?

John: That paper on hallucinations and delusions as being on continua with each other ["Hallucinations and Delusions as Points on Continua Function"] has been very highly thought of. I just learned that about a year ago. And I hadn't realized it, I just did it. So there are some people that appreciate this stuff. There are other people who don't, a lot of people who don't care. Good clinicians, and other people who actually work with patients are more likely to appreciate the ways in which our concepts and theories don't fit real people, more than people off in labs or using traditional theories.

Sarah: So you felt like there were some people who understood and who found this research useful?

John: Well, we got it published, yeah.

Sarah: Do you feel like it was a lot of people?

John: I don't know. I didn't think I had any sense of that. We didn't set out to find what ideas in psychiatry don't seem to be true. You're doing this study, right? You're collecting data that's for the

International Pilot Study of Schizophrenia. And so, you're being a good boy. You're doing what they want you to do, which is collect the data. And I've been terribly lucky in my life, and at NIMH we had lots of resources and some really good people. And I don't know how it happens exactly. But you notice stuff. Like people with schizophrenia were believed not to get better. And we were doing follow-up interviews. And some of the people with schizophrenia were getting better so we developed a prognostic scale and an outcome scale. So we showed that in fact many people with schizophrenia we were seeing were getting better. That kind of raised hell because, I don't know if I mentioned to you or not, but when we sent that paper out to the *American Journal of Psychiatry,* it was rejected. And we knew what we were doing was good science. I mean we were getting good data and we were analyzing it carefully. And one of the reviewers responded "We know this can't be true. People with schizophrenia can't get better." I loved that.

I was working with Will Carpenter, and he's more of a pain or has more courage than I do. We were just beginners in the field, it was our third or fourth paper and we sent a letter back to the *American Journal of Psychiatry* saying that was a terrible quality review.

Sarah: You did?

John: We never heard any more, but yeah, Will was much more gutsy than I was.

Sarah: And then you published it somewhere else?

John: Yeah, it was published in *The Archives*. So, actually a more demanding and more prestigious journal. That period was just at the rise of biological psychiatry. And we were also doing a lot of studies of diagnostic categories. I was very interested in classification at that point following a major and basic scientific principle thinking that we would figure out how to "cut nature at its joints," that is determining what conditions were similar to or different from others. That always seems more obvious in retrospect than it does when you're trying to figure it out. I much later gave up on the idea that that was possible in psychiatry until we learn more about how to understand basic processes of health and disorder. But at that period it was just at the rise of biological psychiatry. And we didn't realize it consciously at the time, but psychoanalysts who had dominated the field in the US weren't all that interested in what we were doing, but the biologists were because they were trying develop a scientific psychiatry, and they needed classification, reliable classification of patients. And they needed measures of improvement. So, we just stumbled into that.

Sarah: What was it like, you said you were raising hell. What was it like to raise hell?

John: Because it was fun. I mean, nobody probably not that many people noticed. But in spite of that reviewer who said that we know this can't be true, we got a fair amount of acceptance for our work. I don't think we recognized this broader context, we were just doing our work and trying to be conscientious about it. We were getting stuff published and papers we submitted to conferences were getting accepted. So it was good.

* * * * *

Sarah: And what did you conclude from the results of your Rochester biplot study?

John: That the concepts of psychiatric diagnosis were pretty clear in terms of symptom clusters, but that the real patients did not fall into neat little diagnostic groups but had all kinds of symptom combinations.

Sarah: And this study was published in what year?

John: "Do Psychiatric Patients Fit Their Diagnosis?" I think it's in the *American Journal of Psychiatry*, and it would have been in the '70s, I think.

Sarah: Do you think people have made use of the results of that study?

John: No.

Sarah: How come?

John: I have a related paper that I like but nobody's paid any attention to. It pissed me off.

Sarah: What's the other one?

John: The other paper is something I published in *The Archives* when I was still in Washington. And that's "Diagnostic Models and the Nature of Psychiatric Disorder." It discusses the many different approaches to thinking about psychiatric disorders such as categorical approaches putting patients into groups and dimensional models that emphasize degree of various symptoms, and the various mixed models putting those two orientations together.

* * * * *

Sarah: People don't want to know what's going on?

John: They don't seem to care.

Sarah: How come?

John: Well, one thing is that I may have an excessive view of my own importance, which is always a problem. But one of the problems I have in pretty much everything I do—and a couple people have told me, which has been very helpful because I constantly have to work on it—is that I don't give answers regarding what people should do. Like "We should be doing X." I don't do that very much partly because I don't know and partly because, it's funny, but I'm not really interested in that. I'm especially interested in identifying what is real and the concepts that help explain the findings. It's that old Yogi Berra thing, "You can see a lot by just looking," but implied in that, you have to know how and where to look. I am, of course, also interested in the implications of our findings for treatment and prevention.

I think with the diagnostic model's paper that I did make some good conclusions, but I'm not sure. Mostly I'm just screwing stuff up all the time. I mean that's what my research has always done. You think people with schizophrenia never get better? Yeah, guess what? You think hallucinations and delusions are totally separate symptoms? Guess what? You think you're doing an adequate job of evaluation, but you're not asking the people do they help themselves? And that's the essence, I do a lot of that stuff. I also see all that as opening up our understanding and developing more adequate concepts, which in turn indicates more effective treatments and prevention.

Sarah: You do do a lot.

John: I do, yes.

Sarah: We haven't talked in the interview about your paper on hallucinations and delusions. What did you say in that?

John: . . . Besides the old Yogi Berra thing, which I love, . . . I also love the Heisenberg idea: What you learn, what you see, depends on the methodology you use, not only on what the reality is. If you're methodology is only built to show you certain things, that's probably all you'll learn about. But he says it much better. That seems so important to me, unbelievably important.

But the other thing is the Yogi Berra quotation that you can see a lot by just looking. The thing with hallucinations and delusions paper was that we were seeing all these patients in Washington for the International Pilot Study and using the beautifully discrete traditional concepts of hallucinations and delusions, that is, voices and thoughts. But then we noticed that some patients talked about . . . yes, it's a voice, but no, it's more like a thought, or no it's not really a thought, it's almost like a voice. . . .There was the range of things people would say like that. So, all you have to do is look, or listen. All you have to do is pay attention to what people will tell you.

Sarah: And what did you make of that study?

John: That there was a continuum between the two, that the perception and the cognition things were not really distinct entities.

Sarah: And that study, you said has been cited many times.

John: I guess.

Sarah: But the other two not as much as that one.

John: "Do Patients Fit Their Diagnosis?" I don't know, because I don't know how to look that stuff up. And I don't look it up so I don't really know. But mostly I don't have any feedback about those studies, any of them.

CONCERNING THE HISTORY OF SCHIZOPHRENIA THEORIES AND TREATMENT

John: . . . How did I spend a lot of time working with schizophrenia? I don't know. I can't tell you. I don't know.

Sarah: Was there an interest in schizophrenia prior to the thesis or was that maybe your first time focusing on schizophrenia?

John: . . . At that time when I was in medical school here at Yale, one of the most famous people, Frederick Redlich was interested in community psychiatry, and two others, Theodore Lidz and Stephen Fleck, were interested in schizophrenia. So those were the leaders. Lidz was interested in families particularly, but also to some extent in cognition. So why have I done so much stuff in schizophrenia? I don't know. What did whatchamacallit say? The guy that robbed banks, why do you rob banks? Because that's where the money is. I mean they were there. People with schizophrenia were patients. It was a big deal. Schizophrenia was big deal in psychiatry. And there was a lot of interesting stuff going on. The Lidz stuff was interesting actually. He could be pompous and overbearing. But it was interesting stuff. Do you know the Lidz stuff?

Sarah: A little bit but why don't tell me?

John: Well, the thing he's known for is schism and skew. There are two kinds of couples he thought who have schizophrenic offspring. And their relationships are described by schism and skew. Schism is when the two parents really aren't on the same team at all. And the skewed couples are where one member has all the power and the other one does not. Looking at families and their interactions was done often in a terribly insensitive way and could give the feeling of blaming the parents. For many reasons looking at family interactions has been essentially abandoned, which I don't think is a great solution. But I really can't tell you why I'm interested in schizophrenia. I think it just mostly happened. I've met some very interesting and nice people with schizophrenia, but as I tried to say, I think my interests are much broader than that.

* * * * *

Sarah: All right, so people were accepting the idea that people can actually recover from schizophrenia?

John: I don't know about "recover," we talked about improvement.

Sarah: You talked about improvement?

John: "Recovery" is a more complicated idea. Recovery involves the idea that you've gotten totally over it, like with measles or pneumococcal pneumonia. First, once you've had schizophrenia I think the fear must linger that it might return. I had severe back problems a few years ago. Once in a while I get a twinge in my back and instantly have the fear that maybe the old problem is coming back. With schizophrenia, I think it must be just like that, only worse. But with schizophrenia the idea of recovery also involves another question. Since we are ignorant of so many things with schizophrenia, we don't know if it involves an underlying vulnerability and if so whether that remains. Thus recovery, at least total recovery, is really not an adequate concept.

Sarah: Recovery is a more complicated idea, that's true. But people improve.

John: Yeah. And they weren't supposed to because that was a major theory in the field of psychiatry. One of the pioneers of modern psychiatry was Emil Kraepelin. He tried to make psychiatry more scientific by defining major categories of mental illness. A major category was dementia praecox, more or less what we call today schizophrenia. Kraeplin described dementia praecox by putting together four different diagnostic groups. He used as the major criterion for dementia praecox that the patients didn't improve. So that became, in a sense, the base for all of scientific psychiatry. Since our work came out there have been many studies around the world showing that our conclusions were accurate, but at first there were many criticisms of our work, some pursuing valid questions and others like "we know this isn't true" based only on unscientific beliefs. In fact, there are still many people, now sixty years later who still hold on to that old Kraepelinian view in spite of all evidence being against it. Kraepelin was a very impressive person, but there were limits to the kinds of methods he could use for his research knowledge.

So the finding of improvement in schizophrenia screwed all that up, which was fun and of course really important for patients and their families and for treatment systems. It meant that these people that were being told and that they had this disease and they wouldn't get better now could be told that they might. And that's been a struggle to this very day. I was in France a couple of years ago. A high-level professor was teaching at the Collège de France and gave a lecture to her students that people with schizophrenia just had a downhill course. And I was going crazy.

Sarah: You were in the lecture?

John: Yeah, I was a special guest. And I said some things. I was very nice, but ...

Sarah: What did you say?

John: I don't remember really. But I think it was something like there are some studies showing that people with schizophrenia could improve.

Sarah: You happened to have conducted many of them.

John: Yes.

Sarah: You didn't mention that?

John: No.

Sarah: Why do you think it's such a struggle even today?

John: I think a lot of people with schizophrenia do have extended problems—that's one thing. I think there are some disorders that go on longer and some that are just acute responses. And some people that have these symptoms continue to have problems that go on longer and some don't.

I think there's also a sociologic problem. I don't have any data for this at all, but I think there is evidence that we humans need to have some people who are different from us, . . . people who are worse off or are hopeless or something like that, like different races, and that helps us feel better. I don't know, but something like that. It depends on the sample, but it's like at least thirty, maybe sixty percent of people who look like they're schizophrenic improve. And the fact is that there are still professionals, a fair number, who are saying people with schizophrenia never get better or they only get worse. There's something weird going on. It's nothing to do with the people with schizophrenia. All I can think of is maybe we need this group of people who are impossible, who are worse than us, who don't belong, something like that.

Sarah: So we need another category.

John: Yeah. And it's interesting because you can take a look at a recent trend. There are a whole group of approaches now trying to treat schizophrenia early in its onset. In fact, it's an issue that is very complex in terms of scientific method and how we define "schizophrenia." But there's an assumption that if you treat these people early you can prevent long-standing disorder. It's not a bad idea, but it's much harder to demonstrate than is often realized. We assume they are early onset. We get them and if you do X and Y, they'll get better. But it may be hard to know early on if a person really has schizophrenia. Or it's also possible maybe the reason they haven't gotten better before or maybe the reason some of these people didn't get better in the past was because they were treated in such a way as to contribute to chronicity. I'm sure that's true, at least partly.

Sarah: What do you mean treated in such a way?

John: Well, were put in hospitals for long periods of time, or given high doses of antipsychotic drugs or treated like non-people. I remember as a kid in Erie, the mental hospital was North Warren, which was, I don't know, twenty, thirty miles from Erie at least. And people would say if you acted, kind of funny, they'd say well you probably should go to North Warren. So, I think there may be something in society as well.

Sarah: Social factors. Well, we've talked about one side of things, which is that there are still these kind of struggles and problems in the field today, and that not everybody in the field has recognized the fact that many people who experience these types of things do improve or do get better or do feel better. And there's the other side and I'm speaking specifically about your work. You work has had a major impact on the field. The work of you and others who have documented these facts about psychotic experiences or experiences that we call psychosis and the fact that they can be transient. What has that been like for you, to make that kind of impact on the field?

John: I don't have any sense of that at all. I just do my work.

Sarah: I had a feeling you would say something like that.

John: I complain when someone says once again, "schizophrenics never improve." When I went to that lecture . . . in France, I was very polite, but I'm pretty polite anyway. But I will say something. Regarding any impact I have had on the field, it's really hard to know. A couple people have told me that my work has had an impact. And that's great. I'm delighted, but I don't feel it directly.

Sarah: You don't have any sense of how it's impacted research or treatment?

John: No.

Sarah: Do you have any sense of how treatment of people in hospitals or experiencing what we call psychosis has changed over the years of your doing this research?

John: Well, I'm certainly aware of the Recovery Movement, especially since I'm very close friends with Larry Davidson. But I would be aware of it anyway. I think things that have led to those changes are more complicated than any impact I had. When I was still at NIMH they had the extramural staff who were the people that handled the federal mental health programs. They would have conferences and they were starting to invite people like

Judy Chamberlain and Esso Leete, who were some of the earliest so-called consumers who spoke out about problems of stigma and the mental health field. I'm not sure what we called them then. They would give lectures and would be participants at conferences given by NIMH. The people at NIMH extramural included some really good people. There really are a lot of good people in the world. I mean there are a lot of bad ones. But there are a lot of good ones. That was a very radical thing for the NIMH people and the "consumers" to do. That was totally separate from us. So there was other stuff going on.

And there were people like R.D. Laing, whom many people did not take all that seriously. But Loren Mosher built somewhat on Laing's ideas and started Soteria House, a small house where psychotic young people were treated with a lot of attention to caring interactions. Loren and I were at NIMH together. We were friends. . . . It was an exciting time.

Sarah: What was it like to be colleagues or friends with Loren Mosher?

John: There were I don't know how many of us, maybe six or eight at NIMH together. We played touch football on weekends. I think he was part of that group. But there was a whole bunch of people, John Davis and Herb Meltzer and Dick Wyatt, a fair number of people who became pretty well known in the field. Loren was always a pain in the ass, but he was very good and creative, and he became head of the schizophrenia center at NIMH. . . . And I liked him. He was a consultant at a halfway house called Woodley House in Washington, which was quite a progressive halfway house for psychiatric patients. I can't remember why, but he left there and told them they should talk with me about being the consultant and I did. . . . It was a good organization. Loren had a very different life style and way of being than most of us, and had some problems that were worse than I knew.

Sarah: Worse than you knew?

John: He lived a very unusual life. He was kind and everything but lived as he wanted to. I didn't realize until after he died, but I learned then that he had a lot of major problems in his life. But he was a real pioneer. I remember we had a big schizophrenia conference in Rochester—that would have been around 1972. He was head of the NIMH schizophrenia center, so he was one of the speakers. He went out on the stage wearing a cowboy hat. Well, you didn't do that unless you were Loren Mosher because everybody else, including me, dressed more conservatively. He would do stuff like that just to aggravate the more straight-laced people. But the Soteria House was a very serious thing.

Sarah: What did you think of it?

John: I thought it was probably a great idea. . . . It was an anti-chronicity thing for acutely psychotic young adults. They would have lots of mostly young people working there to help, and people were treated humanely and like people. Soteria House was a house and it was not a massive institution, so there wasn't a huge group of people. And they weren't in a hospital setting. So . . . it was a very much focusing on human interaction, and I thought it was really good.

Mosher was more anti-medicine than I would have been. But it was a reaction to the heavy focus on medication that had come into psychiatry so his behavior didn't bother me all that much. Will Carpenter, Tom McGlashan, and I wrote a paper on treating people with schizophrenia without medications. So, I didn't have any kind of religious beliefs about meds since I didn't think anyone had the definitive treatment answers. We generally used medications but tried not to depend entirely on them. Because the superstructure of psychiatry was pretty heavy handed, having somebody like Loren involved was a great freeing influence. He was a breath of fresh air.

Sarah: I have some colleagues who started a Soteria House in Jerusalem, and I hope that you'll be able to meet them one day. They're both psychiatrists.

John: Loren died I think it was about six years ago now. There was a memorial conference in Germany which I was at. Luke Ciompi, who started a Soteria House in Bern, Switzerland, was there. And there are a couple maybe several Soterias in Germany. So quite a few of them were set up. I didn't know that about Jerusalem. I think if people get dogmatic in any way, they get in trouble because they aren't open to really look at what's going on. Not being dogmatic I think can be a very good thing because our knowledge is limited.

Sarah: You mentioned alongside Loren Mosier, R.D. Laing. What did you think of his work?

John: He was a little too wild for me.

Sarah: Too wild for you?

John: I didn't know him. I never saw the place in London, but yeah, I think you can get too ideologic in psychiatry in any direction. Did I tell you that at the end of my first year of medical school I was a nursing assistant at the Psychiatric Institute? Did I tell you about that?

Sarah: . . . Let's talk about it a little bit.

John: All right, well I was a nursing assistant, because after the first year of medical school, what do you do? I needed to earn some money. And . . . Bill Radcliff, who was a friend of mine at medical school, said you can get a job as a nursing assistant, I'll tell you who the head nurse at this place is, and you can write them. And I did, and they said fine. So that was a wonderful experience. I had no power. They wouldn't even let me read the records of patients. . . . I did things like count the sharps after meals, I guess knives or forks or whatever. But most of the time I spent taking the patients to the basketball court or sitting with them in the evening and playing cards and just talking. And so, having no power and just being there, it was a great way of seeing the field of psychiatry. I thought about that as we were talking about ideology.

There were two young kids in there, preteens I think. And one was crazy, to speak technically; the other one was clearly not. And they were identical twins. . . . I knew from one of the nurses that they were both there for the schizophrenia study, and they were both considered schizophrenic. The guy that was doing the study was a geneticist, one of the early schizophrenia geneticists whose name escapes me for some reason. One day I said to the nurse I can see how Charlie (I'm making up the names) would be considered schizophrenic, but I can't see why David would be considered schizophrenic. And the nurse said, listen, if they're here on the genetic study and one twin is schizophrenic, the other one always is. And I don't know if what she said was true or not, but I never forgot it.

Sarah: You don't know, you mean, if it's true in the study or if it's true in general?

John: I assume what she was saying is that the investigator wants them both to be schizophrenic to help his genetic theory so they'll both be considered schizophrenic. There were no diagnostic criteria so you could call people whatever you wanted to in order to fit them to your beliefs. It was a great learning experience.

Sarah: What year was this?

John: That was at the end of my first year of medical school. So it would be '55.

Sarah: I guess there were no diagnostic criteria at that time that were really in use.

John: There was DSM whatever, I think DSM-II.

Sarah: I think it was one at that time.

John: Maybe it was. . . . Yeah, in either case the criteria were so fuzzy.

Sarah: And you experienced them as fuzzy at that time?

John: I don't think I paid much attention. That's what she was saying, in a way. We can call them anything we want really. When I got involved in the international pilot study, and especially when Will and I started coming out with some of our findings, Europeans would say, Americans, they don't know how to diagnose schizophrenia, which was true. And so, to adapt to that criticism, we had a method for using the criteria of different European schools of psychiatry. There were many sets of criteria because there were different schools of thought.

Sarah: At that time?

John: Yeah, at that time. We could test all of them in terms of outcome, for example, because from our interviews we had the symptom measures on patients that were essential for making diagnoses with the various systems.

Sarah: This was back in the '50s.

John: No, that would have been the '60s.

Sarah: In the '60s they were on DSM-II . . . DSM-I was '52 to '64.

John: Two was as fuzzy as one, right?

Sarah: Two was actually more psychoanalytic than one.

John: Was it? I don't remember. We had recorded the patients' symptoms, so we could apply our data for several different sets of diagnostic criteria. One of our papers actually described using different diagnostic systems. And then we used also Kurt Schneider's first-rank symptoms. So, we had the capacity to test different concepts of schizophrenia. I learned about the beauties and powers of measurement to test beliefs at that late age as I was working with our data in the International Pilot Study.

CHAPTER 8

REFLECTIONS ON PSYCHIATRY, SCIENCE, MENTAL HEALTH, AND A COUPLE OF OTHER THINGS

People can get better.

My earliest experience with mental illness was, of course, my mother. I have been shocked in recounting my childhood, high school, and college lives, how much I have mentioned my relationship with my father and how little my mother. I do recall things, mostly moments with her, some very lovely and special, but mostly I recall her existence as a shadow, as being there but not being there, or as not being there at all. When she was taken from the house, no one as far as I can remember ever talked to us, my sister or me, about it other than that she had to go to a hospital in New York. There was never a discussion with a doctor or a social worker or even within the family as far as I can recall about what was wrong with her or how we might deal with it. I think we just were supposed to deal with it, to get on with our lives, and so we did—more or less.

So my mother's mental illness—I guess that's what it was—was never part of our conscious existence, and although it most certainly influenced my subsequent life in many ways, it was always part of the background, the matrix, not an object for conscious consideration. Thus, the first time I remember thinking consciously about mental illness was in my college introductory psychology class. We weren't allowed to take psychology until our sophomore year, the idea being—I guess— that it might be too upsetting for beginning freshmen. The professor was Henry Gleitman, who knew everything and was a good teacher. Years later he wrote a popular psychology text, but so far as I know, unlike the other "psych" professors at Swarthmore who were important leaders of Gestalt psychology, Henry never did any special research. When he got to the section on mental illness, he was lecturing on how people became mentally ill and how the illness could be both long-lasting (the concept of chronicity) and recur frequently and I remember raising my hand and asking, "Don't people ever get better?" And Henry, giving that wonderful gentle smile of his, said, "Yes Mr. Strauss, people can get better." I suddenly realized about fifteen years ago, "My heavens, that presaged my whole work life." Somehow, what I have done for the whole time is try to understand whether people get better and if so why and how. All my research has somehow involved follow-up studies, seeing patients over time to see what happened to them.

Our initial research showing that people with even severe mental illness could often get better was a very big deal because there was an established belief that especially people with schizophrenia never did. In fact, schizophrenia was at first called *dementia praecox*, early dementia, and patients (and their families) were often told something like this by psychiatrists: "You have a disease like diabetes. You will have it all your life and have to take medicine for it all your life, and there are many things like getting married, having a family, doing skilled work that you will never be able to do." Imagine being a teenager or in your twenties and being told that! In addition to its practical impact on patients, the theory that schizophrenia was a kind of "dementia" also was an important foundation of modern psychiatric thinking, So the idea that people with schizophrenia get worse or stay the same but never get better was a major thing both practically and theoretically. And, as we showed, it wasn't true.

THE IMPORTANCE OF SCIENCE

When I began medical school I thought I had a pretty good foundation in science. After all I had taken chemistry and biology courses in high school, when I also did a lot of reading in science. Then in college, I took the basic pre-med courses—chemistry, biology, physics, comparative anatomy, organic chemistry—and as a psychology major, I had to take statistics. Med school, though, took me to a new plane, with intensive studies of anatomy, physiology, pathology, and things like that, much more science. The third and fourth years of medical school were on the wards, where I began to add to my mostly book learning the immense amount of practical knowledge that the medical field involves. Internship and the year of medical residency followed—more practical expertise, more science. Then came my psychiatric residency. This was different. In that period psychiatry was heavily based on Freudian thought, and what we learned was a lot of new terminology. Freudian concepts and the various development and pathology theories around them were taught as truth, as part of medicine.

At NIMH I treated patients and worked with their families so continued to learn important concepts and their attendant theories, this time including more attention to the possible role of families in the patient's life context. Then I got involved with the International Pilot Study of Schizophrenia, the goal of which was to develop assessment and diagnostic methods for what we called schizophrenia across the world. Now that might sound simple enough, but wait a minute. As a medical student and then a resident in psychiatry, I had several times asked supervisors, "Why is this patient considered to have schizophrenia?" It was not that I was particularly interested in diagnosis, but in the rest of medicine, when someone was diagnosed, say with pyelonephritis or lung cancer, you knew more or less what they had, what the criteria were for making the diagnosis, what treatments would be used, and what the prognosis was. Once you have a diagnosis, the other things fall in place. In medicine the diagnosis is a very powerful tool.

So what were the answers my psychiatry supervisors gave to my question, "Why is this patient considered to have schizophrenia?" I have already recounted what my med school supervisor said about Mr. W.: "Because he's in this hospital." The answers were not much better during my psychiatry residency: "Because she doesn't relate well to other people" or "Because he's been sick for so long." This was weird.

The overall goal of the IPSS was to find out whether people with schizophrenia could be found pretty much all over the world. That would make it possible to figure out if cultural factors were important, what treatments worked best, and major questions of that sort. But basic to the whole study was the question of diagnosis and diagnostic criteria. Certain symptoms such as hallucinations (hearing voices when no one was present), for example, and delusions (strange ideas, such as "the FBI is trying to poison my food") were likely to be central, but the question came up, how can you find out reliably if these symptoms are present and then whether people in different centers have a cluster of symptoms that could be identified as "schizophrenia." We also planned a follow-up evaluation to see if it would be possible to collect comparable data on a course of illness in the different centers.

Now the question of "reliability" sounds like a particularly boring question. What it boils down to is: Do two or more observers hearing the same response to a question agree, for example, that, yes, this person hears voices. I won't trouble you with how difficult it is to figure out how to ask the question optimally or with the different statistical approaches and the interpretations of their results that are involved with answering that "simple" question, "Yes, these raters agree that the person has hallucinations." Enter our wonderful biostatistician John Bartko. He had to teach us about measurement. All the science courses I had taken notwithstanding, I had never had a clue how beautiful, crucial, and complicated measurement can be. Just that simple little thing, does person X have symptom Y or not, in fact is not so simple. For example, one patient responded to the hallucination question, "Do you hear voices when there is no one there?" with "Do you mean George?" I asked her who George was. George, she explained, was someone who came over in the grandfather clock the family bought in England. All the family heard George. Fortunately (for our need to measure) she also heard voices that the other people in the family did not hear. But the variety of such complicated replies is almost infinite. I did the diagnoses for one multiteam project where the biologically oriented psychologists wanted me to "just tell us who is in which diagnostic group and we'll take it from there." Not always so easy or so obvious in the mental health field. When I was doing all my science courses we never really dealt with these issues. Maybe we didn't need to. But in the mental health field it is essential to make them overt. I think often, after having had these experiences, of supervisors who would tell me "Well, this person has a problem with countercathexes" or "We see here a problem with superego formation." You know in a general way what they mean, but although they talk as though these statements were proven fact, totally reliable judgments, how could they ever be so sure? Hell, we couldn't always tell if a person had something as "obvious" as hallucinations or not.

Measurement is crucial for a science, does a patient have X or not, but in psychiatry it can also be extremely difficult to do. So the question arises, can you have a science of psychiatry if measurement is so complex? I think you can, but that discussion is too complicated to take up here. Maybe later.

SOME THOUGHTS ABOUT THE MENTAL HEALTH FIELD

I'm talking with this middle-aged woman who has a diagnosis of schizophrenia. Notwithstanding the fact that she has trouble thinking coherently, she holds a job as the major secretary in a very busy and confusing office. I ask her with astonishment during our third follow-along interview, having seen her every two months, "But how are you able to work in that situation with the problems of concentration and thinking clearly that you have?" And she answers me, "As I've told you before, Dr. Strauss, when I'm in that setting it's good for me because I HAVE to organize myself." And she *has* told me before, but it has taken this long for it to register because what she has been telling me just doesn't fit with what I have been taught or what seems logical. Now, when I finally hear her, I am surprised. This kind of thing has happened to me many times, and each time I am surprised.

Sometimes my thought after a patient tells me something that surprises me is, "Of course. Why didn't we know that already?" For example, I had been taught and believed that it was not a good idea for one person with serious mental illness to marry another with a major psychiatric problem. Then, however, I had a research patient with severe bipolar disorder who told me during an interview that his wife also had that disorder. I must have looked astonished because he proceeded to reassure me that it was really a good thing because they understood each other's experiences. When his wife said to him, "You're getting out of control" or something like that, he realized she knew what she was talking about and he took the necessary actions to get back to a better state. The lessons I draw from this are once again Yogi Berra's principle that "You can see a lot by just looking"—in this case, you can hear a lot by just listening—and, from another perspective, the idea of one of the founders of modern psychology, William James, that any mental experience is as important as any other and needs to be understood.

As I think about experiences like the contacts with patients I have just described, I am bound to say that the mental health field seems a bit bizarre to me. We go from one extreme explanatory model to another, not noticing the crazy tendency in those wild swings to ignore the very serious efforts of those who came just before us. We lurch from one explanation to another—biological (brain disease), psychological (e.g., poor ego development), social (e.g., social class, family disorder), experiential (e.g., post traumatic), and the much proclaimed but sadly underdeveloped "biopsychosocial"—without the ability to look at the whole thing. Like some retarded chimpanzee, rather than noticing that we can put one box on top another to reach the banana we just continue to climb on one or another box while essentially ignoring the others. Having been both a researcher and a clinician, I have throughout been impressed by how poor the fit is between our theories, concepts, and research practices to the complexity of the realities. Yes, we are like that tired old joke about the drunk man looking for his keys under the corner street light rather than the place he dropped them in the middle of the block "because the light is better here." I'll go a bit beyond Yogi Berra to quote William Osler, who had an idea not so different: "Listen to the patient. He is telling you the diagnosis." The issue then, of course, is how you look, how you listen, what you notice, what is the range of variables and issues you include, and what should you exclude. It's really as simple (and as complicated) as that.

I have learned the most from encounters with research or treatment patients who have insisted on telling me about themselves even though they really had to work at getting me to hear them, to pay attention to their reports of their experiences rather than my preconceptions. From the patient who said, "As I've told you before, Dr. Strauss, when I'm in [my office setting] it's good for me because I HAVE to organize myself," which she had to tell me at three successive interviews before it finally registered with me. From the patient who, after comprehensive interviews about the impacts of her symptoms, treatments, work, family, other relationships, and living setting, asked: "Dr. Strauss, why don't you ever ask me what I do to help myself?" And from the patient who came in looking fine but complaining about her symptoms being more severe and who told me: "No, no, Dr. Strauss, I know I look fine, you've mentioned that several times, but that's why it's such a problem. People tell me I look great but it's always at the time when I am going through emotional hell." Each was trying to get me to see them as they were, not as I had believed, to attend to their feelings, their experience of the world, their desires to act, their deciding upon and carrying out of actions—that's what I consider to be their real subjectivity.

A couple of years ago I watched one of the *Great Courses* on modern social history, "European Thought and Culture in the 20th Century." The course focused on how the context in which a writer or scientist lived was a major influence on his or her work. I began to think, if that way of looking at the world and what happens to the people in it is important, then how has the world in which I live influenced my thinking and my work. It's a bit like Archimedes saying if he had a long enough pole and a place to put a fulcrum he could move the world. If you can somehow get outside your world to look at it, you will be much better able to figure out what the hell you are doing and why—and the meaning of your work, if it has any.

You can see a lot by just looking or listening to the patient, but given human nature, our training, and the need we feel to be experts and know things, it is hard to look and to listen. Of course, much depends on the setting in which you look and listen, your office, the ward, in a coffee house, or while doing dishes together. Much also depends on your situation—having to decide diagnosis and treatment, during a highly structured research interview, in an open-ended research interview, or in a general interaction. And, there is also your personality and mood. I have listened to the recording of one research interviewer, Lisa, who just asked the required questions but somehow elicited unusually frank responses from her patients. I learned from the research director that Lisa had a manner so open and non-threatening that interviewees would tell her things that they had never mentioned previously. In some corner of our experience we all know that such things occur—we have heard of patients who talk to one clinician and tell crucial details they have never shared with others—but these things are rarely taught and may not be "efficient." The data are all there, but we haven't figured out how to see and hear them and then how to correct our concepts and theories in order to put them all together. I guess I keep going "willy-nilly" back to the Kantian model: We receive data from the world and then shape them with our minds, and the process is interactive, including what we notice and how we act to elicit the information, all of which is influenced by the context within which we live.

Still, I ponder whether my fascination with hearing about the diversity and depths of human experiences and efforts to try and figure out their theoretical and practical implications can be influenced not only by my own predispositions and what these patients try to teach me but also, to some extent, by the times in which we live and work. How much we are biased by what we have learned and our broader context may be demonstrated by the piece of history from the mental health field I have alluded to earlier when Will Carpenter, John Bartko, and I published our findings in the '60's showing with careful documentation that people with schizophrenia could improve. Our first paper on that topic was rejected by one major journal to which we submitted it, and one reviewer commented: "We know this [that people with schizophrenia can get better] isn't true." The article was published by the more prestigious journal to which we then sent it. Now, almost sixty years later, some people are still teaching, learning, and writing that people with schizophrenia cannot improve.

In my experience, acceptance of new findings does take place, albeit in this case extremely slowly. A greater percentage of people do now realize that people with schizophrenia may get better. Some of that is due to the fifty-plus studies that have by now been published by researchers from around the world, all with more or less the same results that we obtained. But much of the change in belief is the result of the many patient and family political-action groups pushing, as against a great stone, to have people recognize this more optimistic truth. It has involved a huge amount of work, this evolution of belief, but the evolution has generated many changes in practice and attitude, as reflected in the Recovery Movement. If people's beliefs can blind them and prevent "just looking" and "just listening" then I suppose our social context (which, of course, I share) determines in many ways what we do or don't notice and believe. Somehow, my way of dealing with this has been to rebel against it.

All that generates what I would call a Kantian paradox. If our knowledge of the world involves some interaction between what we see and hear and the structuring characteristics of our minds, what we "know"—our concepts and theories—interacts with what we see, hear, and feel. As part of this interaction, what we "know" can interfere with or otherwise influence what we see and hear. I first encountered that strikingly with an experience I had several years ago. As a child, I would often try to draw a tree. This began when I was about seven and continued on through high school and college, by which time it was a form of doodling in a class that didn't catch my interest. But it was always the same tree. Even when I tried to draw a different tree or draw from nature, I ended up with something that looked like the tree I had been drawing since grade school. Disgusted by my failures, I finally gave up. But then several years ago I took a course on drawing. It had a name like drawing with the right side of the brain. A basic idea was that you drew not the objects themselves but the spaces that surrounded the objects. After many indoor exercises our teacher took us to draw in a park.

At last, my challenge had arrived: Could I draw a real tree? Skeptical and somewhat apprehensive, I started out, following the teacher's admonition to "draw the spaces between the branches, the spaces between the trunk and its surroundings." What began to emerge was a real tree, not the sad non-tree of old! The final drawing was an exciting, long-awaited triumph! It seems to me that this experience was not so different from what I had found in much of my research. If you search for a method and an attitude, it is possible to notice the realities that you had not seen previously; your observations can escape from the errors of what you "knew" before, your previous concepts and beliefs. It's all so simple, so basic.

What I've reported from my research indicates strongly that if you look in more open ways or with new methods at the experiences of people with psychiatric problems, you see and hear stuff that challenges current concepts, theories, and beliefs, and you open things up for new discoveries and concepts—just as the step on the bottom of the float of a seaplane provides a discontinuity that allows the plane to break free of the water on which it rested. But after all, that's just a basic aspect of science, isn't it? True, some of what we have reported more recently in the realm of subjectivity is more difficult to prove than our earlier findings, but if patients report these subjective things repeatedly (e.g., "I decided I had to pull myself together, so I did ") and if they seem to conform to what we observe and ourselves experience, that's worth serious consideration, at least at the level of an important hypothesis—and it can be a hypothesis with major theoretical and practical implications. If we are to include the human in our human science, subjective reports cannot merely be ignored because we have not yet understood how to measure their reality.

INNOVATIVE APPROACHES

I had some critical words to say about French psychiatry earlier in this chapter. But, of course, French psychiatry, like psychiatry elsewhere, is diverse and in some cases quite innovative. I have a good psychiatrist friend in Paris who works with groups. He is terrific. I attended one of his sessions with graduate students, and he had three of them form a temporary "mini-family"—he and they were spectacular. The exercise was an exciting way of modeling family dynamics and also provided a way of commenting on them and exploring their implications. And, of course in community psychiatry, the French developed the ideas of sectors, that psychiatry ought to be set up to deal with geographically defined sectors so that everyone in those sectors could receive adequate care. It was and is a great idea, but in France, as elsewhere, it has proved more difficult to implement than might have been foreseen.

And then there is Sandra. One time while I was in Paris, I heard a striking radio interview with a woman, Sandra Meunier, a clown who worked with older people on a palliative care ward. With the help of my friend in the hotel reception I found her phone number and called her, explaining who I was and how interesting her work was to me. We arranged to meet at one of my café "offices" and then for me to go to the hospital where she worked to watch her. I was so impressed with how, dressed as a clown with the braids of her hair held at right angles from her head by wires, with a large red fake nose and wearing a frilly dress, she could tap into the fantasy worlds of patients, connecting with them in a way that a regular staff person never could. ("How are you?" "Last night I heard the bells." "What did they say?" "They said, When are you coming." "And what did you say?" "I told them I knew I had to come soon but wasn't quite ready.") I also sat in on a session where Sandra (again in her clown getup) was working with nurses, bringing into the nursing class room a hospital bed and inviting the nurses to portray "the patient from hell" and then the "nurse from hell." What a wonderful way to help them express feelings they must have bottled up for a long time. Sandra and I published an article about her work.

The best "mental health" work I have seen in France shows a creativity of thought and action that I have not seen elsewhere. It is also characterized by a remarkable breadth of knowledge. One nurse I met was also a philosopher and scholar. She had written beautifully about the meaning and nature and history of the concept of symptoms for a medical philosophy dictionary, and conducted an empirical study of refugees living in Poland. Another woman, I think she was a psychologist, lectured and taught medical students about the concepts of pathological and normal, starting her talks describing the remarkable work of Georges Canguilhem, a physician and philosopher.

These experiences were fascinating examples of something I often experienced in France, an impressive amount of creativity right alongside some very rigid maintenance of old traditional practices. Because of my own particular situation, I was able generally to avoid what seemed to me antiquated practices and beliefs and greatly benefit from learning about the exciting new efforts. Here's another wonderful example of this juxtaposition: A friend of mine in Paris was involved with something called the "Atelier de Non Faire" ("The workshop for doing nothing"). I think the title was an effort by the people who started it to thumb their nose at some of the traditionalists. The work in the "Atelier" was carried out almost entirely by people with severe and prolonged mental illness who also created and ran the programs and were involved in the administration. When I visited, I was asked to give a talk to a group of psychology interns who were assigned there as a learning experience. My "talk" was mostly a discussion with the interns who told me what a shock it had been for them following all they had learned in their training about how people with severe mental illness were incapable of doing practically anything, to come to this place and see these "incompetent" people run the whole enterprise effectively.

While I'm on the subject of the various kinds of creativity I have encountered in Paris, I want to mention that this creative deviation from the usual may also be common elsewhere in Europe. When I was in the Netherlands, almost by chance, I found out that one center was conducting "horse therapy." Now I know this has been done in the United States and elsewhere for autistic kids and others, but I had not heard of its being done with adults who were dealing with severe mental illness. The horse therapist, Natalie Bryssinck, offered to have a session for me to show how it was conducted. I accepted of course (but was a bit skeptical), and we went to the barn where she led out a horse and then instructed me on how to lead it, feed it, and mount it. I think it's going to be difficult to explain myself here, but I will give it a brief try. Natalie, herself, was remarkably gentle, patient, and understanding. When I was ten I had briefly been given some riding lessons and then when I was hitchhiking in Colorado during that summer in college I ended up one day at a dude ranch, so I had seen horses up close before. But there was something very special and very different about this session. It had to do with paying attention to what the horse needed and expected, for example, holding the carrot to feed him horizontally in my hand and perpendicular to his head. That may sound pretty silly, but horses are very big, too big to be trifled with, and I gather you have to pay attention to what they need, understand and react to. What's involved is so simple, so basic, so important that you learn that you absolutely have to pay attention to those things.

Now, you might think that as a psychiatrist working with a patient, you would just naturally have the same attitude. But as I describe elsewhere, the process of becoming an "expert" tends to lead you away from such simple things and, I think, often leads to major problems by not recognizing the autonomy, needs, and understanding of the patients with whom we work. Does it seem silly to compare dealing with a horse to dealing with a human being? I hope not, it is not meant to be. It's just that horses are very big, and you can't get away with forgetting that!

But horse therapy as treatment for severe mental illness? I have no expertise there, but it could be useful and important as a way of helping the person to get a new start with relating to another being. People with severe mental illness often have major problems relating to other people. The origins of these problems are poorly understood, whether they are connected to genetic factors, early life experiences with trauma or difficult parenting, or something else. Horse therapy, it seems to me, could be a way of starting again to learn how to connect to another being. Horses are different from humans and thus previous human horrible experiences may be less crucial in learning to relate to a horse than to another human. A horse has all kinds of needs that a patient can be taught to recognize and try to meet, and the patient may learn that a particular action on her or his part can generate a very pleasant (or unpleasant) response but that these rarely relate to ulterior motives or other hidden sources. And, of course, with a good therapist such as I had, the whole process takes place under the guidance of a kindly teaching person who is seeking to connect to the patient and help him or her to learn new ways of relating and patterns of behavior and response. And finally, I come back to it, horses are really big. This means that the patient's connection to the horse is a very serious thing, not just a behavioral treatment gambit.

DO PEOPLE GET BETTER? (REVISITED)

So back to the IPSS and what we did with our new respect for the complex, crucial, beautiful issues of measurement. Since the IPSS involved a two-year follow-up, we decided to see if people with schizophrenia actually improved or not. We developed a reliable outcome scale (actually a level-of-function scale that we could apply at the initial interview and then at the two-year follow up) and, while we were at it, a reliable prognostic scale. The latter we rated before we did the follow-up interviews, and the former, the outcome or level-of-function scale, after doing the two-year follow-up interview. We analyzed the results, and, my goodness, we found that a sizable number of the people with schizophrenia we had seen did improve.

As I have described, we sent the findings in to a major psychiatric journal, and the paper was rejected. The reviewer who claimed "We know this isn't true" gave no references, no data. So much for the power of belief over data. (In the seventeenth century Francis Bacon argued for the superiority of bottom-up methodical observation of facts over the top-down approach of fitting facts to established concepts; apparently the thinking he contended with has not entirely disappeared.) Other criticisms were more legitimate, that two years was not a long enough follow-up period, that we were wrong in how we were diagnosing schizophrenia. We wrote another paper using the differing systems of various leaders in the field to diagnose our patients, and the results didn't change substantially. People with schizophrenia at least over two-year period can improve no matter what criteria you use to make the diagnosis. We sent both articles to an even more respected psychiatric journal, which published them. Subsequent research by investigators from many parts of the world and with longer follow-up assessments has essentially uniformly shown that our findings were correct and that people with schizophrenia can improve. This means, of course, that such statements by professionals as "You have a disease like diabetes" are wrong, not to mention cruel and harmful, but even now you still hear them from time to time. In the end, measurement, beautiful humble measurement, beautiful traditional science wins—mostly.

But what do you do if something important resists measurement? That's next.

SUBJECTIVITY

"Why don't you ever ask me what I do to help myself?"

So our work proceeded. My colleagues and I were doing follow-up and follow-along studies, and we were finding out interesting facts related to symptoms and outcome—how diagnostic categories don't seem to reflect the diversity of many important patient characteristics, things like that. Although I was the principal investigator in the studies, I always did a significant number of the interviews myself. (I think it's important to keep in touch with the real world—and more fun, too.) Our follow-up interviews, we felt, were pretty broad minded; we didn't limit our questions to symptoms, medications, and other treatments as was true for many studies but included questions about friends, work, and living situation. We were beginning to realize that one of the fascinating things about methodology is that if you change one thing, often other stuff changes that you had never anticipated. Moreover, since we had started doing "follow-along" interviews, that is sequential interviews over time, rather than a single "follow-up" interview and always had the same interviewer interview the same patients, the patients were getting to know their interviewer. We were all clinicians as well as researchers—and patients began sometimes to ask us or tell us things we didn't even know to ask. So one day I was doing a second or third follow-along interview with one of my patients, a young woman who had been admitted to the hospital with schizophrenia and then been discharged and was living with her parents. I had asked her whether the various aspects of her treatments and surroundings were helpful or harmful, and she suddenly said, "Why don't you ever ask me what I do to help myself?"

The question set me back. It was such a simple, and in retrospect obvious, thing to ask. I have spent the many years since that time trying to figure out the answer to that question and its implications. What she was doing in her quiet way was opening up the whole question of subjectivity. Far from being some cute or academic issue, it is actually a basic aspect of how we understand psychiatric disorder, treatment, and causal and healing processes—how we see "illness" and "treatment." In fact, it takes us back to those old studies by Kohler with the chimpanzee Sultan who figured out how to put one box on top of another to reach the banana, in contrast to the work of people who studied psychology by putting pigeons in boxes with only a lever they could press to get food. It comes down to the question, are people who have what we call a "mental illness" pretty much passive victims of a disease that the clinician must find the right method to "treat" or are we dealing with a much more complex interaction between the person, the problem, and the surroundings where each plays an important role. In other words, is mental illness, even something as serious as schizophrenia, something that the person who has it can actually do something to influence?

Thus, this woman's "simple" question really opened up our assumptions about the nature of mental illness and the processes that influence its onset and course. When a patient says, as some do, "One day I looked around at the other patients on the ward and said to myself, 'I have to pull myself together,' and so I did," is that patient correct? Did he really "pull himself together" or did he just think he did? Without any disrespect, did the chimpanzee Sultan actually figure out the not-obvious solution to getting the banana, or as some suggested did it just look like he did when it was really all chance.

These questions raise two others: What is the nature of the person's experience and what methodology can we use to find out what the "illness" process is? With the woman I described, if we hadn't been doing a follow-along study but only a single follow-up interview, or if I had been following an interview form, as is often true in research, with so many questions that there was no time for anything but yes or no answers, would she have ever asked me her question? And if I had been in too much of a hurry, would her question ever have registered with me? I referred above to the pigeon in a box. Some psychologists have raised the question: If you put a person or animal in a situation such as a Skinner Box for pigeons where all they can do is press one button or lever, or in a maze where all they can do is turn in one of two directions, do you even give them the chance to show that in the right circumstance they can think creatively or abstractly. In psychiatry research do we generally treat our patients like pigeons, severely restricting our learning about their possible ability to act intelligently, creatively, and effectively?

Continuing this methodology question a little further, I want to return to Piaget and what he called the "clinical method" of research. For Piaget, his approach to "clinical research" meant that he had a standard method and a standard question for each of his many tests, but also that after you did the test with the child, you could start to alter it and pose a variety of questions to see the range and the diversity of what the child was thinking. Thus, for example, there is the test with a given amount of water and two glasses with different diameters that I have described. When the water is poured from the glass with a narrower diameter into the wider one, this is the standard part of the test. A young child will say, "There's less water now" (because it has reached a lower height), and an older child will say, "There's no change in the amount of water, all you did was change the container," if not simply, "this is dumb." So here we have the possibility of standardized ratings of responses that are then suitable for statistical evaluation across groups of individual children. But then you can go on with a child and start changing the situation, for example, using glasses with other diameters or posing more specific questions, "What if I . . . ?" "How can it be that if all I did was pour, there's less water now?" "What will happen if I pour it back?" and so on. Especially with children at a transitional phase it is fascinating to have this open "clinical" part of the "clinical method." I'm not sure that Piaget fully appreciated the statistical possibilities of this method, statistics were not generally his thing, but the potential is there. And of course, if you don't ask that "clinical" part, you may have almost no idea of what thoughts are going on in the child's mind.

Growing appreciation for the patient's subjectivity opens up a complex world of issues related to content, theory, and method. It seems incredibly naïve in retrospect that we took so long to recognize that patients have their subjective view of the world and of themselves. I mean how could we not know it. There are some who say, well, psychoanalysts have been doing that all along. I'm not so sure. It seems to me that if you have a rather highly structured theory, as many do, it is really difficult to be open to what is going on in another person's mind. In the field of philosophy this has been beautifully discussed in Thomas Nagel's article "What Is It Like To Be a Bat" (1974), and in biology, in books such as Frans de Waal's *Are We Smart Enough to Know How Smart Animals Are?* (2016).

The subjectivity question raises the issue of methodology. How do I find out what is going on in the person's mind? How do I know if what he or she thinks or does is having an effect, as, for example, when the person says she can "pull herself together? And how can I become more open to hearing and understanding what she is telling me? But the answers to those questions take us beyond the usual concepts of science and scientific methodology. For example, if one wants really to understand subjective experience and communicate its role to our colleagues, should we not attend more to literature, theater, even art and music? For better understanding of the subjective facts of mental illness, the subjective experience, is there really a better way than by reading or seeing *King Lear,* by reading Conrad's *The Heart of Darkness* or Kafka's *Metamorphosis*, or by attending a performance of *Madama Butterfly* or *La Bohème*? I mean King Lear becomes psychotic, after all, and Cho Cho San in *Madama Butterfly* kills herself.

Perhaps I can pardon myself a bit for not realizing all this sooner. The role of subjectivity in the mental health field has most often been handled in a way that is bizarre, not to say, atrocious.

I recently listened to a recorded lecture on modernist literature and what it attempts to notice and describe about the human condition. The specific subject was the work of Joseph Conrad and Ford Maddox Ford. The lecturer talked about the methods they used to show the crucial importance of the narrators, the role their uncertainties play in sharing with the reader the complexities of the situations in which they find themselves, and their efforts to shield themselves from some of the horrors of those situations. He also addressed the ways in which the efforts of these authors differ from those of Victorian authors and how they presage what the modernists will attempt. As I listened, I suddenly thought of an interview I had given a few years earlier. The interviewer was a reporter for an important psychiatry newsletter, and someone had suggested he write something about my work on subjectivity. After some preliminary questions, he said, "Subjectivity, you've been working on that for quite a while, haven't you?" Something about this set my head awhirl, and I came out with some rather tame answer, perhaps: "Yes. Several years. But you see, it's really complicated." He was clearly not impressed. Later I realize what had so totally disoriented me about his question. I think he felt I should have long ago solved the problem of subjectivity, and worse, it was a feeling I shared. I mean this isn't something really complicated like brain function, what was taking me so long? I confess, I still have some of that feeling. When I listen to these lectures on modernism in literature, its roots and its variations, I know cognitively that subjectivity isn't simple. And yet, maybe because of my medical background or perhaps a broader cultural thing, I still have the sense, as my interviewer was possibly implying, "Why haven't you solved this thing and moved on already".

So where are we? While totally accepting the beauty and crucial role of traditional science and relishing my experiences with biostatistics and the traditional scientific method, I have been pulled by patients themselves beyond the belief that those methods can be sufficient in treating people with psychiatric problems. The problem of subjectivity has sent me even into the arts as sources of "data," and those data have suggested that our field has to be a human science. By which I mean that in order to be truly scientific in our field, we have to deal with all the relevant data, including reaching into the arts to learn how to comprehend subjective issues and to communicate them.

My writing groups are a reflection of this reasoning, though when I started them about twenty-five years ago I did not fully realize, as usual for me, what I was doing or why. "Writing Creatively About Clinical Experience" is what I call them. I have two ongoing groups as of this writing and in the past have led single sessions for people in Australia, Sweden, Norway, and France, and, in the United States, at the annual meetings of the American Psychiatric Association, the University of New Mexico, and elsewhere. These sessions provide settings, somewhat varied depending on the situation, where people who work in the mental health field—professors of psychiatry, patients who work with other patients, nurses, psychiatrists, social workers, occupational therapists, whoever—can write about their experiences. The basic "rule," learned from my writing teacher Barbara Turner, is that when someone reads what they have written to the others in the group, the comments of the latter must focus on what works, the positive aspects of the piece, and avoid negativity. This simple-sounding rule means that the writers become less and less defensive, and more and more capable to expand how they write. It does not involve gratuitous "nice" comments, because you can always find something that really does work, that stands out when someone writes about his or her experience. There are a few other supportive rules as well:

Readers may not apologize for what they written before they read it (that's allowed afterwards, but by then no one seems to feel a need to); nor may they respond to comments until everyone who wants to has had their say. This rule practically eliminates the instant tendency to defend oneself and thus not to hear.

Several years ago when I first began thinking of the mental health field as a "human science" that needed to figure out how to bring together traditional scientific methods and concepts with more specifically human subjective aspects involving the arts, I told my friend the psychologist Dan Levinson (author of the ground-breaking *The Seasons of a Man's Life*) that it really shouldn't be that hard to do. Dan responded that it might not be that easy. And he knew what he was talking about! Of course, in one way or another the issue of the divide between arts and sciences is thousands of years old. Because both seem essential in the mental health field, I have struggled with how to bring them together, still falling far short of what could be called success. One problem is that beyond issues of method, they are two ways of being, science involving an intractable logic, the other requiring the subtlety of feeling, and it is not possible merely to slide from one to the other. For example, if you put some "creative" description of a patient or patients in an article as well as numerical data, the latter tend to swallow up the "creative" parts and the feeling qualities they could otherwise communicate. My paper "Uncertainty Theory," in which I presented a traditional "scientific" psychiatric case summary followed by a description of the "case," who happened to be my mother, from my point of view as her son is my most recent effort to combine these aspects. But it still falls short of what I would like to do in putting together "science" and "art," objectivity and subjectivity, to provide a basis for our field as a human science. The problem feels to me like the old jigsaw puzzle with which I started this book: There they are, the two parts, all you have to do is put them together; one day it may be perfectly obvious how to do it, but I just still can't see how. And yet as human beings we put together the objective and subjective all the time.

I want to mention another thing that we see as a dichotomy that makes a conceptual and practical assumption that may be a big mistake. In the mental health field functioning is usually considered as something distinct from the "illness." In people with schizophrenia, for example, the ability to function is often seen in rehabilitation efforts as being essentially separate from treating the illness. I think, on the contrary, that often a person's functioning can help them improve their condition, to get better. In many instances at least, if a person can work, be respected by others, be taken seriously, I believe that can be an important causal factor in the improvement process.

THE NATURE OF TRUTH, A HUMAN SCIENCE

No, this is not going to be a long discourse on epistemology, the nature of inductive and deductive knowledge and so on. I have mentioned that when you enter medical school there are so many things you don't know. And much of what you learn is not just from books, which are actually quite limited in their ability to teach, but from people who've been around for a while, professors, interns, doctors of all kinds, and, of course, nurses. And you need to absorb information like a sponge precisely because you know so little. There are, of course, some people and some books from whom you absorb more knowledge than others. And you become used to learning that way, partly because you just have to.

Also you learn not just the ordinary things, where to find the subclavian artery in your cadaver, the usual course of pneumococcal pneumonia in an otherwise healthy person, which antibiotics work for which kinds of infection, but the unusual things that only a really good expert can teach. When we couldn't find the right subclavian artery in our cadaver, Professor Crelin dug around in the shoulder for a while (where we had already looked) and found it: "Sometimes there's an anomaly where the subclavian goes behind [I no longer remember what]." The same kind of thing happens in treatment: "Yes, X [a certain antibiotic] is not supposed to work for this kind of infection, but in some instances it is actually the best and only treatment."

You learn things like that all the time. In fact, especially if you have access to really good people, the learning never, really never, stops. Of course, patients teach you too. And sometimes you learn positive things from mistakes: For example, a medication given at the wrong dosage may turn out to have a huge beneficial effect. These are not things you want to have happen because you really have to be careful to avoid mistakes, but like it or not, they do happen, and often you learn from them, good things and bad.

So in medicine, truth comes at you from all angles, and you try to absorb it and to weed out non-truth. And the same, of course, happens in psychiatry. The books tell you some things. Your teachers tell you other things, and you accumulate what you consider to be knowledge, truth. And you learn pseudo-truths like "people with schizophrenia never get better" or "the best they can do is get back to baseline." And you absorb that with the rest of the things you are learning, including things that really are true, like "Don't use medication X in patients like that because they can become suicidal."

Hence, when we first sought to publish our findings on

people with schizophrenia getting better and received that negative review, "We know this isn't true," the response, given the way we acquire "knowledge," wasn't all that shocking. Except, of course it was, because we had carefully collected data, and apparently the reviewer hadn't.

And that brings me to the problem of knowledge in psychiatry, the nature of science in our field. I want to suggest that we need two kinds of science: traditional science, with all kinds of important issues of method and statistics, and another kind of science—I don't know exactly what to call it—that allows for other kinds of input. Traditional science first. It's been surprising to me how little people who aren't scientists really get it. I've been over this before, but it seems so elusive, I want to try again. It seems to me that people who have not carried out scientific studies, who have not been subject to critical editors and reviewers, don't really have a sense of what it means to prove something, to decide that something is true. Before I got involved with our work on the IPSS I didn't really have much of a sense of the nature of proof either. It was the wonderful biostatistician John Bartko who taught me what science was, the nature of proof. My experiences with learning how to collect data and analyze it, all that we picked up from the Classification Society, were my introduction to real science—in these cases, the beautiful power and the problems of numbers. I learned that it was really important in judging a scientific project to understand the details; methods without attention to the details were suspect.

But, again, many people who haven't been through such experiences with science often just don't seem to get the importance of carefully collected and analyzed data. When I give a talk trying to describe the importance both of science and of the humanities and subjectivity. I often find that people seem to fall into one of two groups: those who love and understand science but don't seem to understand the issues of subjectivity; and those who love and cherish subjectivity, stories, literature, and the like but don't get it about science and don't understand that almost never does one case definitively prove something. Of course, there are also those, like the "We know this isn't true" reviewer, who just know the "truth" and don't have to bother either with data or observations of subjectivity.

About that second kind of science, the kind that I don't know how to name: Clearly, there are approaches to knowledge that aren't really in the domain of "traditional science," as I define it above. I used to build furniture so know, as does anyone involved in construction of any kind, that triangles are rigid structures and rectangles are not. If you push hard on a rectangle made of wood, for example, you can squash it. You can't do that with a triangle. When you are working with human beings, whole human beings, the problem becomes much more complicated than that. What do you do with intuitions, for example? What do you do when you have interviewed a patient who has told you about A, B, and C, but then your supervisor talks with the same patient and the patient tells him about X, Y, and Z that are far more important for your understanding and decisions about treatment? This happens all the time. You ask your supervisor how she happened to ask those questions, and she says she doesn't really know, it just seemed as though they might be important.

It gets much worse than that. There are so many things you don't think of or don't know. That's where being open to what patients can tell you is so important. But what do you do with what they say? What is the nature of that "knowledge?" "When I looked around me at other patients on the ward, I said to myself, I can do better than this and so I decided to pull myself together." What do you do with a statement like that in light of traditional science and the importance of proof? Try to prove that one! The usual ideas about controlled studies, comparison groups, statistics, and so on are just extremely difficult, perhaps impossible, to apply in a valid way to issues like that.

What should you do with information of this kind? You can say—or more frequently assume, without noticing you're doing it—"That's not scientific" and then ignore it. Or you can assume that it's true, which also happens frequently. Or you can say, "That's an important possibility. How can I deal with it in a way neither to ignore it nor to assume it's true?" And one solution to the question posed by this third option is to accept the patient's statement as a hypothesis, to take it seriously, and to explore it as systematically as possible given the complexity of and problems with exploring that kind of issue. Of course, phenomenologists and others have offered some elaborate schemes to conduct studies of such propositions, but I would say that as a clinician and/or investigator, the main thing we should acknowledge is that it's wrong to ignore such issues of subjectivity. At this point the question of how to go from hypothesis toward proof is completely open to our creativity and desperately needs to be pursued.

MUSIC

De, de, de-de. Why does that music keep going through my head? Hélène Grimaud playing the Brahms' Piano Concerto No. 1. I have a theory about that concerto: I think it was Brahms' first effort at a concerto and is, as a result, a bit awkward. No piano for the first several minutes, kettle drums banging away—I love it. Awkward and so beautiful. People who know music say that's impossible, that Brahms never did anything musical without extreme thought. I don't care. They're wrong. De, de, de-de.

Ravel does something similar with his Piano Concerto in G major. No drums, but in the second movement, like Brahms, so simple, just one single note after another. And so beautiful. Grimaud plays that too.

My father was a terrific piano player. I have described how he would play at night in our living room. Until I was about fifteen, I hated that. Then something happened. I don't have a clue what it was. I started to love listening to him. I also listened to the Met operas on the radio on Saturday afternoons (when it was Puccini or Wagner) and would go with my friend Bob to the Erie Philharmonic rehearsals. As I've mentioned, the orchestra conductor, Fritz Mahler, was a family friend who would come over to the house and play four hands with Dad. Bob knew so much about all kinds of composers. He still does. He lives in California now, and we send each other You Tube links, his of stuff I've never heard of and mine, more common stuff that I love.

In contrast to my sister who played the piano well, I was always a failure as a musical performer. I took about five series of piano lessons, the last my first year at med school. I practiced regularly but never shook off my incompetence. I also took flute lessons. At Swarthmore, where anyone could take part in anything, I was the fifth of five flutists in our rather small college orchestra (large symphony orchestras often have only two flutists). Among that number I could hide safely, but one night of practice the other four flutists didn't come, and during a brief flute solo in the overture to Rossini's *La Gazza Ladra*, there was a point at which I tried and failed utterly to produce a sound. The kindly conductor, professor of astronomy VandeKamp, smiled gently and just went on with the piece. I took my flute to the Island and would play it outside in the evening. People said that the sound coming over the water was beautiful—pretty much my only musical success.

But ever since high school I have loved music with a passion, classical music, popular music, folk music, and especially Brahms and Puccini. My grandfather, Sambo, gave me a player for long playing records when they first came out and a recording of Tchaikovsky's piano concerto. I bought records of *La Bohème*, Edith Piaf, and Brahms, lots of Brahms. I especially loved his concertos piano, violin, double. In the *Academe*, my high school yearbook, they wrote a few lines next to the picture of each of the two hundred seniors. Next to my picture one of the things they put was, "Brahms fan."

My friend Sandra in Paris, the clown, sent me a video she had made of an old guy who could no longer talk sense but who played the piano beautifully.

What is it about music? I know there are all sorts of books about music and the brain, music and mathematics, and so on. But for me the connection is between music and the heart. When I hear "On the street where you live" or the Prokofiev violin concerto, I think of Ann and those wonderful mornings in Trotter when we listened to Prokofiev and studied together. But it doesn't absolutely have to connect with a memory. It can just be hearing a Ravel piece or Brahms concerto. It connects right to the heart.

A SPECIAL PERSON

Not long ago I paid a visit to the Yale Book Store to buy Yale baby T-shirts for my neighbor and a good friend in Los Angeles, both of whom had had babies recently. I walked up to the second floor because I figured that the T-shirts would be there with most of the clothes. They were not readily apparent however among the vast array of Yale sweatshirts, jackets, blankets, socks, sweatpants, and on and on. Nor were any salespeople. Then I noticed at the little alcove off to the right a short woman with her back to me who seemed to be unpacking clothes or taking labels off them. She was hard to reach because of the location of the alcove so, since the place was relatively empty, I called over, "Excuse me." The young woman turned around. She had the face of someone we used to call mongoloid, symptomatic of trisomy X. It's a genetic defect that leaves the person severely limited in what they can understand or do. She looked at me with a rather blank, perhaps confused expression. Should I just say, "Excuse me" again and walk away? No, I couldn't do that, let her know I expected nothing from her. So I asked if she could tell me where the Yale T-shirts for small babies were. Was I pushing her too far? She looked at me for several seconds, perhaps wondering what I had said. Then after ten seconds more had passed, she said, as though still trying to get her thoughts together, "They're over there, at the end of the room." She was apparently not finished and still looking at me as another ten seconds passed. She then raised her arms from her sides until they were held straight out from her body. She looked at one hand and then the other, her mouth seeming to form words to herself, before saying, "They're over there on the [a moment's hesitation as she looked from at her right to her left hand] on the left." I thanked her and followed her directions. There they were, just as she had said. I got three of the T-shirts for eighteen-month infants (one of my friends had had twins) and made my way back to the front of the floor. Before descending the stairs to go to the cashier, I saw my friend again, standing apparently with her supervisor. I called over, "Thank you, I got them" and held the T-shirts up for them to see. I hoped that my friend felt pleased and that her supervisor was impressed that she had been able to help me.

The young woman's effort to give me directions was a particularly beautiful moment. I have tried to explain it to friends, but I don't think they understand. I'm not even sure I do. She was doing something that a "normal" person could do easily. She was putting in so much effort to accomplish it. There was not a second of self-pity, ignoring my request, or anything else, just that determination to do what I had asked. I can't even think of another example to help explain it. Perhaps a man with chronic arthritis who lifts himself at great effort out of his wheel chair to get me something I need when I am sick in bed? No, that doesn't really get at it. It may have been her total lack of self-pity, the quiet determination, the courage, the tremendous courage, to make the effort to respond to my request. I don't know that I can explain it, but my encounter with that young woman was one of the most beautiful experiences of my life. Amazing isn't it?

EXCERPTS FROM MY INTERVIEWS WITH SARAH KAMENS, II

CONCERNING THE RELEVANCE OF EVERYTHING, CASE HISTORIES, AND NARRATIVE

John: I mean that's really weird when you think of it. That taking a little care of a horse for just an hour, and having a therapist there that can talk with you about it can be such a powerful experience. That doesn't make any sense at all. It's not like taking out an appendix. I mean that's horse therapy. And that's one of the things I love about the field is that there's this other relevant stuff. In literature too, in *Hamlet,* for example, when Rosencrantz is trying to find out if Hamlet is crazy and Hamlet says more or less, Do you think I am easier to play on than this flute? There are some psychiatrists who seem to think that people are "easier to play on than a flute." And how about King Lear, Shakespeare's representing his becoming psychotic. But in other areas of human life as well. How does this guy Shakespeare know all this stuff? I mean know some of it, okay. But he knew so much. And how does he do that?

That's literature. I think one of the beauties of psychiatry is that psychology and the biological stuff is important, too. As you know, I'm not all that big on biology in terms of my knowledge, but if you've been knocked out, which I have been, or if you've been sick, you realize that the physical body is really pretty important. I like that everything is relevant. And that includes history. We talked a little bit about microhistory, right?

Sarah: Is that what that book on the table is?

John: Yes, it's a French book, *Penser Par Cas*, edited by Jean Claude Passeron and Jacques Revel. Most of it isn't very interesting for me, but in the beginning chapter they talk about the importance of the way in which the individual case is instructive for history and also about its scientific limitations. So that's what we ought to be talking about in the mental health field, but mostly we're not. These are historians talking about use of a single-case model and how to make it more broadly relevant than just the single case . . ..

John: You have these two worlds, the worlds of large-sample science with special emphasis on the nature of proof, and the single-case histories, which can be wonderful but where proof is very complex. You have the medical world, which uses case histories a lot. And you have the psychiatric world, especially Freud, who uses case histories a lot. Medicine does to some extent, but Freud doesn't consider the weaknesses of the single case. What are its strengths? What would you do to be sure that something is true? What are the alternative explanations? So, I think Freud was a terrible scientist. He was obviously very creative. Piaget was a mix, a scientist and a thinker. Freud was more a thinker and an imaginer, I think. But there are very few people who consider psychoanalysis without either an excessive pro or excessive con approach, who can think about it in a sensible way. But, in contrast, it's interesting that in the field of history there are some people who consider single cases in a creative and still scientific way. We can learn from them.

There are apparently two approaches to history. One is a narrative approach and the other is a social-sciences approach. In psychiatry, we don't know this but these two approaches also exist and need to be considered together. What happens in history, and in sociology too, is that one approach dominates and the other is considered bad, depending on the era. I attended a history conference a while back, and one presenter was almost apologetic about having a narrative focus. But I think we need both approaches.

There's a French historian, Jules Michelet, who's very famous. He was 19th century. There's a street named after him in Paris and there's a lycée named after him as the French do with big academics. So he starts his book on the French Revolution describing in detail what it was like to be at the Place de la Bastille during the time of the Revolution. Well, he wasn't even alive then, but it's beautiful. And it's narrative history. And there's no reason why that can't be part of history in my view. But there's also no reason why it can't be part of psychiatry. In our field, we don't even know that there are these two kinds of possibilities. I mean we do one or the other and we hate, or at least often look with contempt at the people who do the one we don't do. Or we think they're gods. But it is not a thinkable problem for us. What do you do with these two approaches? And microhistory gets to that at least somewhat. In one of its manifestations, Microhistory can go back and forth between the experiences of an individual and the general historical context that existed at the time. Thus, a friend of mine, Pauline Bertrand, wrote her dissertation using historical documents to describe a struggle between a man in the 18th century and the legal-political structures of the period. This made it possible for her to deal with the person's subjective experience and the objective realities of the time, to look at both as well as at their interaction.

CONCERNING PIAGET

John: And then at some point, about fifteen years into our marriage, my wife said Piaget has really influenced what you do and how you think. And I said, oh yeah, you're right. It had never occurred to me. And it really hadn't, so that's my mind. But he did. There's two things. First, he has a clinical method which is unbelievably smart. When you read about it, it doesn't seem like such a big deal. But what it does—which, again, I didn't realize until about twenty years later—. . . it relates to what I've been trying to do these last five or ten years, actually a little longer than that. . . . The clinical method, and I don't even know that he realized this fully, it puts descriptive traditional research, traditional psychological research techniques together with attention to subjectivity and flexibility. For example, you have tests that can combine both, which is very rare—even realizing it is a major issue to consider . . . is rare in the mental fields, although in history and sociology they are very aware of the problem. For example, take the situation where you have a glass of wide diameter and a glass of narrow diameter. You have colored water in one and you pour it into the other asking the child what has happened (the level of liquid changes). So that is a very clear-cut experimental thing where you could count correct answers, is there the same amount of water or not, etc. Piaget talked about that. Somebody asked him once about the people in Montreal who were using his methods. This was sort of an assistant professor in Geneva who said, ". . . The people in Montreal said one of the test results happens at age six not at five." And Piaget said something like, "Well, I'm glad they're doing the statistical thing, the 'cleaning up.'" It was like he was being creative, and these people were doing the cleaning up. And the clinical method allowed you to do that.

Sarah: Subjectivity as well.

John: Yeah, where you could do traditional kind of analysis. I think you could say, people at the average age of 5.73 get this thing about . . . the amount of water not changing—I don't remember the ages— just because the level has changed. But the other part of the research was that you could do that and then you could start fooling around with the situation. You could, for example, pour the water from the narrow tube into the wider diameter glass and you could ask, well, what happened? And the child replies that there's less water now. Then you could ask, "Why is there less water?" And the child replies, "Because it's lower." "So, what would happen if I poured it back?" "It'll be higher" or "There will be more water." So, this is the preoperational level. And Piaget had a lot of theory to explain this thinking, a little like Freud but different of course in many ways, but also a structuralist approach to understanding mental functioning.

But what you can do then after the standard questions is you can start asking all kinds of things. You can say, "Well, how can there be more water? All I did was pour it." . . . You pursue all kinds of questions.

Sarah: What would the child say? Do you remember?

John: It depends on the child. One fascinating instance was a child in between the stage when they don't realize the constancy of the volume of water and the stage when they do. He said, ". . . There's less water now, but all you did was pour it so there shouldn't be less water." And he was obviously perplexed, really beautiful. . . . Then you get an older child and the child looks at you like why are you asking me this stupid question? . . . There's the same amount of water because all you did was pour it. It's like any idiot would know that. It's kind of fun. So that's the clinical method of Piaget, simple, yet so creatively special. It makes you wonder why it's not much more commonly used.

But anyway, . . . mixing structured and unstructured things is almost never done, but he did it. And I'm not sure he fully appreciated the beauty of his method. I don't know how much he knew about statistical approaches to proof that we take for granted. There are not a lot of people who are not specifically trained who know much detail about science. I mean they don't really get it, scientific method. I think I learned most about scientific method when I was involved with the WHO study. . . . For me it was working with the biostatistician John Bartko that was so important.

So, I think Piaget had only a general idea of how special that clinical method was. But I think it really is. It's a way of putting together subjectivity and objectivity which is I guess, that's the search of my life.

Sarah: Search of your life?

John: I think, sort of, yeah.

Sarah: Wow! And when you think back to the comment that your wife said about Piaget really influencing your work, is this what that comment referred to, this combination of structured and unstructured ways of thinking?

John: I'm not great on insight, as you perhaps have gathered. I don't know. I think by then, when she was saying that, I'd started writing papers like about the person with delusions as a person. So, I would think I was starting to get both into the people stuff, which can be infinitely subjective and the objective measure of variables, but even more was the attention to psychological processes that combining subjective and objective focus can provide.

Sarah: But the search of your life?

John: I think so. I mean that's the only way I can make sense of the weird stuff I've been doing.

CONCERNING UNCERTAINTY

Sarah: It sounds like at some point, you realized that there were things nobody knows.

John: And when was that? It's been fairly recently, actually. Yeah, I'd say maybe last five or ten years.

Sarah: How did that realization come about?

John: The image that comes to mind is like opening the windows. The evidence was probably there all the time. But you don't want to know it.

Sarah: You don't want to know that there are things nobody knows.

John: Yeah, because there's too much responsibility. It's hard to communicate that. A big thing for me later on was doing research interviews, especially ones that were not too highly structured. You were free then to be more open because you didn't have to make a diagnosis or decide on a treatment, patients would get to know you because we were doing follow-along studies. So, we'd see people like every month or two months or whatever over four years or something. And you get to know each other. And they'll tell you things that they may not tell somebody else. One of my favorite stories is when I asked someone, "Are you hearing voices? And they said, "Yes, but don't tell my doctor because he thinks I'm doing better." As you get more interested and also, I think more open, and especially with the research approaches we were using, people start telling you things that you didn't ask. You only ask the things that you know to ask, so something that is outside your conceptual structure you don't even know to ask about.

* * * * *

John: . . . About four or five months ago, I was taking off a boot, a very tight boot, and I heard this horrible ripping sound in my thigh and it hurt like hell. I thought I have a torn hamstring. So, I went to the orthopedist and he took about a three-minute history. And then he did a three-minute physical exam and he said you have a torn hamstring. And what you need to do is take it easy for a while for about a week or ten days. It will be better. And I thought it's not possible for something so awful as that to get well so quickly. But I was most impressed that he had done the evaluation, made the diagnosis, decided treatment and prognosis in about twelve minutes or less. And how different that is from psychiatry! And then it turned out he was right. I had made the diagnosis too, but that he was right about everything. That's an unbelievable amount of knowledge.

    Sarah: Why do you think it's different in psychiatry?

    John: Because you can't do that.

    Sarah: Why? Why can't we do that?

    John: Psychiatry is much more complex. I think psychiatry really is biopsychosocial. It could be just a neurotransmitter or a twisted axon or something, like a torn hamstring, but I don't think so. I don't think we know how to think about something of a greater complexity. That's what the uncertainty paper is about that

I finished a year ago. But what really, really, really it is I don't know. I don't think we know enough to be sure at this point.

Sarah: You talked about the idea of the realization some five or ten years ago that nobody knows. I was really struck by the image of opening a window that you mentioned earlier in the interview. Is that the same kind of nobody knows that you're talking about now?

John: It's hard to know where to locate yourself. When I was a resident, people knew, right? And then people knew and they still talk as though they know what they're talking about. And I know that's wrong, they just don't know that much. On the other hand, they know something. It depends which person of course, but they know more than nothing, but less than everything. And so, it's in that middle ground. In the uncertainty paper I say that it's really important not to be too certain.

It's also important of course to know some things. You know certain medications can be helpful for certain problems. It's not like we don't know anything at all, but it's just very hard for people to be in that mid-level of some knowing and some ignorance. The problem is that many people think they know more than they do. I'm somewhat sympathetic with that because as a clinician you have to make all kinds of decisions. But people err too much on the side of thinking they have the answers.

Sarah: I want to come back at some point to this realization that nobody knows and this evolution of your focus on uncertainty. And tell me if you want to take a break or stop for the night.

John: No, I'm okay. I love talking about myself.

* * * * *

John: The sense of not knowing is one of the fun things. It's too bad, but it's also exciting because there's all this stuff, this really obvious stuff that how we think about patients in our theories and teaching is misleading. I mean it's nothing fancy. But you see it. You hear it. And you can find ways of studying things showing that a lot of our concepts are not all that great.

Sarah: Do you feel like other people felt the same way as you did or were also noticing these things?

John: That paper on hallucinations and delusions as being on continua with each other has been very highly thought of. I just learned that about a year ago. So there are some people that appreciate these complexities, especially good clinicians, and other people who actually work with patients.

CONCERNING SUBJECTIVITY

John: What Yogi Berra was saying that is so relevant to us (in the expression I keep quoting, "You can see a lot by just looking") was that in the case of psychiatry, you really have to listen to people. And if you structure your interviews highly, to get back to Heisenberg, you will be limited in a certain way, you won't see stuff that you're not open to seeing. Your interview is a method. If your interview is such that you are not paying attention or allowing for certain things to happen, you will not see them. So, without really realizing the implications we cut down on the number of questions in the interview and allowed for more time. And we used a follow-along structure, which was seeing patients repeatedly over time after they had come into the hospital. The durations between interviews changed over the person's follow-along time, but I think it was two months and then four months and then six months.

What happens, and you don't expect it, because you've never done this before, is that you get to know the patients, and they get to know you. I know that sounds obvious, and it is in retrospect, but none of this stuff is obvious beforehand. You have a research tradition, for example of one or two follow-up interviews and you don't notice that the tradition has a ton of implications of which you have absolutely no idea. So patients, subjects in the study, and each of the interviewers who were also clinicians and followed their particular research subjects over time, the subjects start telling you things you never thought to ask. And so, as Heisenberg (and maybe Yogi Berra as well) might have predicted, in our simple and unsuspecting way, we had made a major change in our method that began to bring out new kinds of information. If you're not just pummeling subjects with questions, you have time to listen and to be more open, and as you get to know each other, they feel free to tell you things you hadn't thought about. You start hearing, for example, about subjectivity and specifically you start hearing things like the woman said who asked, "Why don't you ever ask me what I do to help myself?"

Sarah: Why don't you ever ask me what?

John: What I do to help myself. Which opens up a whole thing, the door to subjectivity.

Sarah: Did she tell you what she does to help herself? Did she also respond to the question?

John: I think I asked her, but really, I may have been so astounded that I didn't. I don't remember. And it took me a long time after that to realize the many implications of that apparently simple question. Subjectivity is a huge deal, and bizarrely in psychiatry, perhaps because we want to be a branch of traditional medicine that understandably values objectivity, we have been very naive about subjective phenomena. I know, people tell me Freud was a master of subjectivity, but I think that if you have a highly structured ideology, which he did, it really inhibits your openness to the unbelievable variety of human experience. In any case, after she asked that, trying without recognizing it to follow more traditionally objective aspects of behavior we started asking people, is there anything they do to help themselves. We then published some papers on their responses. In retrospect, I think our lack of awareness was partly a product of a common basic implicit assumption in medicine that the person is a more or less passive victim of disease, even if they have done something to bring it on. And then it is the role of the doctor to provide the treatment to get rid of that disease. I know, of course, that a lot of people would say that's too simplistic, but I think that is an idea that quietly underlies a lot of what we do, including in research. But I think in psychiatry—and now it's appearing in other areas of medicine as well—that conception is incredibly inadequate and misleading.

Sarah: You've done a lot. And that opened up a whole new door for you.

John: Yes.

Sarah: Have your ideas about subjectivity changed or evolved over time since that?

John: Oh, I've learned tremendously. You want to know about subjectivity, read Victor Hugo. And then if you're really crazy, you'll get into music. See the opera *Madama Butterfly* . . . . You have this story of Madame Butterfly. She's a Japanese girl who marries this American, Pinkerton, who's a sailor. And people are telling her, don't do it. And people are telling him, she's going to take this more seriously than you are. And he leaves. And she has a kid. And he comes back with his wife, with his American wife to Japan. And Cho Cho San, Madame Butterfly, is totally broken hearted and disgraced. And her people say, we told you so. And then you have the Puccini music. It's just mind blowing. And if you want to know something about subjectivity, I mean it's right there. If you want to know something about feeling, you have not only the narrative but also the acting, and the singing and the staging and the music. So if you really want to do a good job with subjectivity, you have to begin to deal with all that. That's what subjectivity is about.

And Victor Hugo, just reading isn't so bad either. There's this whole world there which, I think, in psychiatry we really haven't dealt with. It's just bizarre. So what's the result? It turns out you have two groups of professionals, those who understand science and objectivity and those who understand feelings and subjectivity, but not a lot who really know how to combine both in our theories and research if you are going to do our field justice. . . . There's nobody I know who's teaching these things together effectively. I don't mean together in the same course. But raising the question, how do you deal with studying reliability or sampling or clustering patients' diagnoses, or categorizing, and how do you deal with Madame Butterfly at the same time? Because that's what we should be doing. . . .

Sarah: What's the relationship between Madame Butterfly and the woman who said, "Why don't you ask me what I do to help myself?"

John: Ultimately, I think the most important question is how to have a human science. How do you do that? Madame Butterfly and "Why don't you ask me" are close because they both open the question of what is human experience about, people's feelings, people's decisions, people's actions, and how are they relevant to mental health and illness. I think she was saying "I'm a real person not just a passive blob," and indicating that the questions we were asking about the impacts of her treatments, family, friends and living setting on her were not getting the whole picture. I showed you . . . the Pinocchio statue up on the mantle. . . . There is a part in the Walt Disney version where Pinocchio comes back and has been changed from a puppet to a human being by the good fairy. He says, "Look, Papa, I'm a real boy. And Geppetto says, " No, no, Pinocchio, you're only a wooden doll." In order to be scientific, we're often treating people like wooden dolls, and they're not.

Sarah: What do you think it would take for the field to stop treating people like wooden dolls?

John: And not give up science? Somebody would have to help us find out how to do both together. I've tried, but I haven't gotten as far as I would like. I think I've helped, made some progress, but I don't have the answer. It's a question that in some form goes back centuries really.

Sarah: You have to find a way to do it.

John: Yeah. When I told my friend Dan Levinson, "We need really to put together traditional science and the subjectivity thing, just do both." He said, "Well, it may not be as easy as you think." Was he ever right!

PLACES,
PARIS IN PARTICULAR

I have a wonderful friend named Zheala Qayyum. She was born in Pakistan, lived in Iran, moved to the United States as a child, became a physician then a psychiatrist, joined the army, became a major, then a child psychiatrist. I'm not sure how I met her, but I do recall when I began to realize how special she was. I had invited a woman, Hannah Harvey, to give a talk at the Yale Psychiatry Department. Hannah is a wonderful professional story-teller and teacher of storytelling. After her presentation, Zheala came up to us and invited us to her office to talk further about storytelling and psychiatry. In her office we were surrounded by shelves of small figurines from many different stories of many countries and eras. That's how Zheala and I began our friendship.

After my recent family reunions, Zheala and I were having dinner in a small French-style local restaurant, and around dessert time, I was telling her about the reunion and how strange and totally not strange it was to be in Cleveland. One of the things I mentioned was the fact that you can walk a hotel corridor and meet a family you've never seen before and they'll say "Hi." As I've mentioned, I like to do the same thing at Yale—say "Hi" to people I don't know in an elevator or at the gym—and I get some very wary reactions.

Anyway, I was telling Zheala how strange it was to me to inhabit these two worlds, the one in New Haven and the one in Erie/Cleveland, and a third as well, Paris, and how it feels as though I'm three different people. Without even a pause, she took four glasses that were on the table and placed the big one at the center and the three others around it. "You're the one in the center," she explained. "The other three are the three environments. Each of them is different and connects with different aspects of you, and you connect with them differently." I was moved, overwhelmed, and delighted by the obviousness of her analysis. I'm the biopsychosocial guy after all. Why hadn't I figured that out? I asked her if she would be my psychiatrist, and we both laughed.

But I have to adjust this notion a little. Listening to the radio recently, I heard the English novelist Fiona Mozely refer to "the relationship between a person and a place." That's a perfect way to think about it. Of course, it's a relationship. Now, I don't feel that I have a "relationship" with New Haven, the city where I have lived for much of my adult life, in that sense. There my relationship is with people. There are three *places* with which I have had a relationship: Erie, the Island, and Paris. I have already described in some detail what Erie and the Island have meant to me. Now I'll try to convey my feelings about Paris.

A LETTER

Hi Peter, my profound apologies for not getting back to you sooner! I hope your trip to France and time with your daughter there went well. And I hope she got lots of stuff from her stay. For me, France, like most places I guess, is a mixed bag. But there has been so much wonderful there for me that as you know, I love it and especially Paris, deeply. The cafés there I think are particularly special to me, and that so many people have a deep love and knowledge of history and culture including philosophy is something that for me has complemented the practical empiricism that is so much more developed here in the US. And there are the bookstores, of course. A large one devoted entirely to philosophy, for example. In a more general bookstore that I often go to, in the cellar they have philosophy books along with detective stories and other subjects. Partly just for fun as a kind of test and partly because I was really interested in the rather obscure topic, one day a couple years ago I went downstairs there and asked the clerk with whom I had already been impressed, if they had any books on the history of subjectivity. Without hesitation, he answered, "Yes, we have three. One doesn't have subjectivity in the title but it's about that topic too," and he took me directly to them.

And then of course there was the time years ago, I was twenty-five, I didn't have much money and was living on $21.00 a week, for everything, and was staying in a tiny hotel room with only one window, with wooden bars on it and no glass, giving off onto the hallway. But on the street, on one of the kiosks there was the announcement that David Oistrakh, the Russian violinist, was going to be giving a concert outside of Russia for the first time ever. I owned some of the records he had made and loved his playing. The kiosk said he would be performing a Mozart violin concerto, the Khachaturian violin concerto, and the Brahms violin concerto. I was sure it was a misprint, no one does more than one at any given concert, but I scrounged my money and bought a ticket. At the concert he did the Mozart, then he actually did the Khachaturian. Then he did the Brahms! Superb, all three! I was swept away, overwhelmed.

Although the French certainly can be rude and unpleasant, sometimes even on public transportation there is also a special kindness. A couple years ago, it started that sometimes a teenager or other person on a crowded bus would see me standing, smile at me, and offer me their seat. That has never ever happened to me in New York. (Although French friends tell me how helpful people in New York are when you are lost or are looking for a place.) Another time years ago, I had just arrived at Paris from Geneva on my medium-sized (250 cc) BSA motorcycle and went to a small hotel where I often stayed. The owner said she had no rooms free, but if I wanted to have a shower and clean up before looking elsewhere, that would be fine.

And I have had some very close French friends there. A wonderful woman, the only person I know now who is older than I, still an active painter. An extraordinary man, a psychiatrist, who was like a younger brother to me and who died two years ago of lung cancer. I sat with him at the Salpetrière hospital as he was having the poisons of chemotherapy poured into his body through his chest tube.

And chance encounters (maybe pretty much all encounters are chance). One day about four years ago in one of my two cafés I saw a young woman whom I had seen there several times before. She had kind of wild curly hair and was writing intensely, page after page, with a pen in a *cahier,* a book of blank pages. Finally, I went over and asked her if she was writing a novel. She said yes, actually she was. I said that was very impressive, and she replied that she had already published one. We talked for a while. Afterwards I found her book in a bookstore and read it. It was about a young girl who had been taken by her parents to a psychiatric hospital. The title was *Ils m'ont laissé là* ("They left me there") and was a beautiful recounting by the young girl of being quite lost in that place. Alma Brami and I met and talked several times subsequently, I have most of her books and just recently received an e-mail from her. She is married, living in Japan, has two children, and is just finishing another book.

Years ago, in 1956 in Paris, I had met a young Viennese woman who worked in a small religious jewelry store across from St. Sulpice. (The store is still there, but my friend has moved back to Austria where I have visited her.) In those days long ago, one evening she and I went to the tiny apartment of her cousin where they were celebrating the baptism of her niece. As the evening progressed we drank not very fancy champagne and the couple brought out a small phonograph and many records, records of Viennese waltzes. I have always loved Viennese waltzes, my name is John Strauss after all, but you have never danced waltzes unless you have danced them with a Viennese woman, oh my god! We whirled to that beautiful music in that small apartment, and I became a terrific dancer, for the night. I have never danced so well before, or after. It was still black outside when Traudl and I left to go to my small hotel room not far away to wash up before heading out. A few minutes later as we left the hotel to get on my motorcycle it was still black outside with just the tiniest bit of grey showing at the horizon on our right in the east. As we turned left and drove out along the Seine on the Right Bank with Traudl behind, her body pressed to my back, her arms holding on around me, that grey behind our backs had mounted enough so that it was possible to see the mists rising slowly off the Seine and over its beautiful bridges. "Oh, that's why the impressionists painted that way," I thought. We headed toward the Château Maintenon in the dawn alone on the road along the Seine. The pale light from the just rising sun was at our backs now beginning to bring a golden misty glow to the bridges as we passed surrounded by the soft roar of our engine.

* * * * *

On another occasion, also long ago, 1957 to be exact, a young woman sat on my bed at my small hotel, Hotel du Luxembourg, rue Vaugirard, and we said good-bye. She was American, we had been very much in love in a tumultuous relationship since college. At times it had been unimaginable bliss, at others it had been terrible anguish. She came by one last time to see if perhaps we could try again. We had tried so many times. I said no—with all the resolve I could struggle to find. Ann went off with another man. We never saw each other again for many years.

Almost a year earlier, just after we had both arrived in Paris, after a catastrophic day in our tempestuous relationship, sometimes incredibly beautiful, sometimes quietly heart rending, I was trying to get to sleep in my hotel room in the 6th arrondissement. Around midnight I began hearing the rumbling of the large trucks that came down the streets every night to bring food from all over France to the central market, Les Halles. There the men would work all night long and then in early morning clean up and the food would be taken by the same trucks to markets all over France. That night, hearing one truck after another, unable to sleep, I got up and dressed, went down to the ground floor, and walked to the other side of the Seine over to Les Halles. It was as usual a total bustle of activity with the burly men dressed in cover-alls unloading and loading trucks in the dark, calling and calling back "Ay Beber," "Jacques," lugging sides of beef or crates of lettuce or crates of courgets and all the rest, distributors bargaining, planning, shouting and arguing where the produce would be sent. Around the edges of the huge open square full of trucks and workers were busy workmen's cafes and restaurants. As the grey started to appear in the sky on the east side of the huge place and trucks started one by one to depart, the cafes like the Chien Qui Fume and the plain worker restaurants began to fill with the workmen and a few small groups of tourists to eat, drink coffee and smoke Gauloises or Gitanes, the entwining odors of produce, coffee and the smoke of French cigarettes took over. I found a table and ordered my onion soup and half bottle of wine, and watched all this activity knowing that it happened every night and that as the huge central place got cleaned up by workers by the time the sun was coming up you would never have known that all those trucks, all those people and all that food had ever been there. And a totally different place would be ready for the day to begin.

I realized once again that life was bigger than the sad struggles that Ann and I had, and after finishing and as Les Halles was packing up, I wandered back to my hotel and managed to fall asleep.

For me since I first went to Paris in 1953, I have a long history of experiences there, frightening, sad, incredibly beautiful, that have influenced me deeply and formed a major part of my life.

And then there's that beautiful language. For me its sound when well spoken is like wonderful music (although the French having grown up with it don't know what I'm talking about when I tell them that—poor people), and there are thoughts and feelings in the words and even in sentence structure that I continue to learn that are just not available in English. For example, "I miss you" in French is "Tu me manques" (you are missing to me) which changes from my having an activity (I miss you) to my being helpless and your absence leaving a hole in my life. The English translation of Proust's title "Remembrance of Things Past" from the French À *la recherche de temps perdu* ("In Search of Lost Times") is another example for me. "Remembrance" is such a namby-pamby substitute for "in search of," and "things past" is such a weak copy of "lost times." And then of course there is the wonderful French literature, Victor Hugo, Camus, Saint-Exupéry, and many others, and art, and oh yes music. Have you ever heard the second movements of Ravel's piano concertos, or Barbara singing "Quand reviendras-tu?" ("When will you come back?")?

My travels to Paris have become more rare, I have some wonderful friends here who are French, and being fairly proficient in French (even having published several papers in French journals and having given several lectures in French—some not so great) in talking with them and reading French literature it is still like having a second world, the two worlds that thus emerge have made life so much richer for me, each adding something that is not so much present in the other.

Well, there I go rambling on—but (partly) you got me started. Anyway, I hope you had a terrific time. And again I'm sorry for the delay in getting back to you.

Yours, (In French I could say "Je t'embrasse," see!),

John

THE GIFT

In Paris, at the end of the twentieth century, there was a store called Fauchon. It is still there, but early in the present century they redid it and made it all shiny and glitzy and thus ruined its charm. The old Fauchon was a store of very fine foods, jams, preserved meats, foie gras, sauces, champagne, chocolate, coffee, and other foods of the very finest kind. The store itself was beautiful and the staff dressed in black and white, readily helpful and discreet. Fauchon was on the right bank, next to the Madeleine, and not far from the Opéra, the Café de la Paix, American Express, a store of fine stamps for collectors, and Ladurée, a tea room with some of the finest pâtisserie in Paris, hot chocolate, and something called a Mont Blanc, a purée of chestnut with a topping of crème gentilly.

I rarely went to that part of Paris. It was not my side of the Seine, the side where I had my small hotel, book stores, the Luxembourg Gardens, and my two cafés. But occasionally I would take the bus that crossed the river to a money-exchange store where they had what seemed to me the best rates in Paris or go by Métro to Fauchon to buy a present for friends.

At this time, whenever I was invited to give a lecture somewhere in Europe, I would plan to spend three weeks or so in Paris. Usually I stayed in Room 28 on the top floor of my small left-bank hotel. I was friendly with everyone who worked in the hotel, including the owner who took me out each visit for a fine meal and also gave me a very low price. This time, however, I didn't have even that expense because my very close friend Alain Bottéro had offered to let me to stay in his apartment while he and his family were in the south of France. The apartment was lovely, with many books and a fine kitchen, just across the street from where in the nineteenth century Balzac had lived. It was also perfect for transportation—close to the Passy Métro, not far from Bus 63 either.

At the end of my stay there, I planned to leave a gift for Alain and his family. Although I didn't have all that much money, I was saving a lot by staying in Alain's apartment and I wanted it to be a particularly fine present. He was a terrific cook and loved good food. It was obvious that I should get the gift at Fauchon.

When I entered the store, I told one of the staff that I wanted to make up a basket for a close friend and could spend about $150.00 (of course, I said the equivalent in francs). For that store and its clientele that can't have been much, but she was lovely enough to appear impressed and we went around selecting jams, meats, and other wonderful products from all over France to put in the basket that would be Alain's gift. I had my own ideas of what Alain would like, and she suggested things that had not occurred to me. When we had finished, she said, "Your basket will be ready in two days," and we thanked each other.

Two days later I returned, and someone recognized me. I don't know how that was possible—I'm pretty much a peasant and there are some really fancy people who use a store like that. I think it may be a French characteristic. The woman who takes reservations at the Café de Flore always says, "Oh hello Mr. Strauss," when I come to make a reservation even though I only do it maybe two or three times a year. And at Fauchon the woman said, "Just a minute, I'll get your basket."

It was beautiful, so beautiful, the jars and packets neatly arranged to form a small mountain in a large wicker basket with an arching handle. The whole thing was covered in transparent yellow cellophane with a red bow on top. Now French people aren't allowed to look proud of something, but somehow it comes out anyway, and you could just see how proud she was as she handed it to me. And other people near us looked around and smiled and were very impressed. Me too. I beamed with pride and pleasure as she handed me the basket with great care. She accompanied me and held the basket for me as I paid at the *caisse*. She asked me if my car was there, and I replied that no, I would be taking the Métro. She said, no, you can't take a basket like that on the Métro, would it be all right if they called me a cab. Yes of course, I said.

We walked to the front door of Fauchon, she carrying the basket and people looking on approvingly. At the curb, she insisted that I get in the cab and that she would then hand me the basket. So that's how we did it. We said good-bye to each other, and I thanked her again. She still had that look of invisible pride.

THE HOTELS

My favorite area in my early days in Paris was the 6th arrondissement, an area less chic then than now, filled with students and middle-class people. I stayed in many of its small hotels. I remember the Stella, where there was one bathtub in a small room off the stairway between each two floors and no showers. When I complained that I thought there might be bedbugs in my room to the concierge, she denied it, of course, and then in a rapid countercriticism claimed that I did more laundry in my sink than the *bIanchisserie en face* (the laundry across the street). The François Premier on rue de Condé was where on one occasion, as I describe above, when I arrived by motorcycle from Geneva, the concierge told me that she had no rooms available but that I could take shower and change there. Years later I would stay at the Jardin de l'Odéon, only about a half block from Le Danton. The owners, M. and Mme. Mouton, would invite me for lunch at the very fine Bastide Odéon up the street. One time Madame confided to me, "Mouton [it means "sheep"], what kind of name is Mouton? I shouldn't have given up my maiden name, de Montjean. That's a real name." They finally sold the hotel and moved to the south of France. M. Mouton's cousin owned the nearby hotel where Ann had stayed. And a couple of blocks down was the Hotel Delavigne, where my friend Bob stayed once when we were in Paris at the same time.

My first long stay was at the Hôtel du Luxembourg; I was there for a couple of months in 1956. Madame Angele was the chamber maid there. She had many duties, including carrying up heavy suitcases to the rooms of the overweight tourists since there was no elevator. She called me Monsieur Rossignol (Mr. Nightingale) because I was so often whistling some tune or other, and she would bring me still-vibrant flowers from the rooms of clients who had left them behind.

Now the hotels that I've been describing were all small and relatively simple. Nothing of course like the Ritz. Not even like the Hotel du Louvre, on the Right Bank, where in 1953 I would seek out Henri to exchange francs for dollars at the rate of 450 rather than the official rate of 350. I think he was the doorman or something. I'd go to the lobby and give him a look, then he'd give me a look, and we'd find a quiet corner where the money would change hands.

Eventually, I switched from the 6th to the 5th arrondissement and found a home at the Hotel St. Jacques. Recently, I thought that at last I should send an e-mail to M. Rousseau and the St. Jacques people *pour dire* hello and thank you. After all, I used to stay there several times a year for three to four weeks each, always in the same small room—room 28 on the top floor, with the picture of a horse over the bureau— for what, fifteen years? From the tiny balcony You could look to the east and see the sun come up showing through the beautiful purple,white clouds and if you looked to the left in the evening you could see the sun setting over the Eiffel Tower.

Joe, who speaks six languages, was at the reception when I began going there and until he retired. Brigitte, too, was at the reception when I began, even more regularly than Joe and for an even longer time. She was a very pretty, sparkling blond woman, wonderfully competent, kind, and fun, and after a while we addressed each other as "tu." When Françoise came to the hotel for the first time to pick me up and heard Brigitte and me talking, afterwards said she had never heard a client and a person at reception use "tu" with each other. Françoise seemed to like it. Brigitte left a couple years ago after finally being able to adopt a baby from abroad. At night Aretsky was at the desk. A Berber, he taught me how the Berbers had never lost their culture even though their lands had been taken over many years ago by the Arabs. He spoke Berber and Arabic, French, English, and I don't know what else. I knew Samira, the *femme de chambre,* through two pregnancies and even before. Samira is tall, slender, and so kind, but it is her smile, her wonderful smile, that defines her. And, of course, Romu was the persoon who fixed everything—showers, light fixtures, you name it.

M. Rousseau, Jean Paul, the owner of the hotel, was somehow more enigmatic. As we got to know each other he suggested that we, too, call each other "tu." He asked me one time to recommend the hotel on a travel Web site after someone else had written a negative review, but otherwise he never asked for anything. Yet, on each of my visits he would invite me out to lunch at fine restaurants. The only time I have been to the Tour d'Argent, for example, was with him, his daughter, his son, and his wife, a family party. The Rousseaus had three small hotels in Paris: the St. Jacques, of course, another one quite fancy, and a third that was increasingly managed by the daughter. The son, Pierre—M. Rousseau was sad to say—was into computers and did not want to enter the hotel business. I tried to suggest that maybe someday he would, that sons often had first to break away from their fathers before coming back. I'm not sure Jean Paul was convinced.

For me the St. Jacques was special. I knew the phone number and the address by heart though I hardly ever remember such things. I have a St. Jacques cup, a St. Jacques plate, a St. Jacques pitcher, and several pair of St. Jacques slippers. Samira or someone else there would give me these things without my even asking. Everyone there was wonderful. And I always asked for that same little room, for which they charged me less than one third the usual rate.

Damn, I've known some great hotels—and some great people— in Paris.

A TYPICAL MORNING

Every morning on leaving the Hotel St. Jacques I walk down the hill to the Kayser bakery two blocks away and ask the people behind the counter if they have any croissants that are warm. Someone goes into the back to ask and, if they have them, will bring one to me. I thank them for their trouble, pay for it, walk out the door, and turn right to walk up the hill to my bus, another block away. As I go, I bite into the croissant, being careful to catch the flakes of pastry that fall off, and say out loud, "Damn, there is really nothing like this!" And there isn't. Have you ever eaten a fresh warm French croissant?

Then I take the bus, the 63, the 21 or the 47, whichever comes first, to the stop nearest to a café I have known since 1953, the Danton. The bus (any of them) passes my buddy, Claude Bernard, the nineteenth century founder of physiology, standing in front of the Collège de France on the left. He's the guy who said, "To understand the abnormal you have to understand the normal." Sounds simple doesn't it? But it is incredibly profound, and I don't know about other branches of medicine, but in psychiatry it is almost never noticed—especially in the psychological and social domains. So simple! So important! So forgotten!

Claude is on the left. A block later on the right is the Compagnie bookstore. That's where the guy who works in the cellar pointed out to me without hesitation when I asked, three books that had to do with the history of subjectivity. It's also the place where on the main floor the young saleswoman told me about Augusto Boal and the Theater of the Oppressed. This Brazilian guy, who spent some years of exile in other South American countries as well as in Paris, taught lower-class indigenous peoples to give plays as a way both of learning the dominant language and of having the experience of exercising authority and understanding the differences in power that different people have and ways to deal with that. Terrific stuff.

Now, I've gone about four blocks on the bus, passing the florist, the Viennese pastry place, and the Medical School building. The last is home to an old library where Alain helped me get a membership and has one of those old-fashioned auditoriums where the seats rise in a semicircle in front of the lecturer. I always wanted to be invited to give a lecture there, but it's never happened and is now too late. Half a block later I get off the bus, walk past the medical bookstore, turn left, pass the kiosk where the guy selling the magazines has a brother who lives in Texas and with whom I exchange "bonjour", pass the movie theater, and there I am at the Danton. As I enter, I look to see if the lady who lives around the corner is there this morning (She hasn't been there for a long time. Did she die?). I go to my table, the middle one, there on the right, just behind the *baie vitrée* so I can watch the people and the drivers in the street and the people in the café or read my book or my *Arts et Spectacles* to see what's going on in the city today. Mikel or Dominique, whoever is working today, brings me my *grand crème* without my needing to ask. Monique Guerin, the owner, comes by to hang up the day's menu, and we talk about the day, about politics, the weather, how we feel. I have started an ordinary day in Paris.

ALAIN

Alain, I first met him about twenty years ago. Janis Jenkins was the one who connected us. She and I had done a little work together—she was an anthropologist interested in mental illness—and become friendly. I told her one time that I was going to Paris, and she said, "Oh, I have a friend there, Alain Bottéro. You would like him." I took his address and phone number and contacted him when I got to Paris. We became close friends.

Alain was a wonderfully kind person with a rich sense of humor. He had been involved in the '68 movement of students against the government. And, oh yes, he was a psychiatrist who often worked with psychotic patients. But what was most remarkable about him was the depth and breadth of his thinking. Alain just automatically linked his understanding of psychiatry to his broad knowledge of philosophy, literature, and history. It was his natural way of thinking, which to me was spectacular and so much more valuable because he drew easily from these many sources. He told me about the novel *Aurelia* by Gérard de Nerval, which described for him, and now for me as well, the process of becoming psychotic in a way more impressive than any other. Similarly, he could reach back to the history of psychiatry to the work of Philippe Pinel and Jean Martin Charcot without missing a beat.

Whenever I was in Paris, which I was several times a year for a month at a time, we would get together at least twice. On one of these occasions he would cook a wonderful meal— prepared with vegetables and meat fresh from the market and unusual spices—at his apartment. Alain's father, an antiquities scholar, had written for fun, a Mesopotamian cookbook, and Alain inherited his talent. He would prepare the meal for me and his family—Claire, his wife, Stephan, his son, Milena, his daughter, and Françoise, his sister, who has a permanent post with the French national research organization as a scholar of Chinese and Japanese language. Françoise also became a friend of mine. Alain and I would meet as well for lunch or coffee at the Café Rostand. He would walk there, coming through the Luxembourg Gardens from his office near Métro Vavin on Montparnasse. And we would just talk, about the gardens, about the weather, about George Orwell, about Matisse, about French and American politics and Alain's participation in the student uprisings of '68, and about the small house that he was helping the workers to build for himself on a Greek island.

One time, while Alain and his family were away at their little cottage in the mountains, I stayed in their apartment. It was very comfortable and convenient. As I have already described, I purchased a gift basket from Fauchon as a thank you for their generosity. I left it on the divider shelf between the kitchen and the dining room, with a note. Two days later, Alain called me, obviously very pleased. So my story of "The Gift" came to a very nice conclusion.

Another food story: Some years later, Jeff, my son, offered to pay for dinner for me and a friend at Le Grand Véfour, one of the finest restaurants in France. I don't recall why, perhaps a special birthday present. Naturally, I invited Alain. He knew good food, I mean, really good food. In general, we would eat at a nice restaurant, and it would be okay, but he himself could have cooked a much finer meal. So I was happy to take him to Le Grand Véfour. I seem to remember that they seated us at the *banc* used by Victor Hugo.

It was very fine and very nineteenth century, and Alain and I took full advantage. I figured we'd use Jeff's money for some of it and I'd pay the rest myself. We really did the whole thing, *amuse-bouches,* hors d'oeuvre, main course, salad, and so on and on. And, of course, two really beautiful wines. When the cheese course came around, the waiter brought the huge tray with maybe twenty cheeses on it. I told him I really didn't know very much about cheeses and could he just pick some out for me. He did—helpfully and without condescension, even when he told me the order in which it was best to eat the cheeses. Alain and I ended the meal with a cognac, of course. I knew there were good cognacs and better cognacs, but Alain knew the finest, and that's what we had. I didn't know anything in the world could taste like that.

More than a very close friend and colleague, Alain felt more like a younger brother to me. And then came that horrible day when we met at the Café Rostand and he said, "I've just been diagnosed with lung cancer. They told me I have about a year to live." I was aghast. Slowly we began to talk about it, and soon he said, "You know, your brain just isn't set up to hear that you're going to die in a year." I felt terrible, angry, desolated, and I tried to be there for him. I learned two years later from my own experience that I had had little idea of the feelings he had tried to communicate.

Within a year of the diagnosis Alain was dead. In Paris, I had sat with him for an hour at his outpatient bed as he received poison for the metastasized cancer—the poison which, of course, also affected other vulnerable but normal cells—through a perfusion in his chest. When I got back to New Haven, I would call him on the telephone. One morning his wife, Claire, answered. This was unusual since she is rarely home. She said, "Oh, hello John," then, "Alain can't talk with you, he is too tired," which meant weak and exhausted. But then, "Oh no, he does want to talk with you." We talked for some seconds, maybe a minute, before he was too weak to speak further. We exchanged "Je t'embrasse." We hung up. Ten days later he died

As I think about Alain, about Paris, it occurs to me that when I first went there sixty plus years ago and fell in love with the city, it was not particularly because of its beauty or all the things you can do there. (Three years later Ann and I would often kiss standing on the sidewalk, though people don't seem to do that much anymore.) No, I fell in love with Paris because it said to me, "Oh, you poor fellow, you come to us fine, but they forgot to give you a heart. Here, now you have a heart." Alain, whom I miss so much, helped teach me the truth of that.

CHAPTER 11

PEOPLE,
FAMILY IN PARTICULAR

There are many people who have had a major impact on my life whom I have not written much about, if at all. I don't know why that is. Is it that they are not or have not been important? Not by a long shot! Is it because they have been both intrinsic to and a parallel part of my life? Maybe. But when I think of my kids, Jeff and Sarah, they don't seem parallel to my life at all. It feels more like I am a tree and they are the thickest branches, bending over perhaps to form their own roots and their own two trees. They are part of me. It's weird. And how about the other people whom I have not or only barely mentioned? I have told you a little about Alain, dead, in Paris. I miss him so much. Others in Paris include the hotel owners I have described and Madame G., the *propriétaire* at the Danton. One morning when I said hello over my coffee Madame G. told me that she had a stiff neck, so I got up, asked her permission, and with her agreement massaged it for her, attracting a somewhat amazed look from the waiter. I have been close with my friend Bob since seventh grade, but I have only told you about some of our childhood exploits together. One person I have not mentioned is

Mubahat, who rode from Paris to Vienna with me on my motorcycle, she holding on with her arms around my waist.

But I come back to family, my children, my sister, my father, and my mother. About them I want to add a little more.

MY CHILDREN

I've been thinking about this lately. My relationship with Jeff and Sarah has shifted over the last couple of years from my doing a lot of things for them and being quite independent, to my not being able to do all I used to. As I've become less competent, they've really stepped up. They suggest things I should do and things I don't have to do. And Jeff even said, "Any time you want to come and live with us, you could do that." I had some trouble walking recently, and they're both really good about that. I guess that all sounds pretty normal and as expected, but I had never thought of it, and feeling that transition happening without any fuss is really lovely.

I got married when I was twenty-nine and I remember thinking I would like us to have five kids, but I had no idea what that meant, none. What do you do with kids, how do you act? Basically, you learn from your parents and from what you see.

As I mentioned earlier, Jane and I had what was called at the time a "traditional marriage," that is, she took care of the kids and I worked and brought in money. It was more complicated than that, but those were the basic roles. We just did it that way. I don't think we ever talked about it. If a kid got up in the middle of the night, I was the one to take care of him or her because, ever since medical school, I was accustomed to being called at night. Again, that was just a thing that we did. Our life had a pattern to it, but it wasn't really thought out. I helped with the dishes most the time after dinner. I know I didn't do any psychiatry work immediately after dinner because that was a time to be with the kids. I only worked after they went to bed. On Saturday or maybe Sunday mornings, Jane would sleep in and I would take the kids out for what we called breakfast. I would get a cheeseburger with onions, Sarah would get a grilled cheese sandwich, and I can't remember what Jeff would have. But we usually got milkshakes too in the mornings.

So we built a relationship. I came from a family where you could talk about feelings but not in any great depth. Yet, I've been getting a little better at that sort of thing. Recently I sent an e-mail to Jeff just to tell him that I had had a wonderful time with him when we were at the Tour de France together a couple of years ago, that it was really special. I also mentioned something else. Jeff had his wild side, quietly so, not awful when compared to some other people. And there was one time when he was maybe seventeen or eighteen that he came to our bedroom in the middle of the night and asked if I would come with him. I did. He said, "I'm having a bad trip" an LSD trip, so I sat with him through that. In my e-mail, I told him that I felt really very honored that he asked me to be with him that night.

Sarah has always been very athletic. She was a pitcher for Little League baseball and still plays tennis. She got awards in high school for softball—actually she disliked the game, seeing it as a kind of third-rate baseball—and for basketball and soccer. Sports were just part of her being. She and I used to play catch every day when she was little.

My relationship with my children is like the spirals on DNA. You just connect and you become, in a sense, part of each other's lives. But my work also has always been really important to me, and I tried to see that nothing got in the way of my work. There was one occasion, though, when I had no option. The night before I had my board exams in psychiatry, Sarah got sick, and I got up to be with her. I was really scared about those exams. They lasted six hours or something like that, and I'd studied incredibly hard for them over a year. But you do what you need to do.

I think of my work and my family as forming two separate but interconnected threads. However, that may not do justice to the important role that Jane played in my work. She knew a lot. She read my papers. She came to my talks, and she made comments that were really helpful. For years I struggled in giving talks because I would get really nervous. I never read my talks—I think that is unacceptable—and I learned to use a couple of notes as a starting point, also to begin with smaller groups and work my way up to larger gatherings. But I was still nervous and stared out over the heads of the audience. It was Jane who said, "You're not looking at the people. Look at the people." I finally did, and I mostly conquered my nerves. Jane had practical advice. She was kind, and I could count on her.

As adults, both "children" have my profound admiration. Sarah is a wonderful and creative high school history teacher. I've sat in on her classes, and she's masterful at helping the kids think and express themselves. On the side, she's also a terrific athlete. She is now working on a documentary about women and girls playing baseball (that's right, baseball not softball). Jeff is a television writer, vineyard owner, coffee machine fixer, wonderful cook, and possessor of a lot of other talents. I've attended some of his writers' group sessions and even been a junior teacher to him in a college course he recently gave on writing about characters for television programs and how you portray a human being. I have also accompanied him when he meets with the man who blends his wines.

Both children have always known something of my work. On occasion we'd discuss it at dinner, they'd see me writing and reading, and on occasion they would meet other investigators at our house or when they would come to hear me give a talk. As they became adults I began to send them things that I'd written for their comments. In addition, Sarah is making a film about my life, and she's interviewed a lot of people I've worked with. Several years ago, Jeff did the artwork for the slides I used in a special talk. He came to the event, and when I acknowledged him at the beginning, everyone clapped for him. In the last several years, I've been interested in stories and narratives. Jeff knows much more about stories than I do, and I seek his advice on problems I'm having. He's been very helpful. As Sarah has become involved more recently with making documentaries and the interviews she does for them, we have had great discussions about the experiences of doing such interviews and then turning the results into meaningful narrative. You may find it hard to believe, but both kids are really terrific.

When they were small, the kids knew I was a doctor but not much else. My father, who put it out there sometimes, once asked Jeff what it was like to have a famous father. Dad told me he had asked the question, but I don't remember what Jeff's answer was. He probably didn't know what my father was talking about. After all, I'm a not very shrinky person. There are people who analyze their kids, but I don't think I ever did that. When I'm on a plane and start talking to the person next to me, she or he may ask what I do. When I say I'm a psychiatrist, the reaction is often one of horror: "Oh, You can read my mind." "No need to worry," I reply, "I can't even read mine."

SUSAN

When it comes to my sister, Susan, I don't know how to explain why I have said so little about her. Four years older than I, she was very much a presence in our family home, always there when I was growing up. Even after she left for college when I was fourteen, we were together many times a year. Yet she is not really present in my memories, and this is strange because in many ways she was so important to me. I do remember her teaching me how to ride a bike when I was about six. It was probably her bike, but she was always kind and patient even while knowing that I might fall off a couple of times and possibly damage it. She ran alongside, holding on to the bike as I was trying to push the pedals, and then—wow!— there I was riding a bike. I was not so successful a couple years later. Again riding her bike, I cornered too fast and lost control. As the bike slammed into a curb, I jumped off safely, but the bike went careening along the cement. I don't know if I ever told her.

The bicycle lessons were typical of her generosity toward me. Of course, we argued occasionally, but I don't recall anything serious. They were mostly like the times we would play horses and cows on the car trips from Erie to Cleveland. "A white horse, I get five points!" "No, you don't. He wasn't white, just grey." "He was white." "No, he wasn't." "Yes, he was." Even those fights settled down pretty quickly.

More important, Susan was like an ice-breaker for me. She went ahead, breaking through all the problems of growing up and of growing up in our particular family, while I followed safely and protected in her wake. Now, as I think of it, I realize that this took a toll on her. She was worn down by that role, becoming more and more vulnerable, even while remaining bright and kind. I remember some of her friends in high school, Shirley and Sybil, for example, with whom I would often hang out, especially when I was little. Like Susan, they were kindly and would include me in what they were doing without teasing. During Susan's first year in college, she brought home a friend, Mary Peterson, with whom I fell instantly in love. Well, I was just fourteen. Underneath Susan's kindness and relations with her friends, however, I now detect her vulnerability, maybe even a little shyness.

Susan had a somewhat stormy relationship with our father. As I have said elsewhere, he could be forceful and tough. At dinner, for example, he would often dominate the conversation. I have known other people, German or of German origin, who were like that, and it can be really hard to deal with, to get a word in, to get an idea in, to change the subject. The unremitting onslaught of words and ideas is like a wave that is just too strong to resist. I mostly slipped to one side or another of that wave, but for my mother and for Susan it was harder. Mom often withdrew, although occasionally she would put up verbal resistance. Susan was more likely really to argue with Dad, but she did not often win.

In one way or another, Susan has been rather battered by life.

DAD

Dad's Germanness was not reflected only in his forcefulness. When I was little, some nights he would come in just after I'd gotten into bed to say "Gute nacht" or "Schlaf gut" in his Loudonville-accented German. That was lovely.

Dad was not a community leader. Community leaders were people like the mayor, Rabbi Currick (of Temple Anshe Hesed), the

Catholic bishop, the minister at the Church of the Covenant, the editor of the *Erie Dispatch Herald,* people like that. Dad was active in the community because that's what he thought a person should do. Besides, I think he loved being with people and maybe getting out of the house and out of his tiny office. He was like Superman. During the day he was Clark Kent in that tiny office under the dominance of Sambo, but in the evening he was a wonderful piano player or off to some meeting or other. He was a member of the Temple men's club (where he even served as president), the Temple board, and the Erie Philharmonic board, and he was elected, alongside two more wealthy and powerful men, to the Erie School Board.

Several times a week Dad attended a meeting of one of these groups. Mostly we didn't talk about which. I guess there were a lot of things we never talked about. School board meetings were different, though. A couple of times I even went there to sit in the audience and watch him. He was terrific—quiet, thoughtful, well spoken, and firm. I was impressed with how easily and effectively he fit in with the whole process. Years later I learned that he loved when I attended. I guess it was one of the few times that I saw him as a man independent of home and family.

On the other hand, I don't think Dad was ever that respected by "the Family" (my Mom's family, that is). I don't think he made as much money as my uncles, he certainly wasn't as good as they were at fixing things up at the Island, and I don't think he ever even learned how to navigate among the islands to get from the Island into town.

Dad was not so much a doer (except somewhat in the community) as he was a talker. He loved to tell stories, jokes, whatever. Up at the Island, in the evenings Dad would gather the kids in a corner of the Clubhouse and tell stories about Major Hoople and his forty-seven butlers or Elmer the whale, tales that my cousins and I remember even, now seventy or eighty years later.

Up at the Island, when Dad was not talking with someone or telling stories he was reading. He particularly loved history (as do I and my daughter) and especially the history of the Civil War. He was a little like I am with World War II, though I was alive for that while Dad was born well after the Civil War. Still, growing up, he knew people who had lived through the war, for example, the doctor who used to tell him what it was like to be at the battle of Antietam.

Talking and reading were not highly valued by my mother's family. I'm not sure that my uncles or aunts even had books in their houses. But we had a house with many large bookcases, all full of books. Dad used to joke about one of my aunts, "She has a book, that big one with pictures on her coffee table."

But longevity is important. My father lived until he was ninety-five, and as the uncles and aunts were dying off he started to be recognized as a leader and honored person by my cousins. Dad would have said, "I was just the last of the Mohicans."

A couple of times since his death, I've dreamed that Dad and I were together and could talk for a while. It was terrific seeing him again.

FAMILY AND AUTONOMY

Notre passé et notre avenir sont solidaires.
Nous vivons dans notre race et notre race vit en nous.

Our past and our future are of a piece.
We live in our kin and our kin lives in us.

Gérard de Nerval, *Aurelia,* 1855

I have always been rather quietly and politely autonomous. I have described how my father expected to be listened to, so how did we manage our different tendencies? Usually I just did what he wanted since his desires were pretty reasonable. One incident explains another of our common patterns. Getting ready for a wedding or something of the kind when I was ten, he said, "Put on a shirt and tie." I did but left the top button of my shirt undone because it was so tight. When my father saw that, he told me to button it. Again, I did, but pulled on the button to give myself a little more neck room and popped it off. At that point, my father said, "All right, it's too late to change your shirt now. Just pull your tie up so it won't show." A solution that satisfied us both.

In seventh grade my friend Bob and I would argue with our science teacher (the mayor's daughter), who didn't believe in evolution "because it's not in the Bible." In Sunday School, we'd disagree during the discussions with our teachers who tried to teach us from a book about the Jewish people. Actually, one time when I was about eleven, I was deposited at the school by the car pool and after pretending to walk in, turned around and walked the four miles home, arriving just before my parents set out to pick me up. My resistance to Sunday School ended only when Frank Fox became our teacher and began to teach us about Spinoza, Montaigne, Buddhism, and ethics.

In all this, I never actually thought about autonomy. I just did these things. They made sense to me and felt right. It was the same when I was one of the speakers at our high school graduation and my talk was about how difficult it is for an individual not to be caught up in and overwhelmed by the struggle between big business and big unions.

Then, three years ago, my daughter, Sarah, and I were traveling in Pennsylvania and Ohio as part of a project she was doing on our family history. In Loudonville, the village in Ohio where my father grew up, she searched in the archives for information on Dad and his family. There she found my father's high school graduation speech printed in a 1917 June issue of the *Loudonville Times*. His topic? The relation of the individual to the state and other individuals. How the individual can maintain his identity in the modern world. He had never mentioned to me that he was the graduation speaker, and I certainly had no idea that he would have been interested in such a topic, so close to the topic of my own graduation speech 33 years later. We had never discussed it.

Now, then, I have to think that maybe I got this trait of independence from him. I remember an incident when I was fourteen and riding my bike into the center of Erie and some kids sitting on their front porch called me a sissy because I was wearing shorts. Boys didn't wear shorts in those days. Later, a bit shaken, I told my father about it. "What do you care?" he replied simply and definitively. A great lesson! When someone makes fun of you or puts you down, if they're wrong, if it doesn't change your situation, you can just keep going on as before.

And this feeling of autonomy, it's not so simple. About two years after my grandfather's death, I was up at the Island in Canada and sitting with his widow, Alice, on the large screened porch of the Clubhouse. (After my grandmother died, Sambo had married his secretary.) I was in my early thirties by then, having finished college, medical school, internship, and some of my psychiatric residency. Alice began to tell me how much my grandfather had respected me. "You were particularly special to him," she said. Despite all the time we had spent together over the years, he had never said anything like that to me, and I actually had the impression that I might be one of the few people in the family who didn't necessarily do what he wanted. Then she added, "Did you know, he always had wanted you to be a doctor?"

So proud of being autonomous, yet without realizing it, I had given a high school graduation speech very similar to the one my father gave 33 years earlier and had become a doctor just as my grandfather desired.

ME AND MY MOTHER

You may have noticed—I certainly have—that I haven't written much about my mother, "Mom." In fact, I have noticed that I didn't think consciously much about my mother for most of my life. I didn't realize how angry at her I was. I didn't begin to remember the date of her birthday until I was fifty-five and she was eighty-four. Even then, I had to check to be sure. Only very recently have I begun to grasp the breadth and depth of what my mother's illness has meant in my own life. And for that I must thank Vivian Chan, a Hong Kong social worker who has submitted a dissertation about the children of parents with severe mental illness. I was asked to be an "external examiner" on that dissertation.

Ms. Chan's dissertation includes, among other things, her sensitive and objective histories of four people who had a parent with severe mental illness. She notes that rather than doing the usual scientific analysis to break down the children's experiences into categories such as "relationships," "work," and so on, she decided to look at their "journeys." Not in the sense of Joseph Campbell's "hero's journey," but just to see what their journeys were. This she does. Now, of course, I know what some of the problems are with such an approach, her "constructing" of those journeys from the data she has, problems of reliability of judgments, and all the rest. But she adheres to two of what for me are crucial principles about all research with human beings: my oft-repeated Yogi Berra saying, "You can see a lot by just looking," emphasizing the crucial role of observation; and Henri Poincaré's "A pile of stones is not a house," teaching us to analyze not just the elements of a phenomenon but also its totality as a construction. What Ms. Chan does is really lovely. She looks especially at issues of "suffering" and "creative enduring" of those children who are now adults, and she takes a kind of gestalt approach to look at their "journeys" rather than the usual analysis.

I will return later to the subject of "journeys." More important in this context however, Ms. Chan's work has given me a new perspective on my experiences with my mother. The experiences of Ms. Chan's subjects, their feelings, their reactions, how they dealt with the parent and with other people in their lives, with their need to survive and the guilt, all that was something I recognized immediately for myself. Somehow this gave me license to think about my own experiences and not to feel so harsh, mean, scared, weird, to understand that other people had lived these things as well.

Certainly, her experiences of severe mental illness were terrible for my mother, but—try to be patient with me—they were also hard for me.

I have never really been able to say that before, let alone write it. It involves some element of self-pity, feeling sorry for myself, which I hate. It is also part of a larger feeling: "If you feel sorry for yourself you are weak, and if you are weak you will not survive, perhaps you will succumb to the same thing that has pretty much destroyed her and some of the people around her."

So how do you survive? Well, as my Hong Kong mentors have suggested, you do the best you can. And for me, that often meant separating myself off from her and from the whirlpool that surrounded her and sucked in the lives of others, especially my father and my sister. They didn't really save her, although they, especially my father, helped her survive. But at what horrible cost to them, and maybe even to her. And, of course, living in a family, you are a constant witness to that awful process, the rocks on which lives are washed up and smashed, the lives of those not able to or not selfish enough to try to escape.

I take that image from an experience sailing. One day years ago my wife and I rented a small sloop, a Lightning, to sail in the ocean off of Marblehead, Massachusetts. We were sailing along not far from shore when suddenly an onshore breeze came up coinciding with the rising tide. We were swept closer and closer to massive rocks near the shore. I was worried, but my wife was petrified. She was holding on to the main sheet, the line that controls how closely the main sail is held in. I started shouting at her, "Let it go out! Let it go out." She couldn't bring herself to relax her grip. I had to hit her hand hard and then grab the line as she let go, otherwise, the terrible power of the wind and the incoming waves would have crushed us up against those huge rocks. It has only just occurred to me that life growing up in my family was like that. I learned to loosen the mainsheet, to free myself from those waves and rocks, but of course, at a price. That's the kind of thing my friends in Hong Kong did as well.

The fact that I didn't remember my mother's birthday until late in her life was part of the separation I had "decided" upon. It was not a conscious decision of course. I didn't think about it, I just did it. I led my life at school and with my friends, and I read and listened to music. I was polite to my mother, whether we were visiting her while she was in the hospital or in aftercare in New York and, after she came home, when we were all at the dinner table together. She spent many, many hours in her bedroom after her return, and then I left her alone. She was simply not there for me, and I needed to deal with it.

A few interactions stick with me. One time she and Dad and I were driving me on my way to college, from Erie to Swarthmore. Dad and I shared the actual driving, and on the Pennsylvania Turnpike I had the car up to the speed limit of seventy miles an hour. Mom asked me to slow down, and I did for several minutes, then gradually sped up again. She asked me to slow down again, and the same thing happened. Finally, she said, "If you don't slow down, I'm going to get out." Dad intervened: "Pull over Johnny, I'll drive," he said. I did, and he did. Sometimes when we were eating out, she would put her pills out by her fork, and I would think, "Damn, we all know you're sick. You don't have to do that." Lots of horrible thoughts! It was so hard not to get entangled, to be kind while trying to stay disengaged. I was often unsuccessful. And apparently, from what they described, so were my friends in Hong Kong. There are no winners, only more or less avoidance of total failure.

I think Mom felt badly about not being a better mother. When she was older and starting to develop dementia, she said that maybe she shouldn't have been a mother. I'm not sure that she really wanted to have kids. People just did. She did try to be a good mother. And when she wasn't having problems she wasn't totally self-involved. I remember one occasion when she really helped me. I was on vacation from college, the whole family was in New York, and I was having problems with my girlfriend Ann. My father and sister were having one of their rows. We had reservations for dinner and just as it was time to leave the hotel my sister "had to go to the bathroom" again, where she stayed and stayed while my father went quietly crazy, calling to her that we had to leave. Susan finally came out and we had our dinner at the restaurant, but later that evening, I told my mother that the "thing" between Dad and Susan was killing me because it was on top of my troubles with Ann. Later, she apparently talked to Dad, and he did not quarrel with Susan again for the rest of our stay. Somehow, I felt comfortable talking with Mom about my problem and asking for her help, and she, despite her "mental illness," gave it. There were blessed moments of contact like that. But not a lot. You just couldn't count on it.

That's why I put "Mom" in quotations at the beginning of this section. She wasn't Mom much of the time. Now, in retrospect, when she is long dead and I have my links to the people in Hong Kong, whose experiences were so like mine, I have begun to realize more fully the struggles I had and the struggles she had and to wish that I could have done better. But I also feel gratitude that I could do as well as I did, with tons of help from my father, my sister, Martha, and friends. And, of course, I have spent my life trying to figure out the problems of severe mental illness. That quest has many sources, but one of them—in some way I do not fully understand—must have been to try to help the struggles of my mother.

UNCERTAINTY THEORY

In interviewing me, at one point Sarah Kamens said: "I guess one of the reasons I'm asking you all these questions is because I'm curious given your relationship with your mother in what ways it might have influenced your path to the field." And I had to reply: "Yeah, I assume it does. . . but I don't have a direct feeling connection to it."

I had reached my mid-70s before I even began to think about this. The first time I ever talked publicly about my mother's problem, or even I think with friends, was when I was a speaker at a meeting in Calgary in Canada about fifteen years ago. Among those giving talks, three of us independently talked about our relatives who had psychiatric problems. One of them I knew well but none of us beforehand said that we were going to do it. After that I began to talk more about my mother, not a lot, but on occasion.

Armed with my observations of my psychiatric patients, some of whom I have described, in the last several years my thoughts crystallized around one idea in particular. My mother had a lot of big problems, that's for sure. But at one point I was talking to a friend of the family, a social worker, who said that she didn't have such big psychiatric problems, that she was actually a very competent woman. This was a whole other picture that I had never heard or thought about. She was certainly a very troubled person, but she was also a competent person. She was both. Yes, it's possible to be both. That is what I address in my paper, "Uncertainty Theory," which was published by *Psychiatry* in 2017 (Volume 80, Issue 4). Because it brings together so much in my life and in my thinking, I reproduce it here.

UNCERTAINTY THEORY: A POWERFUL APPROACH TO UNDERSTANDING PSYCHIATRIC DISORDER

John S. Strauss

L'oeil de l'esprit ne peut trouver nulle part plus d'éblouissements ni plus de ténèbres que dans l'homme: il ne peut se fixer sur aucune chose qui soit plus redoutable, plus compliquée; plus mystérieuse et plus infinie. Il y a un spectacle plus grand que la mer, c'est le ciel, il y a un spectacle plus grand que le ciel, c'est l'intérieur de l'âme.

The eye of the mind can find nothing more bright or dark than in a human being; nor can it fix on anything more formidable, more complicated, more mysterious or more infinite. There is only one spectacle more grand than the sea, it is the sky, there is one spectacle more grand than the sky, it is the interior of the soul.

(Hugo, 1862, p 301)

Strange, bizarre really, how the mental health field over the decades has gone through a weird kind of historicism, finding almost total certainty in each era in totally different explanatory models. At the end of the 19th century it was biological, "mental illness is brain disease" (Griesinger, 1861). In the early and middle 20th century it was psychological, especially psychoanalytic: id, ego, superego. Briefly in mid-20th century it was social, social class and mental illness, milieu treatment, families. And now it is biological again: mental illness is brain disease, for example, genetic. Oh yes, there is epigenesis, the effect of experience on genetic expression; there is even neuroplasticity, the effects of experience on neural structures. But these seem to be of interest primarily from a biological point of view. Sometimes it appears that as a field over the years we continue to be in a stage Piaget called "preoperational," a rather early stage in child development when the child can only attend to one aspect of his world at a time (Piaget and Szeminska, 1941).

How have we followed this course of jumping from one explanatory model to another and then back again? "We have not," you may reply. "After all there is the biopsychosocial model." But really that model is like virtue; we extol it, but are not too great in living it. No, I think we have treated the bio, psycho, and social more like a huge cave complex—a cave where after the entrance three passages lead into three cave systems. Although these systems have many links, we tend to get so invested in one or another of them we all but forget the other two. Beyond our problems bringing together the biological, the psychological, and the social, and perhaps contributing to these problems, our field also has the difficulty in combining scientific concepts based on "hard" data with the more subtle and nuanced data of subjectivity—data related to feelings, desires, efforts of the person, data that in order to follow traditional scientific paradigms we have often systematically excluded—an interesting practice, in some ways violating scientific principles of data inclusion.

Is there no way out of these bizarre and limiting practices? In the research conducted with my colleagues we have repeatedly been confronted by findings that do not support a simple model for understanding severe psychiatric disorder, a "disease like any other" model, or any other unitary approach. In trying to classify reliably various symptoms we ran into noting that even two potentially reliably identified symptoms like delusions and hallucinations in fact often represent continua, not discrete phenomena (1969). Then as part of a larger study we noticed that, contrary to the dominant theory at the time, people with schizophrenia, no matter what diagnostic criteria of schizophrenia we used, did not have an inevitable downhill course but could actually improve considerably (Strauss & Carpenter, 1974). Then we noticed that rather than a single "disease process" there were in fact several relatively independent processes in the course of disorder: work, symptoms, social relations, and hospitalization. These biological, psychological, and social processes were related but also had their own trajectories. Subsequently, we noted that not just symptoms but also diagnostic categories reflected continua, not discrete entities (Strauss, 1973; Strauss et al., 1979). To help account for our findings we brought back John Hughlings Jackson's ideas about positive and negative symptoms, separate processes that could be identified (Strauss, Carpenter, & Bartko, 1974). In focusing further on longitudinal aspects of disorder and improvement, expanding on the ideas of Conrad (1958), we noted that, far from a straight line course, there were longitudinal patterns that suggested distinct longitudinal phases of disorder and effective functioning, phases that seemed to be strongly affected by the active role and the subjectivity of the patient him or herself (Breier & Strauss, 1983, 1984; Davidson & Sachs et al., 1974; Strauss, 1992; Rakfeldt & Strauss, 2005; Strauss, 1991, 1996, 1999; Strauss,

Hafez, Lieberman, & Harding, 1985). It was also noted that far from disorder and improvement being influenced only by traditional treatment modalities, aspects of experience such as "someone who cared" and "someone who took me seriously" were noted by patients as central to their improvement. Taken together, these findings suggest that processes that current efforts attempt to view as neatly structured static and discrete phenomena are actually complex and dynamic. Rather than supporting a simple concept such as suggested by "disease like any other," we are dealing with complex, interwoven processes that needed to be viewed from two types of perspective: the biological, psychological, and social perspective and the subjective/objective perspective.

But if we are not to fall back on the old and apparently simplistic explanatory models, how are we to understand this complexity? Rather than remaining at an abstract conceptual level we can proceed to a case history, or rather two case histories, both describing the disorder and its course in the same patient. The first history will take the form of a traditional psychiatric history such as one might find in a case record.

First Case History of Mrs S.
Mrs. S was a 92-year-old woman found dead in her long-term-stay hospital bed. Cause of death was determined to be pneumonia in this debilitated woman. Mrs. S was first admitted to the hospital two years ago following a long history of psychiatric illness. She was first diagnosed schizophrenic at the age of 42, although she had apparently had the onset of psychiatric problems such as anxiety before that time. At the age of 42, suffering from psychotic symptoms, she was hospitalized and treated with electroshock and insulin coma therapy. After several months in the hospital she was discharged to a rehabilitation facility, where she remained several

months. Following that time she was discharged home, and over subsequent years had several relatively brief hospitalizations and was treated continuously with medications and psychotherapy. She did fairly well but then began to regress and, around the age of 60, to develop symptoms of dementia. As these worsened she was admitted for long-term hospitalization where she remained until the time of her death.

Second Case History of Mrs. S.
This case history is of the same person as the one above, namely my mother.

"What? You are recounting the story of your own mother in a scientific article?"

Yes, it is perhaps an awkward sortie into placing subjectivity as a crucial part of our human science. Not just having the subjectivity of narrative as a brief article in a section of a scientific journal, but as a core part of an article where subjectivity—meaning, feelings, intention—allow it to become a basic part of the data. A professor of English literature has noted how what a writer says about a person, or leaves out, basically determines how you see that person (Spurgin, 2006). It seems to me that the idea holds for us as well. What we might consider the objectivity of a traditional medical history has serious limits as well as values. I use my recounting as an example because it is a source of more detailed and varied information over a person's lifetime than is usually available when information is limited to a format that we consider to be purely objective.

An approach to including subjectivity does not, of course, intend in any way to negate the crucial role of measurement and other aspects of traditional science that must also be a central part of our field.

My mother was born in Cleveland, Ohio, in 1903 and did well, graduating from high school and going to Smith College. Near the time of examinations at the end of the first year, she became anxious and called home. Her father, a self-made man of the Victorian era, took the call; he told her she should just come home, since girls did not need to go to college anyway. So she did go home, never completing her first year. She then entered teachers-training school in Cleveland and married my father shortly after graduating. At that time, married women were not hired as teachers because of the concern that they might become pregnant, and it would not be good for the children to see that, so she was not able to find a job. Soon, the national economic situation evolved into the Great Depression of 1929 and the only job open to my father was to take over the management of a small group of apartments in Erie, Pennsylvania, that he co-owned with his father-in-law. My older sister and I had been born, and the family moved to Erie. There, besides her roles as housewife and mother, my mother collaborated with a friend to organize a progressive elementary school, which became very successful. After several years, the school became a favorite of the socially elite and less progressive, so my mother left her involvement with it. The time was early in the Second World War, and I remember fondly working in the backyard with Mom on our victory garden where we grew corn, tomatoes, peas, and other vegetables. Sometimes we would talk, sometimes just work quietly together.

During the summer of 1945, Mom's mother and her especially bright, kind, talented, and beloved younger sister both died of cancer. Our extended family was very close, and this was a major blow in all of our lives. Later that year I remember sitting in our small dining room one day and two men dressed in black emerged from a black car that had just parked in front of our house. They were expected, came into the house and took my mother away with them. Whether that recollection is accurate or not I cannot say, but it is certain that she was taken from our home in Erie to a hospital in New York. Apparently, there was no good hospital of the kind she needed either in Erie or Cleveland. I learned later that she had a severe psychiatric disorder, probably including delusions and hallucinations and was diagnosed as having schizophrenia. She was treated in the hospital with electroshock treatments and insulin coma, and after a few months was transferred to a hospital in the New York suburbs where she received psychotherapy and rehabilitation, learning among other things how to weave with a loom. When Mom came back to Erie she set up a studio where she wove fine table settings and cashmere scarves and sold sophisticated jewelry from Georg Jensen's in New York.

But this was Erie, a midsized rustbelt industrial town, and there was little market for such things. When I would visit Mom's studio there was never a customer there; after about a year she closed the studio. She then opened an office of the American Association for the United Nations. School classes would be brought there, but there was not adequate interest to allow it to stay open. Mom then taught a course in foreign policy at the local college—not bad for a person who had never even completed one year of college herself.

But mostly she hated living in Erie. She found it narrow and constricting, and I remember her saying that the women only wanted to talk about their illnesses. Years later I read Sinclair Lewis's book *Main Street*, in which the doctor's wife, Carol Milford, finds living in a small Midwestern town so stifling she leaves her otherwise happy marriage for a period of time.

Mom continued receiving medications from her doctor in New York, going to that city a couple times a year to stay for many weeks at a time to get psychotherapeutic treatment. We would go to visit, and I recall Mom talking about the volunteer work she was doing at the United Nations with some very famous people and how much she loved that. On one occasion she asked Dad if we could all move to New York, but he said that was impossible since his work at the apartments was in Erie and clearly that could not be moved.

We continued to live in Erie, and in subsequent years, Mom withdrew more and more, and then in her early sixties she began to develop dementia, perhaps contributed to by her having an insulin coma induced in the past. The dementia gradually worsened over the years. Mom spent her final years in a nursing home, mostly in bed, finally dying, demented, of pneumonia at the age of 92.

So why do I give these two presentations here of the same person? Because of the lesson they teach based on the old Yogi Berra statement, paraphrased as "You can see a lot by just looking." If you do not see a huge mass of data, for example, if you do not look for it or do not notice it because your understanding indicates it is not relevant, you will not see that it might be important. In this instance, if we do not tell you about something, as in the first presentation, you will not "see" it (or include it in your understanding). For better or for worse, the first presentation involving valuable brevity and structure is the more traditional medical-type statement and suggests some disease perhaps biologically based and essentially unrelated to experience. The second presentation, on the other hand, suggests the possible interweaving of experience, disorder, social context, and the repeated but unsuccessful efforts of the person to have a life that is meaningful for her. Are we dealing with biological disease or biopsychosocial disorder that includes important subjective as well as objective components? Can we accept the evidence of neuroplasticity and epigenesis, for example, and the data of experiences to allow the current biological model to open up to explore the possibilities of becoming biopsychosocial?

And beyond biopsychosocial as objective data, can we really take the power and nuances of subjectivity into consideration as well?

But why add the focus on subjectivity to the usual objective considerations of biopsychosocial? Subjective data involve attention to feelings, desires, and the active role of the person. Dealing with these involves not merely using the more objective approaches to subjective information as involved, for example, in symptom checklists and life events scales, but also more adequate reflections of human experience generally ignored in our attempts to be scientific. What are we to do, for example, with the psychiatric inpatient who said he realized he had to pull himself together and apparently succeeded? Or the young woman following a psychotic episode who, in what we called "woodshedding," told us yes, she knew she needed to do very little for awhile (which we mistakenly viewed as burning out) before she could go ahead and become more active? Or the young woman who, following her psychosis, found it important to turn on her radio and select a program, as the first experience of being able to exert control over her world? As the Victor Hugo quotation at the beginning of this report suggests, human experience is extremely complex in depth as well as in extent.

As Heisenberg suggested (1958), "What we observe is not nature itself, but nature exposed to our method of questioning." While objective methodologies may be relatively well accepted, there may be several methods to attempt to represent human subjectivity in our field, and it is important to include the special power of the arts as a methodology to explore some of these processes. Traditional scientific approaches in themselves may not be capable of reflecting the power and nuance of experience, feeling, and decisions. In many instances, the subjective data will not even be available to us if during our assessment of a condition we do not have an attitude of being interested in the person, of "being there" with him or her.

An unjustified sense of "knowing" can even cut us off from "seeing" in the Yogi Berra sense. The experience of conducting research interviews is helpful in this regard; if you have a long checklist of questions, you will almost certainly indicate to the subject verbally or nonverbally, and usually without realizing it, "Do not ask me anything or respond in a way not acceptable to our categories since we do not have time for that kind of thing."

To return to the Yogi Berra statement, if we exclude the range, power, and nuances of experience from what we "see" because we assume they are not "scientific" in the traditional sense, we have probably violated the scientific principle of not excluding relevant data before even considering its possible importance. We must value both the power and beauty of traditional science with its attention to methods of data collection, measurement, sampling, and the handling of data, but also utilize methods for reflecting the power and beauty of subjective experience and the active role of the person, even if that means redefining the rules and approaches of our human science. If my mother just finally gave up and sank into her "mental illness," is that a possibility too "unscientific" to consider its possible clinical and theoretical significance?

Rather than accepting a view that our field must be "a science like the others," perhaps we will be better off to view it as a human science in which the traditional scientific approaches and the more especially "human" aspects are both accepted as playing off each other, neither ignoring nor dominating the other. This implication extends even to the type of data we collect and our approach to the collection process

If it is possible that such complexity is also the reality, that bio, psycho, and social, and also objective and subjective in all their complexity, really are relevant to our understanding, how can we possibly deal with all that?

It may be possible to accomplish by using an approach that does not continue the historical trend to focus only on one of the areas and then another in a sequence as noted earlier in this report. Uncertainty theory (Schmidt, 1996) assumes that we are not sure which of the areas interact and are important in a given instance and provides us with the freedom to question and explore. It is not so much a theory as an approach. Especially relevant for complex processes in which many variables are involved, often interacting in complex and nonlinear ways, uncertainty theory proceeds with the possibility that it may not be possible at the present time to find the answer to a given field, but that there are nevertheless ways of proceeding to maximize our understanding and possibility to act effectively. It considers that we are not sure that "mental illness is brain disease," for example; it might be, but it also might not be, or it might be some combination of things.

And that same uncertainty, far from leaving us helpless, provides models and concepts that make more intelligent exploration possible. Uncertainty theory and its many contributors do not, unfortunately, provide the definitive solutions that they sometimes seem to promise, but they do provide important tools for us to use in learning more about our focus of interest. By using alternative explanatory hypotheses, models such as systems theory (e.g., Prigogine, 1977), chaos theory (e.g., Casti, 1994), and complexity theory (e.g., Miller & Page, 2007) allow us to consider such possibilities as tipping points where for an example an accumulation of stresses finally becomes overwhelming, emergents such as new solutions or new decompensations arising out of previous modes of behavior, such as the person realizing that dealing calmly with his or her hallucinated voices changes them from cruel to helpful. With such approaches it is also possible to focus more on phases of disorder onset and improvement, and possible contributions of biology, psychology, and context interacting in ways such as by involving positive or negative feedback loops and new processes of behavior and mental functioning evolving out of earlier ones. Uncertainty theory and these more specific models provide ways of beginning to deal with the kind of data provided in that second presentation of my mother's psychiatric problems, to ask the questions to begin to collect the data and explore complexities that the single domain models to understanding psychiatric disorder just cannot even approach.

Biological, psychological, and social interactions? Did she have a genetic predisposition to certain psychiatric problems (as well perhaps as a genetic predisposition to particular effective coping styles)? Data including such information as her earlier severe anxiety problems suggest that the answer may be yes. Did the recurrent disappointments and failures generated by social contexts that repeatedly blocked her aspirations perhaps generate a "tipping point" into psychiatric disorder, set off by the death of her mother and younger sister, which finally overwhelmed her strengths, desires, and sense of a competent self? Had she felt that she could no longer keep on trying when every time, over all these years, there has been nothing but failure and defeat again and again and again? How does a formulation involving that kind of despair compare to alternative hypotheses? Did my mother have a biological disease, a brain disease, not importantly influenced by her experiences, coping styles, and social milieu? Uncertainty theory gives us many tools to think about this wider world in our considerations of the possible complexities of our field. Not being certain about the nature of psychiatric disorders actually is a potential source for learning the possible complexities involved. Being "certain" in our theories, research, teaching and practice, if we are also wrong, can prevent us from such learning.

References

Breier, A., & Strauss, J. S. (1983). Self-control in psychotic disorders. *Archives of General Psychiatry, 40*(10), 1141-1145.

Breier, A., & Strauss, J. S. (1984). Social relationships in the recovery from psychotic disorder. *American Journal of Psychiatry, 141*(8), 949-955.

Casti, J. L. (1994). *Complexification : Explaining a paradoxical world through the science of surprise.* New York, NY: Harper Collins.

Conrad, K. (1958). *Die beginnende Schizophrenie.* Stuttgart, Germany: Thieme Verlag.

Davidson, L., & Strauss, J. S. (1992). Sense of self in recovery from severe mental illness. *British Journal of Medical Psychology, 65:* 131-145.

Griesinger, W. (1861). *Pathologie und Therapie der psychischen Krankheiten.* Stuttgart, Germany: Krabbe.

Heisenberg, W. (1958). *Physics and philosophy: The revolution in modern science.* London, United Kingdom: George Allen and Unwin,.

Hugo, V. (1862). *Les Misérables.* Paris, France: Pagnerre. (2015), Vol 1, Paris: edition d'Yves Gohin Gallimard.

Miller, J. & Page, S. (2007). *Complex adaptive systems.*Princeton, NJ: Princeton University Press.

Piaget, J., & Szeminska, A. (1941). *La Genese du Nombre chez l'enfant.* Neuchatel, France: Delachaux et Niestlé.

Prigogine, I. (1977). *Self-organization in non-equilibrium systems.* Hoboken, NJ: Wiley.

Rakfeldt, J., & Strauss, J. S. (2005). The low turning point: A control mechanism in the course of mental disorder. In L. Davidson, C. Harding, & L. Spaniol, (Eds.) *Recovery from Severe mental illness* (pp.316-326). Boston, MA: Boston University, Center for

Psychiatric Rehabilitation. (Reprinted from *Journal of Nervous and Mental Disease,* 1989, *177*(1): 32-37.)

Sachs, M., Carpenter, W. T., Jr., & Strauss, J. S. (1974). Recovery from delusions: Three phases documented by patients' interpretation of research procedures. *Archives of General Psychiatry, 30*(1), 117-120.

Schmidt, C. (Ed.). (1996). *Uncertainty in economic thought.* Brookfield, VT: Edward Elgar.

Spurgin, T. (2006) *The English novel.* Chantilly, VA: The Teaching Company.

Strauss, J. S. (1969). Hallucinations and delusions as points on continua function: Rating scale evidence. *Archives of General Psychiatry, 31,* 581-586.

Strauss, J. S., (1973), Diagnostic models and the nature of psychiatric disorder. *Archives of General Psychiatry, 29,* 445-449.

Strauss, J. S. (1991). The person with delusions. *British Journal of Psychiatry,159*(Suppl. 14), 57-61.

Strauss, J. S. (1996). Subjectivity. *Journal of Nervous and Mental Disease, 184*(4): 205-212.

Strauss, J. S. (1999). À Maryanne: Le Contexte, la Personne et la Maladie Mentale. VST: Revue du Champ Social et de la Santé Mentale. No. 64, pp. 8 à 13. *Réedité Dans Psychothérapies.* 2001, *21*(4), 235-242.

Strauss, J. S., & Carpenter, W. T., Jr. (1974a). Characteristic symptoms and outcome in schizophrenia. *Archives of General Psychiatry, 30*(1), 429-434.

Strauss, J. S., & Carpenter, W. T., Jr. (1974b), Prediction of outcome in schizophrenia: II. Relationships between predictor and outcome variables. *Archives of General Psychiatry, 31,* 37-42.

Strauss, J. S., Carpenter, W. T., Jr., & Bartko, J. J. (1974).

Speculations on the processes that underlie schizophrenic symptoms. *Schizophrenia Bulletin, 11,* 61-70.

Strauss, J. S., Gabriel, K. R., Kokes, R. F., Ritzler, B. A., VanOrd, A., & Tarana, E. (1979). Do psychiatric patients fit their diagnoses? Patterns of symptomatology as described with the biplot. *Journal of Nervous and Mental Disease, 167,* 105-113.

Strauss, J. S., Hafez, H., Lieberman, P., & Harding, C. M. (1985). The course of psychiatric disorder: III. Longitudinal principles. *American Journal of Psychiatry, 142*(3), 289-296.

* * * * *

Recently, I was talking over lunch with a young psychiatrist about careers, the mental health field, what we were doing, and so on. All of a sudden she said, "I'd like to change the subject, if that's all right." I said, "Sure." "Well, I know you've started to write about your mother who had severe mental illness in your papers, and talk about that in your lectures. I have the same problem with my mother." You know, in all my eighty-six years, no one—unless we knew each other very well—has even shared the existence of mental illness in his or her family with me. And no one has ever asked me for advice about it or even wanted really to reflect about it together. No one. I felt this ray of sunshine, this great gift, that another person in the world wanted help with this, like I was her older brother or uncle or something. No one! So we talked about it. I told her what I'd tried, how much I just denied or avoided, how hard it was. Not once, never in my life, have I had that conversation before.

All these connections, these revelations, so late in life!

CHAPTER 13

GETTING OLDER AND A VIEW OF THE PAST

My travels are pretty much behind me. My hitchhiking trips in the United States and in Europe are long behind me, as are my motorcycle trips. I no longer fly off to New Delhi or Ibadan or even to London, Geneva, or Aarhus in Denmark, or to the wonderful islands off the west coast of Norway or Tromsø way north of the Arctic Circle. I haven't been to Paris for over a year now. And I stopped going up to the Island around the age of seventy-eight because I had slipped off the deck of my Sunfish sailboat, something that never ever would have happened to me before I got so old.

Part of the reason I'm not traveling much is that people rarely invite me to give talks any more. But don't feel sorry for me, I feel more relief than bitterness over that. In fact, I really like much better now having breakfast with Larry, lunch with Maria or Joe, fondue with Claude and Linda, talking with my kids, or sometimes just lying on my couch.

When I am on that couch, of course, I travel too. To some Aegean island that I have been to many years ago, where I understand now a little more than I ever did before how Daedalus felt, or even more how Icarus felt, zooming up to the sun, down to the very wave tops, flying at last. And then, of course, crashing into the sea. It is hardest, though, to grasp how it was with me and my mother. I think I am getting little by little to feel how it was to be her, a queen of sorts, but an unrecognized one, living in Erie, Pennsylvania, with her fancy gloves, gold-rimmed plates, ornate sterling silver. Running the local organization for the UN, teaching foreign policy, never really recognized, always in the wrong place, maybe even with the wrong husband. But how it was for her and me, that's more difficult. I've made a stab at describing it, but it's too personal and troubling to get below the surface, to tell you or maybe even to tell myself. These things take a lot of thinking. I don't really have time to travel all around the world, even if people did invite me. I should be here lying on the couch, thinking, watching the eagles that live in Edgewood Park soar by sometimes, not moving a wing, way up there in the cold winter air.

It's not after all as if I have all the time in the world. One day looking out onto the backyard, I saw a huge bird—one of the eagles?—sitting over the mangled body of a squirrel. That squirrel had probably just been running around in the yard, looking for acorns, and then, whoosh, it was all over. There's so much to try to grasp. What did it really feel like—or what would it have really felt like had I been able to feel it— standing out on the west end of Erie with my thumb in the air, at the beginning of my three-month trip out west? My father in great kindness had taken me there. We'd said good-bye. And now I was standing out there all alone. What was that like? What was it about?

And what is it about now, lying on my couch, with thoughts like these? Somehow I am now seeing more and better but still only a little tiny bit—that eagle up there, Daedalus, Icarus, Mubahat, my kids, Mom, Dad, Susan. And Walter Strauss, the kindly young refugee from Nazi Germany, who joined the U.S. army and left me his Bakelite radio and his sergeant stripes, then was killed on Omaha Beach.

WHAT'S IT LIKE

What's it like to be getting older? I never thought about it much before this year. I probably had an image of a bunch of shriveled people on rocking chairs outside of a big old house, an old people's home. But that's not my experience. My father, for example, lived to the age of ninety-five, was still driving into his nineties, cracking jokes with the young women who were life guards at the swimming pool in the retirement center where he lived, and giving piano concerts to "the old folks"—the advantage, he said, was they fell asleep so didn't notice when he made mistakes. The last time I saw my grandfather alive I was helping him nail boards onto our boardwalk at the Island. Then he was dead and in his coffin in Cleveland.

Talking with Sarah Kamens has prompted me to take the long view of my life. And it's a really weird experience, maybe a little like being in the space station and looking down at the earth. For one thing, your life is too big—or rather too complicated—to really grasp. There are all those "nooks and crannies," as the English muffin package says, or, as on a rocky beach, quiet recesses and pools swarming with life but hidden under rock shelves.

We see in the movies and read in books of old guys just reliving the past or asking themselves what it all means. For me it isn't like that at all. It's more like wonderment. How the hell did I ever do that? How did I ever not get killed in one of the near-calamitous incidents when I was riding my bike or my motor-cycle or hitchhiking?

What does it mean? It's a silly question. What's it mean, those hundreds of books in my bookshelves—*Dave Dawson in the RAF, Out of Africa, Antigone*? What's it mean, my hundred-plus sets of *Great Courses*—"The Plays of Ancient Greece," "The Piano Concerto," "Philosophy of the Enlightenment?" What's it mean, the death of my parents, of my grandfather, of Alain from lung cancer, or Sara Lee when she was only thirty-seven? Or even what's it mean, the woman who ran the red light and totaled my car with me in it and Pat from Ernie's Pizza coming out to see if I was all right. This constant unfolding of experiences, of people, of places, of encounters. The beauty of knowing people, some fleetingly as on my hitchhiking trip and others, like my children, for their entire lives. My daughter, once a tiny baby, now listens to my problems and gives me advice. My son, whom I have also known since he was born, now tells me, "You know, if you decide at any time you would like to live with us we would be very happy to have you."

What does it all mean? You just see it lying there all around you, before you, after you, above you, wherever. And you're just amazed.

In *Wild Strawberries* the Swedish director Ingmar Bergman depicts the story of an elderly and somewhat rigid but also kind professor who is taking an automobile trip with his son and his daughter-in-law to the city of Lund to receive a major award. On the trip you see the current actions and interactions of the three along with frequent scenes of the professor's recollections evoked by events that happen on the trip or by the places they stop or the people they encounter. I think Ingmar Bergman has captured perfectly my own experience of how it is when one becomes older. Daily life goes on, just as in the past. But at moments when there is space for reflection during the day or when going to sleep at night or awakening in the morning, those experiences and probably other things as well, recall events earlier in one's life—a phenomenon that allows one not only to see those events again but to gain a richer understanding of their importance and role.

I resist the word "meaning" because it implies a final and complete truth, and I don't think like that at all. I recently remembered my father telling me as an adult of a time when he had taken me, aged about three, for a walk at the "Peninsula" in Erie. He felt guilty because he had hidden behind a tree so I couldn't see him and I started to cry and call out for him. I think the episode lasted only a few moments, but I remember his telling me, more than once, about it. I have had my own, varied feelings about it: "Those things happen, we all have pieces of ourselves that do nasty things like that"; "Maybe he was angry at my mother and took it out on me"; "That was really cruel"; and I relive the terror of a little boy feeling lost and alone in a totally unknown space. On the recent night when I thought about it I was feeling all of those, kind of a conglomerate feeling. I neither passed off the incident as too bad but not so important nor felt that my father was terrible, but I also felt that what he had done was cruel, sad, terrifying, all of those things.

And yet I feel now that one can put all those things together, that as diverse and contradictory as they are, they form a unity. You know how when you're doing a jigsaw puzzle you put together some pieces that are sky pieces, you put together some pieces that are farmhouse pieces, some pieces that are man plowing pieces, and then after a while you realize, "Oh, I see they fit together!" It's like that. The sky pieces are still sky pieces, the farmhouse pieces are still farmhouse pieces, and the man plowing pieces are still man plowing pieces, but they now also come together to form a whole. It's like that.

A DIFFERENT ERA

One thing about getting older is coming to terms with how much things have changed. There are the things and places in your own life that have changed, sometimes in such a way as to make you question the accuracy of your memories. And then, of course, there are the broad aspects of culture, the things that formed a backdrop to your life in earlier eras.

I must get one unsettling final trip to Euclid Avenue out of the way. When Dad was getting pretty old, eighty-nine or so, and living in a retirement community in Shaker Heights while Mom was in a nursing home, I thought I'd better ask him to drive me to Sambo's old Euclid Avenue house before he himself got too old and it would be lost for good. I certainly could never have found it. All I had were the vague memories of the big curving stairway, the sliding doors, the tree in the backyard, and the ghosts of Herb and Ethel, Sambo, and Nanny. Dad agreed, which surprised me because I thought maybe he would rather let those old memories go. I had forgotten how much of an adventurer he was, in his own way. So we went. We started driving down this wide street with a lot of medium-sized houses on it, set back a little. He stopped. "There it is." "Where?" All I saw was a little grey house, well not little exactly, but not all that big. "That's it?" I almost cried. "That's it," he said in the firm gentle way of his that meant a million things, including this time, "Isn't it surprising how you remember things? 10650 Euclid." (Dad had this incredible memory for numbers.) "Do you mind if I get out?" I asked. "No, go right ahead. I'll wait for you here." Even Dad had his limits. I walked slowly up to the house. I was able to peer through two big windows, one on each side of the front door. The windows were greasy, there were no curtains. Inside it looked pretty bare. On the left I looked into what must have been the dining room in the old days; four scruffy-looking guys were sitting around a big table, like a ping pong table, drinking coffee. On the other side I saw nothing except the floor and bare walls. No sliding doors—I wondered if they had ever existed. The stairway, if it existed, would have been behind the front door. The Rudds' house next door was still there, not as big as I remembered but nice. I wonder what happened to them. I walked down the walk, back to the car, away from the greasy windows and the dull grey middling sized house. I was stunned. I opened the car door and let myself in. "Thanks, Dad," I said in what must have been a very muted tone. He looked at me as though half to say, "I'm sorry it's like this, life is hard isn't it?" and maybe a little as though to say, "I miss the old days too. They were so long ago." Then he started the engine, put the car into gear, and we drove slowly off.

So what I remember of Euclid Avenue is gone, if it ever really existed. But other aspects of life in those days can be revisited with the help of the movies. For example, I recently watched the movie *Cheers for Miss Bishop* with Martha Scott. It is the story of a girl from the Midwest who becomes a beloved teacher at a midwestern university. The movie was made in 1941 and covers a period from the late nineteenth century until about 1938, and it captures the feel of much of my early life. My parents sometimes tried to describe what it was like to grow up at the turn of the twentieth century—my mom in Cleveland, my dad in a small central Ohio village—the advent of electric street lights, cars that at first had buggy-whip holders in order to make the transition from horse drawn carriages more acceptable, and the arrival of radio and the telephone.

Although *Cheers for Miss Bishop* depicts a time mostly before I was born, it made me feel, "Yes, that's how it was." For one thing, when it came out, which is probably also when I saw it for the first time, it was an entirely usual kind of movie for me. Now you can't even imagine that such a movie would be made, even less that it would be accepted for distribution. Why? It is just too nice, too cozy, too simple, too unencumbered. It is in black and white. It shows things like a horse-drawn sleigh. No, they were not common when I grew up, but I have ridden in them. When I was little, kids would often have a sleigh ride as part of their birthday party, or in summer, a hay ride in a horse-drawn wagon. But it is mostly the feel of things being slower, more personal, less complicated than would be acceptable now. When I am at the Yale gym and coming down the stairs of that large building, students and young faculty coming up don't see me because they are looking at their I-phones. When I say "Hi" (sometimes to be friendly, sometimes out of irony), they don't hear me because they have ear-pieces in their ears. There is no contact. That is different and so alien—also, I have to say, aggravating—to me coming from "my time."

But my point here is not to grouse but to try and convey how different it was. Another comparison might help a little: When I was in my second year at med school I bought a second-hand 125cc (small!) motorcycle. Among other things, I used it to go and see my girlfriend in New Rochelle. I took the Merritt Parkway, a highway with many big hills that my low-powered motorcycle could only ascend at about 25 mph. But the traffic was not heavy, and the cars there were managed to navigate around me. My children just took me for a two-day birthday vacation on Cape Cod. Going and coming back there were solid lines of traffic both ways. When I was growing up there were a hundred and thirty million people in the United States; now there are over three hundred million. That makes a big difference in everyday crowding, the nightmare of parking (we didn't have any parking meters in Erie). To continue my litany, when I was growing up, three cents would send a letter, one cent a postcard, eleven cents would buy a quart of milk, and three cents would buy a newspaper. And an ice cream cone, it cost a nickel.

One more thing: I love to listen to Rogers and Hammerstein, songs from *South Pacific, Carousel* and their other musicals. When I was about ten or so, maybe a little later, the family went to New York a couple of times. We stayed at the Madison Hotel. Once I remember when we were in the lobby, this rich-looking older guy stepped off the elevator with two tall, young, beautifully dressed women, one blond and one brunette. My father gave an unusual look and made a comment to my mother that I couldn't hear. So this was New York. You never saw anything like that in Erie.

But mostly I remember the great things we did in New York. We went to really nice restaurants, although my favorite was the automat. I loved the food in little glass cases, one dish per case, and you put a quarter or whatever in the slot next to the case, the door opened, and you could take out your *schnecken* (cinnamon bun, probably to you), your peanut butter sandwich, or whatever you had selected. We also went to some musicals, *Oklahoma,* I think, which premiered in 1943, and a few years later, *South Pacific.* Songs like "Some Enchanted Evening" were so perfect for the time, simple and melodious; you could leave the theater singing them. They were naive, even when treating war and racism, but that's how those times were. On our New York visits I discovered a great model shop on Fifth Avenue in midtown. When I was a little older I bought a wonderful model of a gas-engine plane there. The model itself consisted of just sticks of balsa wood and the plans. You bought the gas engine separately—I got an Ohlsson and Rice,

.025cc I think. Eventually I would go farther downtown to the huge used book stores and get books by people like Montaigne and Spinoza really cheap.

Communicating how different that world, that life, felt is hard, just as it was difficult for my parents to convey the feel of their growing-up world to me. You sort of can and at the same time you can't. My writing group brought home this paradox to me. About two years ago I was sitting in a session of one of the groups I have been leading for about twenty years, and I suddenly realized how each of these people sees the world in different ways and expresses her or himself about it in different ways, each way being consistent and characteristic for that person only. How is that possible, that we both can and cannot communicate across such differences?

HUMAN BEINGS AND UNDERSTANDING OTHER TIMES

Cultural historians try to teach us how to put ourselves in the place of people who have lived in eras before ours. They try to teach us that living in the nineteenth, fifteenth, or seventh centuries was a very different experience from our own, that the way people believed, that their understanding of reality, of their environment, family, the world and the universe were vastly different from our own and that for us to understand those times, how people thought and lived, we need to appreciate that. I think such a perspective is right, but it is also hard. The fact is that when my parents tried to tell us about their lives at the beginning of the twentieth century and their wonder at how much had changed, I would listen politely and then get back to doing whatever I had been up to. What they tried to communicate was not of much interest to me, although it clearly was for them.

Now I find myself in the same position. I try to tell younger people what it was like before television, before jet planes, when we crossed the Atlantic by ocean liner, which took five to seven days. I tell what it was like each day when the clocks on the ship were changed forward by one hour, so there was no *décalage horaire,* time lag, and what it was like after days of meeting new people, eating good food—even in tourist (third) class, and watching the sea and the sky, to begin, like Christopher Columbus (going in the opposite direction of course), to begin to see a few birds, then branches and leaves in the water, then a faint line on the horizon, land! All of that is gone now, and it was really not that long ago, not even a century ago.

The same *décalage annuaire,* but in the other direction, tending to neglect the past rather than be stuck in it, also holds. I try not to be too judgmental of the Yale students glued to their phones and oblivious to all around them. I try to put myself in their places and experience, as one student explained to me, the relief he felt from the pressures of his life while looking at his I phone and listening to music through his ear buds. I tried, but it was really very hard to put myself in his place, other than perhaps for a fleeting minute or two.

In his paper "What Is It Like To Be a Bat" (mentioned earlier), Thomas Nagel describes how difficult it is to put oneself in the place of another being, human or other animal. I think that's true. In doing interviews with psychiatric patients, talking with friends, talking with my kids, I have to really work to get where they're coming from. It is always worth the effort, but it is also so easy to forget.

And yet.

Sophocles wrote *Antigone* thousands of years ago. I do not find it difficult at all to put myself in Antigone's place, or in the place of her sister Ismene either. The two of them disagreed on what was a life-shattering decision. Antigone was dedicated to giving her dead brother some of the rituals of burial. There was no way she was going to leave his body out there beyond the city walls, to be devoured by dogs and never be able to find his final rest in the world hereafter. She would bury him even if it meant violating the law of her uncle, King Creon, who condemned to death anyone who would try to bury that brother whom he deemed to be a traitor to the kingdom. Ismene tried to convince Antigone that their uncle's decision was best for the state and that such laws needed to be followed. Why have yourself be killed for violating a law that in the end was decided by authorities who were in a position to know best?

I'm having some trouble walking these days. I can get around, but certainly not as easily as I could some few years ago. On a cold winter day I sometimes think of the French army retreating from Moscow as the Russian winter moved in. I imagine myself, corporal or private, needing to walk through the snow the countless miles toward France but only lasting maybe a mile or two. Then, even if someone tried to carry me or pull me along, very soon they would have to leave me on the side of the road, to freeze to death there.

How strange it all is! I can put myself in the place of a French soldier in Napoleon's army in 1812 or of a girl portrayed thousands of years ago as living in ancient Greece, but not of a young man, my father, growing up in the United States a century ago or another young man, a student sitting across from me at the table at Atticus restaurant trying to explain why he does what he does. Perhaps there are certain basic human experiences, for example, feelings of vulnerability, decisions about basic morality conflicting with authority, that transcend time whereas specific aspects of situations including belief systems and understanding of concrete realities change over the years.

CHAPTER 14

FURTHER REFLECTIONS

A CONCEPTUAL FRAMEWORK

What we need is a conceptual framework for the human psyche within which we can place our experiences. And, at last, I have one. A while back I started working with a personal trainer. I had always thought personal trainers were for rich women who had nothing better to do and rented someone to pretend to get a more perfect body. Then a couple of years ago I decided that since I had been lifting weights for many years, maybe I should get a personal trainer to show me how to do it right. I did for one month. She was very helpful and corrected many things I had been doing wrong.

More recently the Yale gym changed all their weight machines, and I got a personal trainer to help me with these new machines. I hired a woman called Tania Quinones and I told her what I wanted. She ignored me entirely and said I should warm up on the elliptical stair climber, which I had been using for years anyway, and then we would proceed. What we proceeded to was stretching, doing all kinds of movements, and holding my body and limbs this way and that. I didn't lift one weight but ended up exhausted. It was so aggravating. I couldn't or could barely do movements I thought I should be able to do. She had me trying to move in ways that I had never noticed that I wasn't doing and discovering that I couldn't. And she had me trying things that I had never even thought of. I couldn't do those either.

It's been aggravating, as I said, very hard but great. I often ask Tania what I'm doing, and why, what's it supposed to be helping with. She's very good at explaining. And I think what she's telling me is also a great model for thinking about psychiatry!

She says the origin of my many limitations (which I never realized I had but are now obvious) is difficult to discern but is probably interactive (my word, not hers). For example, she says I may have had a pain from a certain movement that could have been a result of many possible causes, stopped making that movement, causing the muscles used for it to weaken, and pretty soon I no longer could make the movement even if I wanted to. Furthermore, she suggests, when I needed to make that motion, I may progressively have tried to use other muscles and joints in ways they were not meant to work and thus compounded the problem. Beyond that, in areas of the body such as the shoulder joint, many muscles are involved, including some in the back and chest; as a result, a lot of parts may get distorted and go wrong for a problem in which they were not originally involved.

Let's see how that might apply to psychiatric problems. Take the notion of the unconscious. "Unconsciousness" can be of many types. It may be just lack of awareness, which I could argue is the source of many of my physical issues. Or it may involve more "depth psychological" processes based on meaning and/or early childhood experience. Such explanations might have implications for the possible choice of cognitive behavioral therapy (CBT), psychotherapy, medications, and so on, to help overcome a particular problem.

An example of one possible type of process could be that a person's tendency to overvalue certain kinds of thoughts such as feeling vulnerable and victimized might be genetic. Early life experiences, such as parents who tended to devalue certain things or being bullied in grade school, could exaggerate a tendency to blame more powerful people. In adulthood, a situation—for example, being fired from a local paper as part of a reduction in staff—could generate a major stress that would be "explained" by a paranoid delusion ("It's not my fault; they are out to get me"). The continuation or worsening of that stress might result in the delusion's becoming "chronic," first as a face-saving explanation of the ongoing stress and then as an unrecognized "habit." But, especially if the "stresses" become greater, the use of the delusion as a kind of protective explanatory device could begin to cause major alienation from people around you and thus really start to get you in trouble. Tania says that with the problems she deals with she thinks, "Oftentimes, it is the overload finally taking its toll." Yes, exactly. That's perhaps just what often happens in psychiatric conditions.

A tendency to think or react in a certain way (e.g., blaming other people) might, under severe psychological stress such as inability to earn a living, become so exaggerated that the person begins to explain everything by blaming others. He or she will see them as picking on him or plotting against him, eventually to a delusional degree. Parenthetically, such a description of the process of becoming "mentally ill" also connects easily with ideas of Henri Bergson and more recently, complexity theory, both of which illustrate such features of human functioning as sudden non-linear change, emergents (behaviors or attitudes unlike any the person has had before that seem to come out of nowhere), and tipping points, the idea that certain levels of stress, for example, lead suddenly to major changes.

There are an infinite number of possible variations, of course, but the main point is that what we call "symptoms," implying that we are dealing "with an illness like any other," could actually be exaggerations of "normal" behaviors or ways of thought and feeling that arise through many possible paths. These exaggerated ways of behaving and believing might sometimes require various "treatments" (to use another term originating in medical theory), things like medications, working, or psychotherapy of some kind, singly or in combination. Furthermore, the appearance of the "symptom" in one aspect of a person's psychology, such as cognition or emotion, doesn't necessarily make that aspect the origin of the problem any more than my inability to do pushups arises from my laziness rather than having had a rotator cuff tear. Like the body, the mind is a complex "organic" thing with many aspects interacting in complex ways. Of course, these interactions also can involve many different environmental factors and relationships so that a wide range of possible social and experiential factors needs to be part of the conceptualization and possible approaches to change as well.

THE HOUSE BEHIND MINE
OR A THEORY OF THE CONNECTION BETWEEN BEING
HUMAN AND MENTAL ILLNESS

There is a house behind mine whose front gives on to the street one block over. That house and mine are separated by our two backyards, which in turn are separated by an old fence, some bushes, and a few small trees. I don't see much of the people there. The man and I wave at each other when he is out working on their small garden patch, and his daughter called over to me once asking if she could come and get her ball, which had flown into my backyard. I said, "Certainly," and before I could add, "I'll just throw it to you," she had left their yard and was on her way over. She came, tall and thin, and said her name was Siobhan. I'd say she was about fourteen.

It's not the neighbors but their house that worries me. You see, there's a big part of the wood siding where the paint has all worn off. It's been that way for several years. Otherwise they seem to keep the house and the yard very carefully, so what's the deal with that large patch? The reason I'm worried is that if the siding stays unpainted like that for much longer the wood is going to rot and then they'll be in real trouble. Clearly, that needs to be taken care of. I mean, it doesn't matter to me personally, but you really need to take care of a house.

Thinking about this recently, the phrase slipped into my mind, "It's like life." I had been trying to figure out what the hell the auto-biography I'd been working on—and you are now reading— is all about. What have I been trying to say?

Well, a human life is like that house. If I don't take my pills or work out, I'll fall apart or even die. And watching one of those sur-vival programs on television has reminded me of the basic fact that it's a real deal to get food and water. We take them for granted, of course. But we're spoiled rotten. For billions of people over the course of history and right down to the present, getting enough food and water has been difficult and often required both skill and luck. And without them, you're going to die. It's as simple, and cru-cial as that.

So one thought leads to another. If we don't take care of our-selves, for whatever reason, we've had it. Life involves constant maintenance, just like my neighbor's house. Of course, the house is a passive object requiring someone to care for it. Humans, on the other hand, can and must take an active role, hunting and gathering or going to the grocery store, seeing the doctor, taking their pills, going to school so that, at the very least, they can learn to read and, later on, probably earn money so they can have food and shelter and whatever else they need—to say nothing of growing, developing, and thriving more generally.

Because we require other people in order to be born, grow up, and to exist, we have to figure out how to deal with them, learn language, deal with our emotions and theirs, and so forth. But if like that house, for whatever reason we have a bare patch, a thing that makes us vulnerable to decay, falling apart, whatever, that could be a real problem. What if we get so anxious that we aren't able to care for ourselves, or hear voices that confuse and disorient us, or can't sleep at night, or don't want to eat enough? Then we're in real trouble. And how could such unhelpful things come to pass? Well, there are millions of ways.

Say that house isn't a house but a Ferrari. Not only does it need gas and oil and air to work properly, but it's very temperamental and high strung and needs an expert mechanic to keep it functioning. Or what if, as a human, you've had a difficult childhood, or a severe illness, or some genetic problem, or disastrous or long-term stress? Unlike the house or the Ferrari, neither of which can adapt to different situations, you can, and you do. There are many possibilities, some good, but some, that if they get out of hand, will court disaster. Say you deal with anxiety by smoking or driving fast. Not great, potentially fatal. Say you do it by denying problems or even not noticing that certain realities exist. Say that the problems get worse, and that your means for handling them can't keep up and are overwhelmed. At that point you may collapse, refuse to get out of bed, stop eating or sleeping, become psychotic. Is that what life and mental illness involve? You make efforts to survive, to adapt, to enjoy life, prosper, and sometimes, progressively perhaps, things may go wrong, you become overwhelmed, and then need certain kinds of help to get out of a terrible situation? Is that what mental "health" and "illness" are about, and what "treatment" is about as well?

I wish my neighbor would paint his house before it's too late, but he seems pretty smart and hardworking and maybe there's a reason he hasn't done anything. I would say something, but I think he might resent it since he must have noticed the problem. But I worry about him and his house.

FEELINGS

I have told you something of my friend Alain and the great pain I felt—and still feel—at his premature death. When he first told me of his cancer diagnosis, he said, "You know, your brain just isn't set up to hear that you're going to die in a year."

Two years later, one year after Alain's death, I saw my cardiologist regarding my irregular heartbeat, which was only moderately well controlled at the time. She told me somberly that the results from the biopsy of some tissue had come back and that it looked as though I had amyloid cardiac disease. She was not clear on the type, treatment, or prognosis, since it was not a common disease, and she recommended that I go to Boston to see an international expert on the disease at Brigham and Women's Hospital. She added, "It's too bad you didn't have a coronary." On returning home I looked up amyloid cardiac disease on the Internet and learned that the maximum life expectancy after the diagnosis was about one year.

During the subsequent month, as I waited for my Boston appointment, I finally began to understand what Alain had meant when he said, "Your brain isn't meant to hear . . .." It turned out, as I learned later, that the Internet did not know the whole story. According to the Boston specialist, there is a whole range of outcomes for amyloid cardiac disease. Mine is not getting worse, which means, as he told me in response to my question, when I die it will probably be from something else.

Feelings are hard to communicate. It is even harder to comprehend what an experience feels like when someone tries to tell you about it. Not so long ago, a woman ran a red light and crashed into the front part of my car, totaling it. I was not hurt physically but was profoundly shaken up by the incident. The instant of seeing a huge vehicle come hurtling toward me, the crushing sound of collapsing metal—that I can describe, but my feelings at that moment—much harder. More recently, I was trying to work out a collaboration with a colleague who has also been a very close friend of mine for many years. He seemed just not to get a point I was trying to make (about feelings) that was, from my point of view, a central issue in our proposed collaboration. I couldn't even describe to myself my feelings in that encounter except that I was aware of an awful hollowness in the pit of my stomach, as well as disillusion, sadness, frustration, anger, at what seemed to me to be his total failure even to be interested in what to me was so important.

You would think that as mental health experts we would be good at understanding and communicating feelings. I'm afraid that more often than not the opposite is true. Especially in the research and academic areas, in our writing, and even in much of our training we are often severely deficient. We talk about "affects" or sometimes "emotions" rather than "feelings" and generally translate any consideration of feelings and their power into intellectualized ideas. Even "old" Freud in his analysis of Wilhelm Jensen's novella *La Gradiva* (*Delusion and Dream in Jensen's* Gradiva) essentially says at the very beginning of his commentary that this is a beautiful story, now let's analyze its meaning. He never again discusses its "beauty," as though somehow that is not relevant. For many years, when patients told me that they heard voices, I would respond with questions such as "What do they say?" Eventually, after listening to some audiotapes simulating auditory hallucinations and from really listening during research interviews, I realized that it was much better to say something like "Wow." That reaction, depending also on the tone of voice (something I learned from my acting classes not my psychiatry training), reflected a feeling, something far more connecting to the patient than a prefabricated cognitive inquiry.

From a conceptual point of view, I think our frequent incompetence in dealing with feelings means that we vastly underestimate their power in determining what we call psychiatric symptoms and illnesses and our consideration of treatment needs. When patients tell us (perhaps more often in research interviews when we have limited power) that the most important thing in their getting better was "someone who cared" or "someone who took me seriously," they are letting us know that factors closely connected to feelings (and human connection) are of major importance. These connections to the other people do not simply fall under the oft-used (by academic professionals) simplistic and demeaning rubric "common factors," which are generally considered not central to "treatment."

The problem that mental health professionals have in dealing with feelings in our theories, concepts, and training is compounded by that time-honored and common assumption that we "do it already" or "know it already," which, of course, prevents us from noticing and learning that we don't, and doing better.

Yet the solution, at least from a practical point of view (in contrast to the needs of our own psyches), is not very complicated at all. Questions like "How have things been going?" or "How has that been for you?" can be extremely helpful. Human responses like "Wow," "That sounds hard," and other such "ordinary" comments of feeling by the clinician can also be important. Even silence. I have served as a preceptor in a relatively new medical school teaching program where we taught the medical students that after delivering bad news to a patient (a severe diagnosis, prognosis, or the like), they should not necessarily say anything right away but rather let the patient respond in the way natural to him or her.

Feelings are central to our understanding of the links among bio, psycho, and social factors and are exemplified by things like the effects of feeling alone, vulnerable, even happy. Although we may never know all about feelings—their nuances, what causes which feelings, and what things feelings cause (think of Anna Karenina or King Lear, for example)—still our attention to them, and some humility on our part, can go a very long way.

IDEAS ABOUT HUMAN DEVELOPMENT

Journeys of Life

"Life can be very complex," as Lord Willoughby said to Arabella Bishop (Olivia de Havilland) in the Errol Flynn pirate film *Captain Blood* (1935).

When Joseph Campbell wrote about the "hero's journey" it

sounded really simple. The hero has to leave home for a reason. He has to go through many challenges during his journey. Then he reaches the goal and, the implication seems to be, "lived happily ever after." Neat, isn't it?

The literature on adult development (Erik Erikson, Dan Levinson) mostly assumed that the evolution of a life, as earlier outlined for the child by Freud and others, was best described as defined stages. In the cognitive domain, Piaget and others have also focused on defining stages of development. Hard to fit such concepts into the idea of a journey, but wait.

Victor Hugo, as one might expect, sees it differently. In *Les Misérables* he writes:

"Toutes les choses de la vie sont perpétuellement en fuite devant nous. Les obscursissements et les clartés s'entremêlent: après un éblouissement, une éclipse; on regarde, on se hâte, on tend les mains pour saisir ce qui passe; chaque événement est comme un tournant de la route; et tout à coup on est vieux. On sent comme une secousse, tout est noir, on distingue une porte obscure, ce sombre cheval de la vie qui vous traînait s'arrête et l'on voit quelqu'un de voilé et d'inconnu qui le détèlle dans les ténèbres."

"All things in our lives are perpetually fleeing ahead of us. The confusions and recognitions intermix; after a revelation there is a blackness, we hurry, we reach out to grasp something that is passing, every event is like a turn in the road; and then all of a sudden we are old. You feel a sudden shock, everything is black, you see a dark barely visible door, this somber horse of a life that was pulling you along stops and you see someone who is veiled and unrecognized unhitching the horse in the shadows." (My translation.)

How is it possible that three such different orientations, the ideas of a journey, of life stages, and of a horse that pulls you along, exist and yet at the same time pretty much ignore each other, as though they didn't inhabit the same world, as though only one deals with the realities of a human life?

Not really being able to make any progress with that puzzle I posed the question to my friend sculptor and psychiatrist Joe Saccio, who seems so often to have ways of thinking that would never come to me. Instantly, he said, it was like with a piece of sculpture, you can look at it, at a life, from many different perspectives, each with its own reality, the observer can move around the piece to see those different perspectives, all together represent the reality. Then I realized that view was complementary to the view of my friend Zheala, whom I mentioned earlier. When I asked how I could be so different when I was in Paris from when I was in New Haven, she assembled three objects on a table around a central glass and explained that I was that glass while the other objects were the different environments. The combination of each of the objects with the glass in the middle is a combination of that object with the part of the glass nearest to it. Together they all relate to the unity of the one glass, but each combination in a sense is different from the others. Joe, then, emphasizes perspective while Zheala notes the role of context, the environment, as bringing out different aspects of the object in the center.

All these thoughts are really the fault of Vivian Chan and her study of the children of parents with severe psychiatric disorders. I have described earlier how that excellent study affected me in considering my own relationship with my mother. However, her gestalt-like approach of looking at the "journeys" of her subjects, rather than the usual analysis of specific variables, has prompted me to look at my own life in that way.

As I have worked on my autobiography, I have begun to ask myself, did I even have a "journey?" When I spent three months after my second year in college hitchhiking around the country I ended up in San Francisco. Was that the goal of the journey? Well, yes and no. My goal was really to hitchhike around the country for three months—yes, that was my real goal. But I did really want to end up in San Francisco. Or was the real point of the journey to come back to Erie, where I had started, or to Cleveland, where my father drove from Erie to pick me up? Thinking about it now, I conclude that the real "goal" of that trip was the trip itself, not just getting to San Francisco. If my goal had been to get to San Francisco I could have done it a hell of a lot faster, even by hitchhiking. When I headed back home from San Francisco, I made it in five days.

When I was in college, I suppose my "journey" was to succeed, to get through it and do well. Yet now I think back to Miss Hilda Cohen, my kind, bright, young German teacher who had us read Schiller, Hesse, and Heine, and regret that I never took "time out" enough to go talk with her. Aged eighty-something and in Paris, it suddenly struck me how great the book *Knulp* was and how sad it was that I had never reached out to Miss Cohen to talk about how she chose it. *Knulp,* by the way, is the story of a guy who kind of wanders through life, has many experiences, and makes meaningful connections with a lot of people; then he dies.

Did I reach my goal at college? Well, yes, I graduated with high honors. Was that what my "journey" at college was about? No, not really, but I didn't know what my goal should have been. Was the goal I accomplished perhaps the only goal I could have managed at the time? Or have my goals changed? No, in my right mind, I would have identified the goal of talking with Miss Cohen, even then—if I could have relaxed enough to realize that was a goal of the "journey" I would have wanted to have.

A Coda

According to my *Webster Collegiate Dictionary*, 1943 edition, the fourth definition of coda is as follows: "Music. A concluding passage, the function of which is to bring a composition or a division to a proper close." Here's my effort, with regard to "journeys" at least.

Was Joseph Campbell wrong? No, I don't think so. But he was incomplete in that he focused on just one aspect of the journey. How about the theories that define stages such as the theories of psychoanalysis, Piaget or others? The journey of a person's life is much more complex than any of these theories. You may need to take many mini-journeys while making your main journey. Perhaps even conceptualizing a "main" journey is incorrect.

Furthermore, maybe as in my hitchhiking, your journey is affected by the rides you get or don't get and the people you meet or don't meet, and by your decisions, your feelings, or the decisions you don't make or feelings you don't allow, maybe it's more or less purposefully wandering through life. In retrospect, I believe the ideas of Campbell, Freud, and Erikson are relevant, but if I had to choose, I think Victor Hugo best captures the complex evolution of a life.

To me, Hugo's description captures the unpredictability, the intrusion of unexpected or uncontrollable events, and the efforts of the person to pursue his or her life interacting with this changing picture. My very close friend in Paris, Alain, who was like a slightly younger brother all of a sudden around age sixty was diagnosed with lung cancer, told he would die within a year, and then did. "Each event," says Hugo, "is like a turn in the road."

Consider my mother's journey. What if she had finished her college degree and been able to pursue her professional dreams? What if she had not become a mother? (Toward the end of her life she mused that maybe she should never have been one.) Did these turns in the road contribute to her illness, perhaps the ultimate turn in the road? And, of course, that turn in the road for her was one for us all, a part for all of us of our journeys.

I think the various theories all have validity but only within the broader framework as described by Hugo. Of course, there are stages of a person's life, more or less, and even fairly tidy stories of a life's evolution. To some extent, these theories are efforts to introduce some predictability into what otherwise is an evolution so much dominated by one's desires and actions, life context, accidents, and diseases.

And this brings me to a final point: The concept of "Uncertainty Theory" is an effort to bring some order into the problem, as in the field of economics, of understanding the possible evolutions of a multivariable phenomenon involving interacting processes. "Uncertainty Theory," as noted earlier, is not so much a theory as an approach to dealing with complexity that surpasses neat prediction. I think that best captures my understanding of a life.

I have had the rather unsettling experience of finishing my four-hundred-or-so-page autobiography and then realizing all the people and experiences I had left out. In many instances, these people and experiences were central to my life. It seems to me that without really intending to, I had written pieces that constructed more or less of a coherent story, and that it would be easy to start all over, focusing on the events and people I had left out and construct a very different story. Dear reader, don't worry, I'm not going to do that, the possibility is too overwhelming even to consider. Maybe some day, and then I can think of how it might be possible to deal more effectively with the idea that we are living several journeys. It's a pretty interesting possibility actually. I mean I've never told you what it was like to have our research team meet every week over breakfast at Chuck's Lunchette; or what it was like to be a speaker at an international meeting in Moscow and go to that inhuman and empty immensity of Red Square and feel like nothing, like a meaningless ant; or to be in Cali, Colombia, when army trucks stopped in front of our hotel and a squad of soldiers with machine guns drawn jumped out as a small revolution was going on; or to fall in love with a wonderful Canadian woman—none of that.

And From the Inside?

From the inside, my life feels much more like a weird mix of continuities and changes heavily influenced by me but also by the situations in which I found myself. Yes, my hitchhiking experiences relate easily to Joseph Campbell's ideas about the hero's journey, but my feeling about those trips was "I need to do this." How could you predict (not postdict, those processes are very different) that I would get my finger smashed by a gear wheel while putting a Ferris wheel together at Frontier Days rodeo in Cheyenne? Or that a garage mechanic, after advising me where I could put my sleeping bag and go to sleep in a small park nearby, insisted I take five dollars from him, saying, "When I was doing what you're doing someone gave it to me and I'm just passing it on." The beauty of his kindness, and the sense of a continuity of human kindnesses and caring, probably existing in links across centuries is enough to make me weep even today so many years later.

The ideas of stages and goals are useful I guess, but also, as my acting teacher Doug Taylor taught us, "Life is in the details, there is nothing general about life." I took an acting class some years ago because my friend Mary Barnet had said that I should. I had been a chronic failure whenever I had tried to act in a play. It was not a big deal for me—I never had an idea of going into the theater—but it still bothered me. So at Mary's suggestion—and she is rarely wrong—I signed up for Doug's course. Doug was from the Actor's Studio. He started out by pairing us up and having me say to my partner, "You have brown hair," to which she responded, "I have brown hair." We went back and forth saying exactly the same words until Doug yelled at me, "But John, you're not listening to her!" I realized what he meant, but I had thought we were just supposed to repeat the words. I started listening to her and began to hear the changes in the tones and emphases in our voices and in the looks on her face and the movements of our bodies as we really listened to each other. A miracle. There was so much there I had never noticed, and it had been there all the time! I began to lose my self-consciousness and entered more and more into what Doug was teaching us. After a couple weeks (meeting once a week), I did my first improvisation. My partner this time was a man somewhat younger than I, and following Doug's guidelines to portray a key specific incident, we decided that I should be a lawyer planning to take my first vacation in many years while he would be my ne'er-do-well son who had once more gotten himself in trouble and needed me to stay home to help him get out of it. We started our improv, but Doug quickly called out to stop us. "John, where did you go to law school?" "Doug, that's not relevant. That was years earlier." "John, where did you go to law school?" "OK, Harvard." "How many children do you have?" "Three" (I had decided to go along with Doug just to get to our improv). "Good, start again." As we restarted, I realized that once again Doug was right. The mere sense that I knew where "I had gone to law school" and how many children I had, although totally imagined, made me feel much more grounded in my struggle with my "son." As Doug said, once again, "Life is in the details. There is nothing general about life."

MEMORIES

It is early summer as I write this. When the sun starts to come up around 5 o'clock, I find myself waking sometimes around 4:30 or 6:00. It isn't unpleasant. I lie there in bed and memories and thoughts flow through my mind, days at the Island, Paris, Ann, all kinds of things. It strikes me that the belief that old people have nothing to do so they just call up old memories is totally wrong. My experience, anyway, is that from this perspective of looking back, and forward, I'm letting this stuff float around to see what happens. It's a bit like a jigsaw puzzle that could be completed in an infinite number of ways, some with a better fit than others but none of them perfect.

Why am I thinking so much about the Island, about Paris, about hitchhiking across the United States? Those things took up only a tiny fraction of my years, and yet they seem, for now anyway, of huge importance. They are dominating my mind, the sailboat or something at the very center of this million-piece puzzle.

Like this morning. There I was, lying in bed, thinking of the Ojibways who would come up to the Island in their canoes, bringing things to sell, especially the small baskets they made of birch bark, porcupine quills, and sweet grass. Those little baskets smelled so good, and were so beautiful. I have one old one, very faded, left. The Ojibways would come in the evening, perhaps once every couple of years. We'd be sitting in the Clubhouse, talking, a couple people playing cards, Dad reading, and there'd be a kind of bustle and maybe someone coming in to say, "The Indians are here." A few minutes later some Ojibways—always women, I think—would come in with their wares, and we'd all get up to welcome them, look over what they had, and buy. Then they'd leave, and one or two of us might go down to the dock with them to say good-bye. Everything would go back to where it was just twenty minutes or so before. The occasions may have been short, but they have been stamped clearly on my mind for ever.

THE PSYCHIATRIC INTERVIEW AND HITCHHIKING

Right off the bat, let me say that "the psychiatric interview" is a horrible and misleading term. Even the word "interview" isn't great. What we are doing, or at least should be doing, is simply finding out about a person's life. I've done literally hundreds of these interviews, maybe thousands, and in thinking about them recently I have begun to liken them to the experience of hitchhiking. Think about how the latter works: Someone slows down and stops, you run to get to the car, put your pack in the back seat, get into the front seat, and the driver starts up and you're on the road again. You exchange names, the driver asks, "Where are you going?" and then you start finding out about each other. He (more commonly than she) may ask, "How did you happen to be doing this?" You tell him, then ask about him, and you're off. Each one of you finding out more about the other, and, depending how long you're both going in the same direction, twenty minutes, five hours, whatever, you and this total stranger are finding about each other's lives.

I think it's in the *Harzreise* that Heinrich Heine speaks about the freedom of "Ich komme nie wieder" (essentially, "we'll never see each other again") to be found in the brief encounter. That effect can be truly liberating. It depends, of course, on where the two of you are in your lives, how things have gone that day, and so forth, but it is not rare that the two of you can share experiences and feelings that perhaps you have never shared with another person. And it works because neither really knows who the other person is and you know you will never see each other again. If psychiatric interviews, "intakes," therapy, and related encounters could be seen in those terms, how honest and forthcoming the two participants could be. Of course, for psychiatric purposes, the format needs to be altered somewhat. The professional may share much less of his or her feelings and experiences and may want to provide some guidance, but that basic sense of freedom should form the heart of the experience. The more we are trying to conform to some structure, to reach a goal, to fill a role, the less we are likely to succeed in any of these unusual endeavors. The more that we can have a sense of "being there" with the person, the more likely we are to be effective, to make the connection that is really the most crucial part of encounter, the encounter we call a "psychiatric interview."

WHAT WOULD YOU DO IF YOU HAD THE CHOICE?

My friend Pauline is from France. She has a doctorate in history from a French university, awarded for a thesis that explores the issues of linking two kinds of narratives—one about an individual and the other describing in detail the social and political context of that person's country and period—into a third iterative narrative going back and forth to explain the interaction of the person and the social context. Pauline came to the United States two years ago on a temporary visa that allows her to support herself (barely) on two part-time jobs, one as a research assistant in an American university sociology project and the other working with people released from prison. She loved the latter job, getting to know both the just-released prisoners and their "peers," others who have had the same experience who are helping them to live once again on the outside, and trying to be of help. When she described this work, her eyes sparkled. But she was also trying to figure out how to get on with her own life.

"So, in looking for your next job, what do you intend to do?" I asked her. "Well, first I have to write some articles for some books based on data I already have." She replied as though she were somehow chained to that project. "What will you write about?" I asked. "Something that fits into what they want about what the data show." She looked even more bored and discouraged. "What would you write if you had the choice?" I asked.

I love this question and have often asked it of myself when working on something and starting to hate it, knowing somehow that I am free to do what I want but also that I tend to fall back into what has been expected of me and of the other people involved in a given research project. How do I get involved in such traps? I'm like a lobster in a lobster pot. Without realizing it, I go further and further ahead only to find myself in a narrower and narrower space from which there is no escape. It's mostly my own problem, I do it to myself. But also it's because—and I see it often in my field—that path is viewed as acceptable and is rewarded, paid for.

At some point, I realized how stupid this was. If you're a lobster and you know there are these traps all around, just avoid them. Not so easy! You just don't notice them. Maybe they're hidden in some way or maybe you're too used to them. But then I discovered this magic question, "What would I do if I had the choice?" Instantly, the door swings open and I walk out. Once out in the open water again, I can consider whether I really do have the choice or not. Even more wonderful, I can think about what I really want to do and pursue it. I no longer feel constricted, stifled, resentful. Somehow, now I'm free and excited.

Pursuing this approach with Pauline, I asked, "What would you do with those articles you need to write if you had the choice?" A slight gleam appears in her eyes, but she still feels trapped: "I don't have the choice. They will want just the usual kind of thing that fits in with the other articles." I know that feeling. But there are other questions to be asked: "Are they paying you for writing the articles?" "No." "If you do what you really want, would it give you a bad reputation that will hurt your plans for the future?" "No." Her eyes are really sparkling now, and it is a pleasure to behold. But I let it go at that point. I have found that it doesn't help to push farther at such a moment, for myself or for someone else. There is a danger that the person will get scared and negative and retreat back into the lobster trap.

What will Pauline do? I don't know. It depends who she is, where she is in her life, and probably on a bunch of other things. She is very bright and wonderfully creative, and now it is like watching a butterfly trying to free herself from the constraining strands of her chrysalis to escape and fly free or a young eagle approach the point where she allows herself the freedom to soar into the skies. Will she? I so much hope so.

Of course, the issue of human choice runs very deep, as deep, for example, as Sophocles takes it in *Antigone* or Euripides in *Iphigeneia at Aulis* or Victor Hugo in *Les Misérables*, all powerful and profound explorations of the whole world of making a choice.

WHAT IF NOTHING WORKS?

A young friend has told me about a terrible period in his life when he had almost constant anxiety attacks. He saw one therapist, then another, then another. He was given medication, Cognitive Behavioral Therapy, told to exercise, to meditate. And he said, looking at me in anguish: "But nothing worked! I told them, 'Tell me what to do, I'll do anything, but help me escape from this horror!' But nothing worked. Well finally, I hung on and hung on and finally after months, little sleep and much misery, barely able to work, it finally started to get better. All by itself. It had been horrible. Nothing had worked." Except perhaps time.

Long ago, I saw a depressed patient in private treatment. I tried psychotherapy and medication. In those days there was no CBT or the idea of work or exercise to help, and, dammit, she would just sit there in the chair opposite me and tell me how miserable she was, unable to do most anything. Nothing I tried helped. Then I started to feel that she wasn't really working at it, at getting better, and you know how that kind of feeling grows. I started seeing her in couples therapy with her husband. That didn't help either. Finally she just stopped coming. I have to admit, it was a relief. But I felt awful.

Another case: A psychiatrist friend of mine told me of working with a lovely kid, a college student, who had become psychotic. Hospitalization, meds, psychotherapy, the kid got better. Two months later he was crazy again. Same thing, slowly getting better, then whammo, psychotic again. My friend was worried, said the kid was beginning to look chronic. Awful. And nothing worked.

In the village where my dad grew up there was a doctor, "Old Doc" somebody (I don't remember his name), who had been at the Battle of Antietem. When Dad and his friend Paul Kuhlman were about ten or twelve and needed money, they would go to the old doctor's house, and he would pay them each a nickel to listen to his battle stories. He told them about sawing off the arms and legs of wounded young soldiers, their severed limbs then piled high outside the medical tent. No anesthesia, just "bite on this bullet." The screams, the misery, the pain. Nothing else they could do. And the wounds often became infected, killing half those kids anyway.

Recently, I had a very minor surgical procedure, in the doctor's office. The surgeon injected my arm with lidocaine or something, nice guy, and asked me if it hurt when he started cutting. "No, it's perfect," I said, then told him the story about Dad and the old doctor. "How lucky am I," I said. "In those days, they did what they could, but it was horrible."

At my car dealership, where I went to collect some touch-up paint and get additional instructions about my new car, the salesman volunteered: "By the way, did you know that there's a lever under the steering wheel that allows you to change the angle of it?" Actually, I had been having a little problem with the position of the wheel and hadn't known I could do anything about it. With the seat adjusted properly for me to use the foot pedals the steering wheel was too far away. I could only reach it with straightened arms, feeling a little like the Frankenstein monster. Now I could adjust the steering wheel and solve the problem. Everything was just right. It worked perfectly.

Some things work. Others don't. I guess you just need to know where the lever is and how it works. For some things, if you don't know about the lever or can't find it—or there isn't one— it can be a living horror.

EARLY IN THE MORNING

I love the early morning. When I awake around 6:30 it may still be black out except for a tiny sliver of grey on the horizon in the East. I watch through my bedroom window as the blackness of the night begins to lighten to a soft grey and the silhouettes and forms of black begin to acquire color. And then as the grey shifts into blue, a yellow glow arises on the tiny branches of the trees and on the sides of the church and house across the street.

When I was a medical student, this was the time of day when, having begun work almost twenty-four hours earlier, it was finally time for me to check the patients on the danger list and the IV's one last time before putting on my coat and walking outside into the cool air of the half-night, half morning. As the grey took over from the black of night, I walked home to the apartment on Dwight Street I shared with Dave, another student. Sometimes, lured by the smell of fresh bread, I went into one of the Jewish bakeries on Legion Avenue and called hello—there was never anyone out front, they were all in back baking. A round fellow would come out, I'd ask for a loaf of rye bread, and he'd fetch it from the back, returning with a smile. Not many people besides us up this early in the morning. I would walk through the empty streets, the warmth of the rye bread tucked between my arm and my side, the grey light growing in the sky. Back at the apartment, I tossed my coat on the couch, went into the kitchen, took the butter out of the fridge, took down the breadboard and the bread knife, and sliced two pieces. The butter would soften as I spread it. The smell of the fresh bread spread in the small apartment. Dave would shout out from the bedroom, "Oooh, bread", and we'd sit down to eat. Four slices of warm bread and butter later I'd throw off my clothes and fall into bed. Out the window, the sky was no longer black, only the blue grey and the yellow glow of early morning as I fell asleep.

Or, in Paris, after another of those horrible arguments with Ann, when I watched the dawn at Les Halles. I had been in agony, but the day was now coming. It would be better with people in streets and in the cafés. Life all around. People, warm bodies, smiles, problems, people hurrying, having coffee with other people, people and their dogs. I wouldn't be alone any more, for now.

THE OUTDOORS

I was watching a Ken Burns program about the national parks on PBS. I wasn't expecting much, but I was agreeably surprised as they started talking about Jim Bridger, John Muir, others. These guys, and the commentators too, really cared. They talked of the importance of the outdoors to their very lives, the meanings of their life, of how the outdoors represents something so deep in us, combining beauty, wonder, danger, and the unknown with a profound sense of feeling at home there. As the program showed the history of the parks, the struggles of the supporters against commercial development, the peace that the wilderness can bring to people, I thought of my time at Swarthmore and how much I have loved running in the woods on the path next to Crum Creek. It was partly a relief from the pressures of college, but even more, it was a thing in itself. Running felt like flying, really, gliding above the roots crossing the path, away from people, the creek on my left, trees above me and on my right, bushes everywhere.

When I was hitchhiking across the country, I spent two days in Glacier National Park. The family that had given me a ride left me off as we crossed the path I was to take up to a glacier. I walked up, alone in the woods. No one in the world knew where I was and I saw no one. As I got higher, I encountered mountain goats, with hairy faces and immense horns; they were not in the least afraid of me. Finally, I came to a small turquoise glacier lake. I slept by the side of the lake and woke to find a deer nearby quietly drinking its water. Total calm.

And, of course, I have had the Island in my life, every summer since the age of three. When I hit my teens and had my own canoe, I knew my way, even in darkest night, through the passages between the islands. I could paddle without making a sound. Listening to the call of the whippoorwills as the sun set. On rough, windy days keeping my canoe on its course. The islands, mostly without owners and houses, the rocks, the trees, only a rare boat to be seen. Going through the woods with Joe.

I have told you the story of how my grandfather, the patriarch, Sambo, bought that island in Canada. The most beautiful place in the world, he said. One of two or three of the most beautiful places, I think, up there with the Taj Mahal. What was he looking for? What had he found? He is dead now, of course, has been since 1959. If like Dante I get the chance to talk with people who are now dead, I will ask him. Chances are he won't have anything to say about it. Except, "Most beautiful place in the world. It's right here. What did you need to go to Paris for?" Well, I needed to go to Paris too, but he wasn't completely wrong. "Whatever guided you to come up here?" I will ask him. He will probably just say, "We came up here for the fishing." Then he will add, "Most beautiful place on earth."

I DID NOTHING TODAY

I awoke just before the alarm went off and shaved, after covering my face with foamy lather from my lovely soft badger brush. I stretched my shoulders on the doorframe as my mind went out the window somewhere to fly around in the blue sky.

I got downstairs in time to hear Amy Goodman say, "From free speech radio, this is Democracy Now." And to listen as she talked about the protests at the time of the Vancouver Olympics about public money going to corporations rather than for the needs of the Vancouver citizens and her discussion with a Vancouver doctor talking about how the mind and the body affect each other—all that while I was pouring orange juice, foaming milk for my coffee, toasting my New York bagel "with everything" from Edge of the Woods, then slathering it half with butter, half with peanut butter that I had made myself.

After Amy and breakfast I had to hurry to get to the gym, where I wanted to be finished in time to attend a lecture at Kirkland Hall by a psychologist from Colgate University on the relationships between body gestures and the spoken word. I brushed my teeth with my electric toothbrush, got in the car, and drove downtown, even more green lights than red today. The short, somewhat pudgy man who is in charge of the gym shook my hand, and I said how good it was to have him there, that I knew he wants to get back to teaching but in the meantime it's a pleasure to have him running things. He looks after us users, bought some stretch bands for me last week, checks on the equipment, and doesn't play zombie drum-machine music on the speaker system.

I did the elliptical stair climber and then the six machines for working all parts of your body, once again reassuring myself that

I am still using heavier resistances than most of the people who use these Cybex machines even though they are much younger than I. I showered, stretched my shoulder, and walked to the lecture. Young people all around, a pleasure. A young Chinese woman sat down next to me. She said she is a graduate student from the University of Maryland, working on a dissertation on cultural differences in patterns of prejudice. I am very interested in that, and she will send me a draft and a poster she has presented.

The conference was good, a young thoughtful nondogmatic professor who studies whether bodily gesture and language are separate channels for communication and learning. His work, as I had hoped, is very relevant for the paper I am writing on human science. I just don't know yet exactly how to work it all out. I asked him whether his ideas connect with ideas about different ways of knowing, experience compared to discursive verbal means, and whether he has worked with theater people. He hasn't, well just a little.

I returned home, picked up Barbara's paper from the front of her house so that passers by won't know she's away, had a slice of frozen pizza (to which I added hot peppers) heated up in my little toaster oven for lunch, and read my e-mails. There were ten from centrist causes (there is no left any more, no socialists, no communists), three from newspapers, and one from Cecile, who is French and lives in Houston and called responding to the personals in the *New York Review of Books* I had placed last week. Naturally I answered her.

I lay on my couch for a little while, once again letting my mind fly out the window to do whatever it chose among the snowflakes. (I write of a winter day in a year when there was a real winter.) Margarita, a Spanish graduate student whom I had met the previous year at the Yale Cabaret, called to set a time for coffee and ask if I knew a therapist for her former boyfriend. Robert called to confirm our lunch at the Union League Club. Neither of us had been there for years, but we both thought, "What the hell, why not a little class in our lives from time to time." Later, as I was fixing dinner, I finally listened to a poetry CD that I had bought years ago but never listened to before.

I ate my dinner, fried shredded wheat with bananas—a meal that my father's mother had taught him to make—then sat down and wrote this.

I did nothing today. I applied for no grant, attended no meetings, mailed off no paper, received no invitation to give a lecture. I did nothing today. What a charmed life I lead.

THE MOVIES

I like to watch *The Rachel Maddow Show* on television, but the commercials drive me crazy. One of the virtues of the Turner Classic Movies is that there are no commercials except a few between the movies. I like that, and I like the channel, where lately, the movie line up has been like tuning in to *This Is Your Life*.

Maybe you young folks don't know what that program was. It was on the radio when I was a kid (though later a television show), and the idea was to present a regular person to the audience and then recount the life of that person. They would bring to the microphone the major people he or she had encountered during the course of his/her life: "Now, here is that second-grade teacher, Miss Ripley, that you so adored" or "Here is Mr. Mifkovic, your swimming coach and geometry teacher who gave you the A you hadn't really earned." Things like that.

So, recently, TCM has been like that for me. They're doing a hundred years of Oscar winners and there's one movie after another that has marked my life. Now you have to realize that before television, before cell phones, before computers, the movies were pretty much it. My mother took me to see *The Wizard of Oz* when I was about five, and apparently I was so scared by the flying monkeys that I cried and we had to leave. When I was older, Bob and I would go to the movies on Saturday afternoon and afterwards to Polako's for a hot fudge sundae. Later when I started dating girls, we would go to the movies. That's what I did with Marilyn Larson and Suzanne Carlson (though not Barbara Love, my goodness!).

I saw *Captains Courageous* with my mother when I was about seven. It starred Spencer Tracey, whom I think she really liked. I just saw it again on TCM and realized that it's a very good movie. It's about the rich bratty kid, Freddie Bartholomew, who falls overboard near the Grand Banks during an ocean voyage across the Atlantic and is rescued by a fisherman, Spencer Tracey. The latter, with a heavy Portuguese accent, is working aboard a fishing schooner, and Freddie has to stay aboard the boat until the fishermen finish their several-week long fishing run. During this time with the stern but loving Tracey and other members of the crew Freddie learns to accept the basic food, the hard life, the lack of luxury, and to become as you might say "a real boy." It's moving to see him change and develop a loving relationship with Tracey, as it is when the trip is over, to watch Freddie and his Dad struggle, ultimately successfully, to get to know each other.

And what else on TCM? There are so many. *Mutiny on the Bounty*, with Charles Laughton, Clark Gable, and Franchot Tone. Laughton calls out to Gable, "Mr. Christian, come over here!" And, of course, Errol Flynn in *The Sea Hawk*. Treated unjustly, he becomes a pirate and falls in love with Maureen O'Sullivan, saves the British town of Port Royal from the Spanish brutes, and is given his freedom. And *Casablanca,* I don't need to tell you about *Casablanca:* "Here's looking at you kid," "Play it Sam," "You must remember this, a kiss is just a kiss, a sigh is just a sigh," and "We'll always have Paris."

That wartime classic reminds me of others, not quite so well known, that resonate for me. *Hanover Street* is not a very good movie, but it starts with scenes representing London during the blitz of World War II. I was pretty young then, ten in 1942, but on the radio we heard Eric Severeid reporting from London and in the movie newsreels we saw pictures of the bombing of London, the explosions, the collapsing buildings, the fire hoses aiming their streams of water at buildings engulfed in fire, the beams of search lights trying to find the Nazi planes in the black sky.

When I first went to Europe eleven years later and visited London, the rubble was all gone, but there were still huge gaps where destroyed buildings had not yet been rebuilt. And in Paris, I saw bullet holes in the walls of the Comédie-Française Rive Gauche (now called the Odéon-Théâtre de l'Europe) left by fire fights between the resistance and the German troops. *Hanover Street* reminded me of all those sights, and its love story reminded me of yet another and much better movie, *Waterloo Bridge,* which also took place in London during the Blitz. In the latter, a young British woman (Vivian Leigh) in love with an American soldier (Robert Taylor) becomes so distraught when she hears he has been killed that she turns to prostitution. He reappears, however, and they are reunited, but filled with guilt, she kills herself by jumping off Waterloo Bridge, where they had first met. Such sadness turns my thoughts once again to Walter Strauss, killed on Omaha Beach, buried in the Normandy American Cemetery. I finally visited the cemetery sixty years after his death and was overcome with sobs at the sight of his grave.

And then there's *The Razor's Edge*, which also happens to be, sort of anyway, the story of my life. It's not a very good movie, as I've mentioned before, but it does have the song "Mam'selle," which I will never forget, and stars Tyrone Power, Jean Tierney, John Payne, Anne Baxter, and Clifton Webb. I first saw it when I was about sixteen, maybe with Bob, maybe with Suzanne Carlson, and even then had some inkling of its significance for my life. The real Tyrone Power had been a Marine pilot during the Second World War, and *The Razor's Edge* was the first movie he made after returning to civilian life. He plays a man traumatized by an incident in the First World War who is one of a group of friends all from very rich Chicago families. He is in love with Jean Tierney—man, she was beautiful—and she wants him to take the fancy job offered by a friend so they can get married and live the good, rich life. But much as he loves her, Tyrone Power knows that's not right for him and that he needs to find something, find himself. Jean is miffed, but she loves him and thinks if he takes a year, that should do it. He goes off to Paris, where he meets people from all walks of life. He has rich friends, but he prefers to go off and work in the mines. One thing leads to another, and Tyrone goes off to India to find himself even more. By this time Jean has had enough and marries their rich friend (John Payne). They have lots of money and two kids, but John Payne has headaches.

A year or so passes. Tyrone, having found a guru in India and spent time alone in a Tibetan mountain cabin, comes back much better than he had been. He's not totally enlightened but pretty good. He uses some Eastern mysticism to help John Payne get rid of his headaches and then tries to help their friend Anne Baxter. She had been married to a great guy and had a baby, but both the husband and baby are killed in a car crash, and Anne turns to drink, frequenting seedy Paris cafes. To cut it short, Tyrone does help her and plans to marry her, but Jean, who is terribly jealous, undermines Anne Baxter's cure and Anne, drinking again, goes off and gets killed by some Paris thug/lover. The last thing we see is Tyrone working as a common seaman on the lurching deck of a freighter during a storm on his way back to America.

Obviously, the parallels to my life are not very close, and I can't quite figure out why this feels like the story of my life, "sort of." But it does. In some ways I am the boy from Erie, Pennsylvania. In others I am like a wandering Knulp or Tyrone Power in *The Razor's Edge* (I am not delusional, I know I never looked like him) in the sense that I can feel close to and have an ability to put myself in the place of other people, even (maybe especially) people I encounter only briefly and in strange situations. It happened so many times when I was hitchhiking and often talking with a waitress or a fellow customer in a restaurant, like that guy who joined me at the table in Delhi. When comparing hitchhiking to the psychiatric interview earlier, I cited Heine's "Ich komme doch nie wieder" (I will never be coming back) and the freedom that allows. I think the sense of not being in one's usual world accounts for the special intensity of such encounters.

I didn't go to India when I was young, like Tyrone Power did in the movie. I have described how I wanted to take a year off from college to go and study there, but my parents wanted me to finish college first and I got the same advice from my Swarthmore teachers. So I stayed put. Later, when I was working on the IPSS, one of our centers was in Agra so I did finally get to India. I went two days early so I could spend time by myself there. At the Oberoi Hotel in New Delhi, I awoke very early in the morning because of the *décalage horaire* and asked the man at the desk if it was safe to walk around in the town. He said it was. When I went out, I saw people preparing their meals over little stoves. And here I may be conflating two memories, but as I was about to cross a street, I realized that everyone was waiting for a wedding procession to pass. Is it possible that the bride and groom were riding on an elephant? I was standing there in wonderment, and a man behind me put his hand on my shoulder and said kindly, "You've never seen anything like that before?" It was the next day that I met and shared my table with the gentleman with whom I discussed god. Hadn't done anything like before, either.

I must mention one other movie, one I just watched: Ingmar Bergman's *Autumn Sonata*. The nub of the story is the relationship between a mother (Ingrid Bergman), who is a professional pianist, and her daughter (Liv Ullman). It is a very difficult relationship. Near the end of the film Liv finally lights into her mother with passionate fury about how the mother always ignored her and treated her as practically nonexistent, a nuisance. The mother then described her own difficult and deprived childhood. There was no real resolution.

That's right, Liv Ullman! I know those feelings! Although, unlike you in the movie, I never expressed them. Having a parent like that is like having a family member whose job it is to keep your iron lung working properly but who wanders off frequently leaving you there gasping for breath. But you're not allowed to replace this person, you're not allowed even to notice.

As Liv was exploding with anger, I knew, I know, exactly how she felt. Of course, my situation was much better than Liv's in the movie. Although my mother was almost always distant and preoccupied, and then physically absent, she really did try. And I had my father, who was left to manage his work, our household, everything, was always caring, so too were my sister and Martha, our housekeeper.

But I never had any understanding of the totality of these things, only the sense that I needed pretty much to take care of myself, which I did. Seeing *Autumn Sonata* now, I get some sense of the fury I felt, the helplessness and inability to do anything about it, and the feeling that my mother was just not someone I could count on or who was even very interested in me. Recognizing my feelings these many years later is frightening, almost overwhelming.

So that's "This is your life," courtesy of Turner Classic Movies.

TIME

Another Ken Burns series that shows up on PBS periodically is the one on the Civil War. It starts out with a bunch of skinny old guys all dressed up and riding in the back seats of open cars in a parade. Now the funny thing is that I have seen those guys, or ones just like them. Mine were in Erie. I was eight. My dad had taken me to see the Decoration Day parade, and we watched from the corner of State Street and Tenth, amid a crowd of other people up and down State Street. The open cars and their bony occupants came, and Dad says "You know who those guys are?" I say, "No." And he tells me, "Those are the last living veterans of the Civil War." I can still see them clearly in my mind all these years later.

Dad was big on the Civil War. I always remember him with *Lee's Lieutenants*, the big three-volume set of books by Douglas Southall Freeman, but he read lots of other books on it as well. And I've told you about the stories he and his friend heard from that doctor in Loudonville about the Battle of Antietam. Something like 23,000 men were killed and wounded in that battle, said to be the highest single-day battle casualties in American history. Photos actually show the heaps of amputated arms and legs outside medical tents the doctor described. I wonder now if he told his Antietam stories as a way of trying to give himself a little therapy for the PTSD he lived from his experiences there.

I didn't know the old doctor, but I did see those guys in their cars. And you know what? Those guys might just have known veterans from the American Revolution, which creates a chain from me then back through the First World War, when my Dad was a soldier, all the way to the War of Independence and forward through the Second World War, which I lived through on the home front, and on through later wars to the present.

No, this is not a piece about wars, it is about time. The history of this country, as an independent nation, can be encompassed in a short chain of people from only four generations, from 1776 until 2019. What is that, 243 years? Of course, that's not very long compared to the 3,000-year history of ancient Egypt. But it's exciting to think that we are part of a string, if only a teeny, short part.

Apparently, the Egyptian idea of time changed over the course of their ancient history. They thought at first that it was linear but later decided that it was cyclical, more or less repeating itself over the centuries. Nowadays we don't think much about time at all. Our perspective is like one of those weird photographs taken through a fisheye lens in which the center is hugely expanded and the two sides vastly reduced in size. For us today, the present (perhaps the last few through the next few days) is huge and seems to go on forever while the days before and beyond that recede rapidly toward the extremes of the past and the future.

And how about people's lives? They too disappear after being so large while lived. Jennie Post and I had lunch at Atticus about four years ago. She had often had big troubles, but when you were with her she was full of life. Her arms and hands talked as her voice did.

She died recently, maybe from a heroin overdose—it wasn't immediately known. She was in her 30's, I think. About a hundred people attended her memorial service. People said wonderful things about her—her brother, her sister, her former roommate, people she had worked with—and the things they said were true. The minister was very respectful but also funny, as were other speakers. Jennie was full of fun and life.

But after the memorial service, she was gone, really gone. Except, not completely. Many of us hold her in our memories, in our beings even. Yet, gradually, those memories will go and once we are dead, who will remember her? Certainly in the distant future, if there are still people then, no one will have heard of her. Yet, I like to think that somehow tiny traces of her laughter and talking with her hands will have continued on, ripples in the oceans of time, like the connections that link us to the soldiers of the Civil War soldiers and the American Revolution and even to the people of the ancient Egyptian kingdoms.

PATTERNS OF A HUMAN LIFE

In writing about the painter J. M. W. Turner, John Ruskin spoke of "the deep final truth." Let's see if we can find any of that.

Writing an autobiography has been much more complicated than I had anticipated. It has made obvious things that somehow I hadn't expected or even known. I have been puzzled by some of the things of which I have become aware from the writing—for example, how rarely I write about my mother, at least in the early narrative, and the ways in which I seem to have compartmentalized my work and the other aspects of my life. Though sometimes it has felt like that, and sometimes not.

And, as I think about compartmentalization or the notion of leading separate, parallel lives, I realize that it doesn't really hold. I prefer the image of life as a braided cord. A braided cord—didn't the Greeks have that idea?—because there are so many intertwined threads, some running the whole length of the cord, others going on for a while and then perhaps ending or disappearing but then reappearing.

Take music, for example, one of the longest threads. My grandfather, as I have said, played the violin in the Cleveland Symphony, and my mother's family was very musical. My father told me he married the family as well as my mother, and I think music was a big part of that. He, of course, loved to play the piano and played it well. I would listen to him for long hours. Music became a passion for me. I was the "Brahms fan," remember. I learned from one of my *Great Courses* that Brahms combined the rigors of classicism and the feelings of romanticism. No wonder I love his music. I too have been attempting to bring together two seemingly contradictory things, in my case, the rigor of science and the feelings expressed by romanticism. We're all in this together, although I have not quite reached his level of success.

In writing this autobiography, too, I am braiding threads. I have included a chronology of my life, excerpts from my interviews with Sarah Kamens, an article about "Uncertainty Theory" and my mother, and assorted informal reflections on my experiences. This is all material I know. Except it doesn't feel like that at all. The me who writes the chronology, the me who writes both articles and pieces I just feel like writing, and the me in the interviews with Sarah seem like very separate sources. The one that is most perplexing is the me in interviews with Sarah. I think her warmth, her intelligence, her kindness, and her patience drew out from me things different from those found in self-examination. The magic of being with someone you value and trust opens up that "source" in you that is not otherwise available.

So what more can I say about this braid? I have expressed my astonishment at how much I didn't know about myself. Yet perhaps the most fascinating part has been the overall sense seeing and realizing so many pieces together. Is it too self-serving to try to resort to the ideas of Gestalt psychology and of Bergson and the concepts of emergents? Both orientations deal with the issues of totality, of the whole as being different from the sum of its parts. I love the observation of Poincaré that a pile of stones is not a house. Whatever the reason, pulling together so much of my life in one place has been a powerful experience. Rather than separate threads braided together, I finally have a sense of the elements of my life flowing together at least somewhat. It is an experience totally unexpected, weird, nice, scary, all of the above.

I have discussed these various metaphors for the complexity of an individual life with my friend Joe Saccio, a sculptor and psychiatrist whom I mentioned earlier. After I explain to him my idea of life as a cord with many filaments, he asks what holds them together. "Me," I answer, but what does that mean? He also asks what the filaments are made of, a great question. Different materials have different qualities, more or less permanent, more or less flexible, subject to mold or rust, and so on. The more I get into this the more I realize I don't know, the more I learn. Excuse the grandiosity, but I feel a little like Magellan, discovering new lands, new people, new worlds, and at the same time since this process is going on primarily in New Haven, like Kant who never left Königsberg. Not bad models to have, though, of course, poor Magellan never made it all the way. Well, so be it. I feel more like an empiricist and explorer, than a narrator. No, really! What is a person? Complicated, *pas evident*, fascinating!

Another conversation with Joe, who constantly gets me to thinking about new things. Now, I'm trying to explain to him why working on this autobiography has had such an impact on me. I think of the poem "Die Lorelei" by Heinrich Heine. It begins, "Ich weiss nicht was soll es bedeuten dass ich so traurig bin" (I don't know what it means that I am so sad). I'm not sad, but I remain mystified as to why it has affected me so much. It's not that I'm closer to understanding the meaning of my life. Yes, it's true that I can see some of the themes more clearly and as more constant than I could before: my tendency to try to put things together that must be together but just aren't (yet); the tendency to want to solve the questions around my mother (and to help her); the love of diversity in thinking and knowledge; the love of being a pain in the ass, of noticing the obvious and telling people, often to their annoyance, about it; the mix of being a romantic and, in the musical sense, a classicist. Those are some of the big ones. Joe suggests the idea of a collage. I like that metaphor too. I have the sense of all these tendencies and experiences being sort of plastered there, a mix of randomness and structure at the same time. Whatever, there's kind of a power of seeing all this stuff more or less together, that certainly never existed for me before.

CHAPTER 15

CLOSING THOUGHTS

FATE

I receive the *Swarthmore College Bulletin* periodically. Toward the end of the magazine are the reports from the classes where there is at least one living member. I graduated in 1954. As of 2019, sixty-five classes had graduated since me!? Sixty-five. One, two, three, four, count up to sixty-five, that is a hell of a lot of classes since me. And now, to think of some of the friends from my class. Some who were very close are dead. Some even died long ago. One close friend died of ovarian cancer over forty years ago; another wonderful friend, who had also been my roommate for a year and then visited me in Geneva, died of a heart attack while walking in the woods about ten years ago now. Not a bad way to go actually.

Thinking of these people, as well as many other friends currently and from across the years, reminds me of a little game we some-times got at the Atlantic gas station when I was about ten. (Atlantic stations don't exist anymore.) It was called Horse Race and, as I recall, consisted of a thin piece of paper three inches square with a thin cardboard backing. A small circle at one edge of the paper was marked "Start," and beside it were the numbers 1, 2, 3. The game was for each of three players to pick a number and then for an adult to touch a lighted cigarette to the circle. The paper had been treated with some chemical so that three numbered lines would start to smolder as though headed to the opposite edge of the paper. But then one smolder would start to head off to the left and just stop. A second smolder might head off toward the goal at the other end of the paper and then, half way or so would just stop. The third smolder would reach the goal and that, of course, was the winner. But there was absolutely no way to know beforehand which of the three smolders would do what. Lives seem to me to be something like that.

Just one more game. Have you ever played clock solitaire? You deal face down the cards to take the places of the twelve numbers of a clock and place one more in the middle. There end up being four cards at each place. You take the top card from the middle pack and if it is a three, for example, you put it face up at the bottom of the number three pack; then you take the top card from that pack and continue this process, putting any queen cards in the middle pack. The goal is to get the cards in all the packs face up except for the queen pack. When all the cards in the queen pack face up you have lost. It is almost impossible to win this game and, in fact, losing has a kind of inevitability about it. Which makes the game what? Oppressive, daunting, exasperating, a real challenge? Almost like life, except in life, sooner or later, you always "lose."

So that's where I am in my autobiography—and, indeed, my life. My luck in life has been good, but I am necessarily close to the place where all of our tracks burn out and all our center pile cards are face up.

THE FUTURE

I have just learned about the NAMI (National Alliance for the Mentally Ill) program in which people with severe mental disorders describe in several phases the evolution of their situation. They finish with the final phase entitled, "The Future." It seems a fitting way to end my autobiography too. Of course, at my age, there isn't going to be that much of a future, which is scary for me.

I hope for a fast death and one without pain. Die in my sleep? Well, perhaps, but I'd rather be awake. Before that? Well, I am happy to continue pretty much with my life as it is: meeting every Friday morning with Larry; talking several times a week on the phone with Jeff and Sarah; meetings over lunches and dinners with Joe, Maria, Sarah K., Pauline, Tom, Stan, and others; planning presentations; working on and hopefully completing my autobiography; and last but not least—though with much more ambivalence—going to the gym three times a week. And, of course, I want to continue sleeping in my own bed, watching the UConn women's basketball games on television, and taking my *Great Courses*, so many of them are outstanding. Maybe I'll even get to read a bit more of *Les Misérables* to find out what Jean Valjean decides to do about the judgment regarding the man who has been mistaken for him.

Yes, and one more thing: solve the problem of mental illness. Really? No, not really. As Fred Wertz noted and I realized, I wouldn't trust any such definitive solution even if I thought for a minute I found it. The idea of a definitive solution for me assumes that you've fooled yourself. There's always something more to question and to understand. That's the way it should be, and that's

the way it is, always some further challenge to face with the pleasure that involves.

AN ENCOUNTER

I was sitting at my usual table at the Café Danton, looking out
through the huge window that forms the front wall of the café
looking out onto Boulevard St. Germain. Mikel had brought me
the *café crème* (coffee with steamed milk on top making a beautiful little design) without my even needing to ask and Mme. Guerin
(Monique) had hung up today's menu on the post behind my table.
I was just sitting, sipping the hot coffee, and thinking how wonderful it was to be here and to have known this place since I first came
to Paris in 1953.

There are three small tables in a row just behind that huge front
window, mine the one in the middle. As I was musing, a young
woman, nice looking and neatly dressed, apparently in a hurry,
sat down at the table between me and the front entrance to the
café. She took out an appointment book from her purse and was
writing something in it when Mikel appeared. She looked up for a
minute and said "Un café crème, s'il vous plaît." Her French was
actually pretty good, but it was clear from her accent that she was
Américaine. I was going to venture a "Do you come here often?"
question but decided that was too corny even for me. Instead I said
"I really like this café." She turned toward me and said, "I like it too.
I just discovered it yesterday. It's perfect for me." She had blue eyes
and a lovely smile. We started talking, she put her purse and the
appointment book down on the table, and said "Do you live here?
In Paris I mean." "No, but I come here often and just love this city.

I'm working on an autobiography, and it's so good to do it here where I have many memories—and the time to write."

"I just got a job with a branch of the UN on rue Dauphine" she said. "I've wanted to do something like this for so long. We're trying to work on a program where countries who are getting into a confrontation can step back, talk, and find some common ground for discussion. I know it sounds idealistic, but it's really important to try."

"Will you be staying long?" I asked.

"Well, it's not clear yet, but I really hope so. We certainly aren't going to be able to develop what we need in just a couple of weeks."

She signaled to Mikel, said *"L'addition, s'il vous plait"* with that nice accent and a kind tone, and turned to me, "Excuse me," she said, "I need to rush off. We have a big meeting this morning." As she got up I asked her, "What is your name?" "Augusta," she replied. "That's strange," I said, "That's the name of my mother."

"I know," she said and, as she got to the door, "Maybe we'll meet again" She smiled at me and rushed off.

I woke up.

* * * * *

Since you are now at the end of this book you might want to listen to the end of the first act of *La Bohème,* where Rudolfo and Mimi are introducing themselves to each other by singing their answers to the question, *"Chi Son?"* ("Who am I?"). It's on YouTube of course.

As for me, I think I'll have some homemade peanut butter on a cracker.

A F T E R W O R D

by S a r a h   K a m e n s

"What is this book?" That is the question that, as John tells us, he struggled with while creating this work, which went through many different iterations before reaching its present and final form.

What is this book? The question is larger and more existential than it might at first seem. Those of us on the outside can answer relatively concretely and rapidly: It's the autobiography of a renowned psychiatrist, a series of *pensées* or reflections by someone who, when it comes down to it, revolutionized the foundational assumptions of his field. It's also a collection of reflections on art, music, and literature. On growing up, on getting to know the world. Contemplations on how and what to write – indeed, the very meaning of writing about one's life, and of writing itself.

Perhaps as a result of the philosophical gravity of these questions—and most certainly as a result of John's humbleness and kindness—this book project began and ended with striking humility. Indeed, in in its first iterations, this book was not one that one would open and initially understand as the work of a renowned psychiatrist. Proceeding through the first pages and chapters—starting with John's birth in Cleveland and his move to Erie—the reader would encounter the glorious memories of his childhood, perhaps with a brief, enigmatic allusion to a later conference or two, never realizing that this author changed the way the world thinks about mental illness, and schizophrenia in particular. It took some convincing before John agreed to mention his work as a psychiatrist earlier in the book. This is because for John, the everyday experiences of one's life growing up—playing with cars on the front porch, going to the Island in the summer—are just as, if not more meaningful and important than the later accolades and accomplishments.

Even here, in the book's final manifestation, John tells us that he is still trying to figure out how best to write about his life, how to think about and express human experience. What he does not tell us, at least at first—what he leaves to the reader to figure out—is the fact that this question also underlies his life's work. John describes his life as if he is any other person not because he is making an effort to be modest nor because, in some literary sleight-of-hand, he's delaying the reveal of his identity. He is doing so because he genuinely believes that he is no different from any other person, and that by exploring his own life, he can better understand something about what it means to be human.

What is this book? This book is not only the story of someone reflecting back on his own life, but also that of his mother. In that regard, it is the story of a mother who defied all odds, who—in the days when women were barely permitted to do such things— attended college, established a progressive elementary school, set up a crafts and jewelry studio, opened an office of the American Association for the United Nations, and taught foreign policy at the college level. It is the story of a woman with a bright child, a child who did not know why, as he was sitting at the dining room table, the black cars pulled up to his house to take her away. It is the story of a woman who was institutionalized due to now-outdated ideas, ideas about the nature and treatment of schizophrenia that her son would go on to challenge and reshape as an adult. It is the story of a mother whose son—although he didn't realize it at first—spent his life trying to get to know her condition, and the scientific institutions that wholly misunderstood it.

This book is also the rare portrait of a psychiatric researcher who has become more uncertain and humbler about his expertise over time. As he has accumulated knowledge—an impressive, wide-ranging trove of knowledge—the more hesitant he is to make truth claims, and the more hesitant and provisional his ideas. The more he learns, John once explained to me, the more he questions what he once knew.

This openness to the contradictions and heterogeneity of our empirical world lies in stark contrast to the tendency of many clinical researchers to increasingly narrow their ideas about the nature of humankind. As clinicians are trained in diagnosing people's distress using the *Diagnostic and Statistical Manual of Mental Disorders* (DSM), more and more of human experience comes to be interpreted through this lens, and the more other lenses fall away. Philosopher of science Thomas Kuhn once explained in so many words that most researchers labor to support the existing scientific paradigm, even if it is faltering. That paradigm is upheld as much by popular belief as it is by the empirical details—details which, often enough, eventually come into question.

John's guiding principle is not faith, but doubt. In this way, John is an authentic scientist, following the steady route to truth— even if that truth is the fact of biopsychosocial complexity and uncertainty—rather than succumbing to the siren of conviction. He not only acknowledges empirical anomalies—the true uniqueness of every human being, despite which DSM box they might seem to fit in—but he stares at them with wonder, admires them, tries to understand them. This is what led him, decades before other researchers, to discover the fact that people diagnosed with schizophrenia can and often do feel better. He noted, also decades before other researchers, that psychological distress is not a dichotomous division between those with and without mental illness, but rather exists on a continuum. We all experience it, at different times in our lives, to some degree, and even those who experience it the most don't all experience it in the same way. That distress is not random, but deeply entangled in the meanings of our life experiences and the social world. Understanding the experiential intricacies and complexities of human suffering solely through the lens of the DSM is, as John once told me over dinner, "like trying to open a pistachio with a hammer."

What is this book? It's the story of a psychiatrist who wants to learn from his patients, who acknowledges his uncertainty about the nature of mental illness. It's the story of someone who teaches his colleagues that psychiatric patients are fellow human beings who deserve respect just like any other. And it's a book that tells us something about the history of psychiatry, and a psychiatrist's explorations through that history. When we first started the interviews John mentioned, one of the reasons I was enthusiastic (and honored) to do them was that it was a rare opportunity to hear about, and to document, someone who had lived through and participated in the circuitous evolution of psychiatry, its historical turns and about-faces. He had lived through the psychodynamic era, conducted family therapy, studied with Piaget in Geneva, witnessed the return to a staunchly biomedical psychiatry. He had participated in some of the most well-known—and controversial—international studies of schizophrenia. And he had eventually come to reshape the ways that we think about the condition, and mental disorder more broadly.

But that history of psychiatry presented in this book is also a visionary history, a history of how psychiatry should have been and could be. That history is as much the story of John's life, start-ing with his childhood, as it is the later tales of higher education and renowned institutions. In other words, the history of psychi-atry, according to John, should be the history of human beings. It should not be a didactic and doctrinaire explanation about how human beings are, but a set of questions, humbly posed, along-side a careful listening that allows one human being to learn more about another. John demonstrates this stance in this book by ask-ing questions about his own life, and in doing so, showing us how his life has been one of asking questions and learning about others.

What is this book? It is the story of different ways of telling a story, and different ways of knowing about human life. It's a book that shows us that psychiatry should be a lot more like writing—like understanding the unique individual experiences that make up a life—and that writing, by attending to medical knowledge about human pain, can also be a lot like psychiatry. It's a book that is, in itself, a hybrid demonstration of *doing psychiatry through writ-ing,* and *writing through the practice of psychiatry.*

In telling us about his effort to integrate the sciences and human-ities, John quotes Bob Spitzer, architect of the third version of the DSM who is often seen as revolutionizing the way that mental ill-ness is diagnosed. As John tells the story, his colleague tells him, "John, you are always trying to put two things together that are difficult to join." Fast-forward several decades, as clinical research-ers have amassed extensive evidence that the DSM-III diagnostic system, rather than "cutting nature at its joints," is characterized by extensive comorbidity (simultaneous diagnoses) and overlap-ping symptom profiles. Efforts are underway to develop new par-adigms—new diagnostic systems that reflect the commonality of cross-cutting symptoms (symptoms that cut across traditional diagnostic categories). It seems that while he was critiquing John for putting two things together, Spitzer was busy separating things that should have never been split apart.

That is to say: John's attempt to combine psychiatric thinking and narrative writing, here and in his other work, is an effort that should be taken in absolute seriousness. In an era when mental health professionals have more stigmatizing beliefs about mental illness than the general public, and when there is widespread belief that there are fundamental differences between those diagnosed with mental illnesses and those who are not, John's attempt to merge the sciences and humanities may seem like something of an anomaly. But history will tell that it is the techno-mechanistic beliefs of this era—and not John's insistence on a more humanistic psychiatry—that was out of place.

This book is not only a story, but a demonstration of how stories comprise human life, and how they can be used to understand a person. Indeed, it is John's belief in the value and meaning of everyday experience—as well as a genuine wonder and existential curiosity about others—that define him as a psychiatrist and a writer, as a psychiatrist-writer. John went into psychiatry because of an authentic love and appreciation for his fellow human being. And that is his vision of psychiatry in the future: a humanistic profession of respect, care, awe, and love. A profession that cares about each and every person, that documents not only the technical terms for their maladies and troubles, but also the meaningful narratives that make up a human life. This book is a book of those narratives. The same narratives that are—and always have been—the very 'stuff' of human experience.

REFERENCES

Breier, A., and Strauss, J. S. "Self-control in Psychotic Disorders." *Archives of General Psychiatry* 40, no. 10 (1983), 1141-1145.

Davidson, L., and Strauss, J. S. "Sense of Self in Recovery from Severe Mental Illness." *British Journal of Medical Psychology* 65 (1992): 131-145. Reprinted in *Psychological and Social Aspects of Psychiatric Disability,* edited by L. Spaniol, C. Gagne, and M. Koehler. Boston: Center for Psychiatric Rehabilitation, Boston University, 1997.

_____"Beyond the Biopsychosocial Model: Integrating Disorder, Health and Recovery." *Psychiatry* 58 (1995): 44-55.

Harding, C. M., Zubin, J., and Strauss, J. S. "Chronicity in Schizophrenia: Fact, Partial Fact, or Artifact? *Hospital and Community Psychiatry* 38, no. 5 (1987): 477-486. Reprinted in *Psychological and Social Aspects of Psychiatric Disability,* edited by L. Spaniol, C. Gagne, and M. Koehler. Boston: Center for Psychiatric Rehabilitation, Boston University, 1997.

Meunier, S., and Strauss, J. "Une Clown-thérapeute en USP et en gériatrie: rêve ou réalité?" *La Lettre du Psychiatre* 3 (2007): 107-111. Reprinted in *La Lettre du Cancérologue* 2007: 477-481 and in *La Lettre du Pneumologue* 2008: 26-30.

Piaget, J., and Szeminska, A. *La Genese du Nombre chez l'enfant.* Neuchatel: Delachaux et Niestlé, 1941.

Rakfeldt, J., and Strauss, J. S. "The Low Turning Point: A Control Mechanism in the Course of Mental Disorder." *Journal of Nervous and Mental Disease* 177, no. 1 (1989): 32-37. Reprinted in *Recovery from Severe Mental Illness,* edited by L. Davidson, C. Harding, and L. Spaniol. Boston: Boston University Center for Psychiatric Rehabilitation, 2005.

Sachs, M., Carpenter, W. T., Jr., and Strauss, J. S., (1974). "Recovery from Delusions: Three Phases Documented by Patients' Interpretation of Research Procedures." *Archives of General Psychiatry* 30, no. 1 (1974): 117-120.

Strauss, J. S. "The Clarification of Schizophrenic Concreteness by Piaget's Tests." *Psychiatry* 30 (1967): 294-301.

_____"Hallucinations and Delusions as Points on Continua Function: Rating Scale Evidence." *Archives of General Psychiatry,* 31 (1969): 581-586.

_____"Classification by Cluster Analysis." In World Health Organization, *The International Pilot Study of Schizophrenia,* vol. 1. Geneva, Switzerland: WHO Press, 1973.

_____"Diagnostic Models and the Nature of Psychiatric Disorder." *Archives of General Psychiatry* 29 (1973): 445-449. Reprinted in *The Psychology of Adjustment: Current Concepts and Applications,* edited by W. Katkovsky and L. Gorlow. New York: McGraw-Hill, 1976.

_____"A Comprehensive Approach to Psychiatric Diagnosis." *American Journal of Psychiatry* 132, no. 11 (1975): 1193-1197.

_____"Social and Cultural Influences on Psychopathology." *Annual Review of Psychology* 30 (1979): 397-415.

_____"Complexity in Psychiatric Disorder: The Need for More Clinical Input into the Research Endeavor." *Journal of Clinical Psychiatry* 41, no. 9 (1980): 293-294.

_____"Subjective Experiences of Schizophrenia: Towards a New

Dynamic Psychiatry." *Schizophrenia Bulletin* 15, no. 2 (1989): 179-187.

_____ "The Person with Schizophrenia as a Person." In *Psychotherapy of Schizophrenia: Facilitating and Obstructive Factors*, edited by A. Werbart and J. Cullberg. Oslo: Scandinavian University Press, 1992.

_____"Subjectivity." *Journal of Nervous and Mental Disease* 184, no. 4 (1996): 205-212. Reprinted as "Subjektivitet" in *Dialog* 9, no. 3 (1999), 37-50; translated into Norwegian by Soren Rimestad.

_____"À Maryanne: Le Contexte, la Personne et la Maladie Mentale." *VST: Revue du Champ Social et de la Santé Mentale* 64 (1999): 8-13.

_____"Diagnosis and Reality: A Noun is a Terrible Thing to Waste." *Psychopathology* 38, no. 4 (2005): 189-191.

_____"La réalité et le concept de maladie mentale." *Psychiatrie, Sciences Humaines, et Neurosciences* 5 (2007): 25-130.

_____"Subjectivity and Severe Psychiatric Disorders." *Schizophrenia Bulletin* 37 (2011): 8-13.

_____"Uncertainty Theory: A Powerful Approach to Understanding Psychiatric Disorder." *Psychiatry* 80 (2017): 301-38.

Strauss, J. S., Bartko, J. J., and Carpenter, W.T., Jr. "The Use of Clustering Techniques for the Classification of Psychiatric Patients." *British Journal of Psychiatry* 122 (1973): 122: 531-540.

_____"New Directions in Diagnosis: The Longitudinal Processes of Schizophrenia." *American Journal of Psychiatry* 138, no. 7 (1981): 954-958.

Strauss, J., Bernard, P., and Harper, A. "Towards a Biopsychosocial Psychiatry." *Psychiatry* 82, no. 2 (2019): 103-112.

Strauss, J. S., and Carpenter, W. T., Jr. "Characteristic Symptoms and Outcome in Schizophrenia." *Archives of General Psychiatry* 30, no. 1 (1974): 429-434.

_____"Prediction of Outcome in Schizophrenia: II. Relationships

Between Predictor and Outcome Variables." *Archives of General Psychiatry* 31 (1974): 37-42.

_____ "The Prognosis of Schizophrenia: Rationale for a Multidimensional Concept. *Schizophrenia Bulletin* 4, no. 1 (1978): 56-67.

_____ *Schizophrenia*. New York: Plenum, 1981.

Strauss, J. S., Carpenter, W. T., Jr., and Bartko, J. J. "Speculations on the Processes That Underlie Schizophrenic Symptoms. *Schizophrenia Bulletin* 11 (1974): 61-70.

Strauss, J. S., Gabriel, K. R., Kokes, R. F., Ritzler, B. A., VanOrd, A., and Tarana, E. "Do Psychiatric Patients Fit Their Diagnoses? Patterns of Symptomatology as Described with the Biplot." *Journal of Nervous and Mental Disease* 167 (1979): 105-113.

Strauss, J. S., and Hafez, H. "Clinical Questions and 'Real' Research. *American Journal of Psychiatry* 138, no.12 (1981): 1592-1597.

Strauss, J. S., Hafez, H., Lieberman, P., and Harding, C. M. "The Course of Psychiatric Disorder: III. Longitudinal Principles. *American Journal of Psychiatry* 142, no. 3 (1985): 289-296. Reprinted in *Psychological and Social Aspects of Psychiatric Disability,* edited by L. Spaniol, C. Gagne, and M. Koehler. Boston: Center for Psychiatric Rehabilitation, Boston University, 1997.

Strauss, J., Staeheli-Lawless, M., and Sells, D. "Becoming an Expert." *Psychiatry* 72 (2009): 211-221.

CPSIA information can be obtained
at www.ICGtesting.com
Printed in the USA
LVHW092149271120
672814LV00006B/129

9 781951 937553